EVERAFTER

THE UNSENTIMENTAL EDUCATION

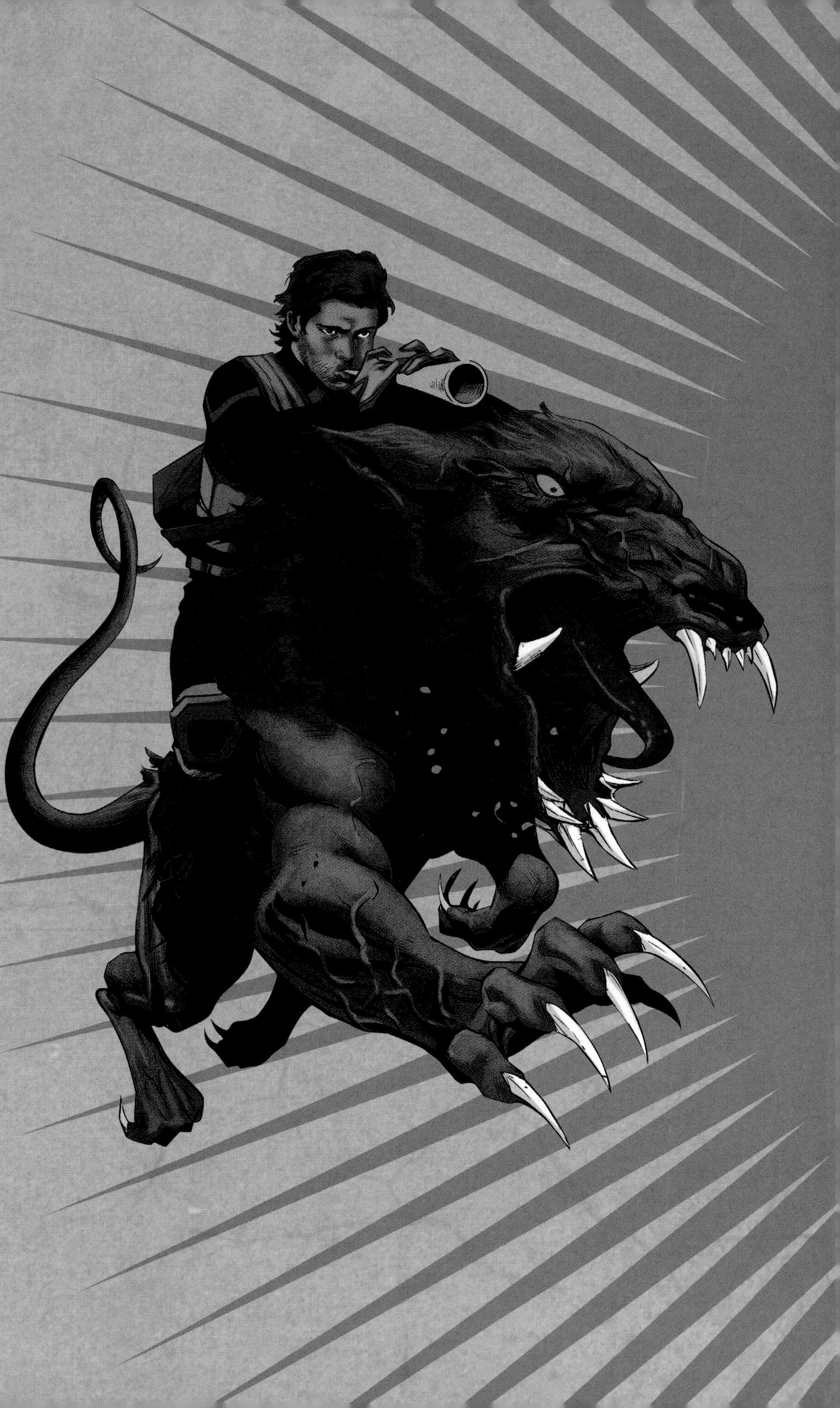

EVERAFTER
THE UNSENTIMENTAL EDUCATION

DAVE JUSTUS & LILAH STURGES
writers

TRAVIS MOORE
artist (issues #8-12)

MARK BUCKINGHAM
artist (issue #7)

MICHAEL WIGGAM
colorist

TODD KLEIN
letterer

cover art and original series covers
TULA LOTAY

FABLES created by
BILL WILLINGHAM

ELLIE PYLE JAMIE S. RICH Editors – Original Series
MAGGIE HOWELL Assistant Editor – Original Series
JAMIE S. RICH Group Editor – Vertigo Comics
JEB WOODARD Group Editor – Collected Editions
SCOTT NYBAKKEN Editor – Collected Edition
STEVE COOK Design Director – Books
DAMIAN RYLAND Publication Design

BOB HARRAS Senior VP – Editor-in-Chief, DC Comics
MARK DOYLE Executive Editor, Vertigo

DIANE NELSON President
DAN DiDIO Publisher
JIM LEE Publisher
GEOFF JOHNS President & Chief Creative Officer
AMIT DESAI Executive VP – Business & Marketing Strategy, Direct to Consumer & Global Franchise Management
SAM ADES Senior VP & General Manager, Digital Services
BOBBIE CHASE VP & Executive Editor, Young Reader & Talent Development
MARK CHIARELLO Senior VP – Art, Design & Collected Editions
JOHN CUNNINGHAM Senior VP – Sales & Trade Marketing
ANNE DePIES Senior VP – Business Strategy, Finance & Administration
DON FALLETTI VP – Manufacturing Operations
LAWRENCE GANEM VP – Editorial Administration & Talent Relations
ALISON GILL Senior VP – Manufacturing & Operations
HANK KANALZ Senior VP – Editorial Strategy & Administration
JAY KOGAN VP – Legal Affairs
JACK MAHAN VP – Business Affairs
NICK J. NAPOLITANO VP – Manufacturing Administration
EDDIE SCANNELL VP – Consumer Marketing
COURTNEY SIMMONS Senior VP – Publicity & Communications
JIM (SKI) SOKOLOWSKI VP – Comic Book Specialty Sales & Trade Marketing
NANCY SPEARS VP – Mass, Book, Digital Sales & Trade Marketing
MICHELE R. WELLS VP – Content Strategy

EVERAFTER: THE UNSENTIMENTAL EDUCATION

DC Comics 2900 West Alameda Avenue, Burbank, CA 91505
Printed by Solisco Printers, Scott, QC, Canada. 11/24/17
First printing. ISBN: 978-1-4012-7502-0

Library of Congress Cataloging-in-Publication data is available.

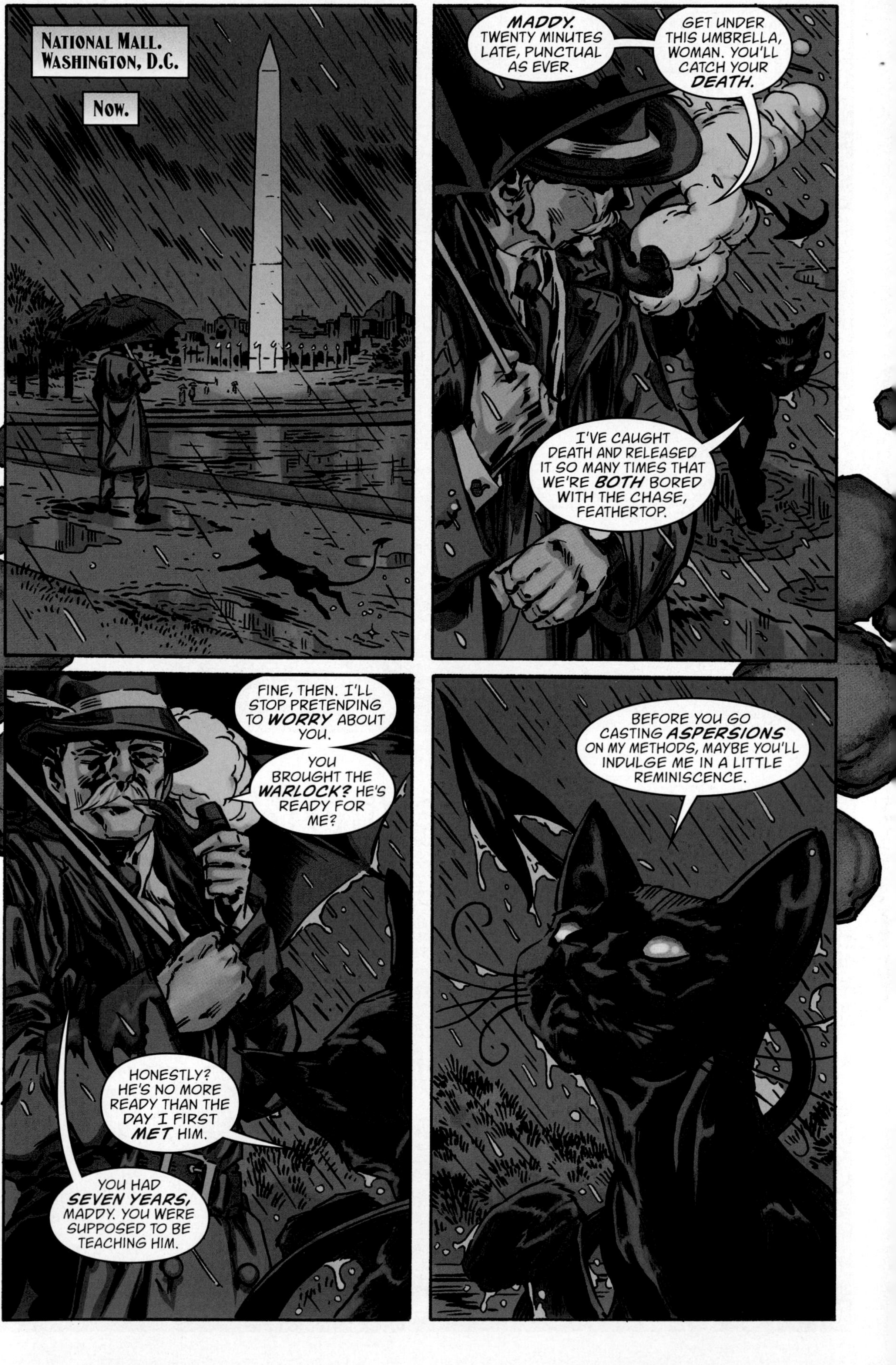
NATIONAL MALL. WASHINGTON, D.C.
NOW.
MADDY. TWENTY MINUTES LATE, PUNCTUAL AS EVER.
GET UNDER THIS UMBRELLA, WOMAN. YOU'LL CATCH YOUR DEATH.
I'VE CAUGHT DEATH AND RELEASED IT SO MANY TIMES THAT WE'RE BOTH BORED WITH THE CHASE, FEATHERTOP.
FINE, THEN. I'LL STOP PRETENDING TO WORRY ABOUT YOU.
YOU BROUGHT THE WARLOCK? HE'S READY FOR ME?
HONESTLY? HE'S NO MORE READY THAN THE DAY I FIRST MET HIM.
YOU HAD SEVEN YEARS, MADDY. YOU WERE SUPPOSED TO BE TEACHING HIM.
BEFORE YOU GO CASTING ASPERSIONS ON MY METHODS, MAYBE YOU'LL INDULGE ME IN A LITTLE REMINISCENCE.

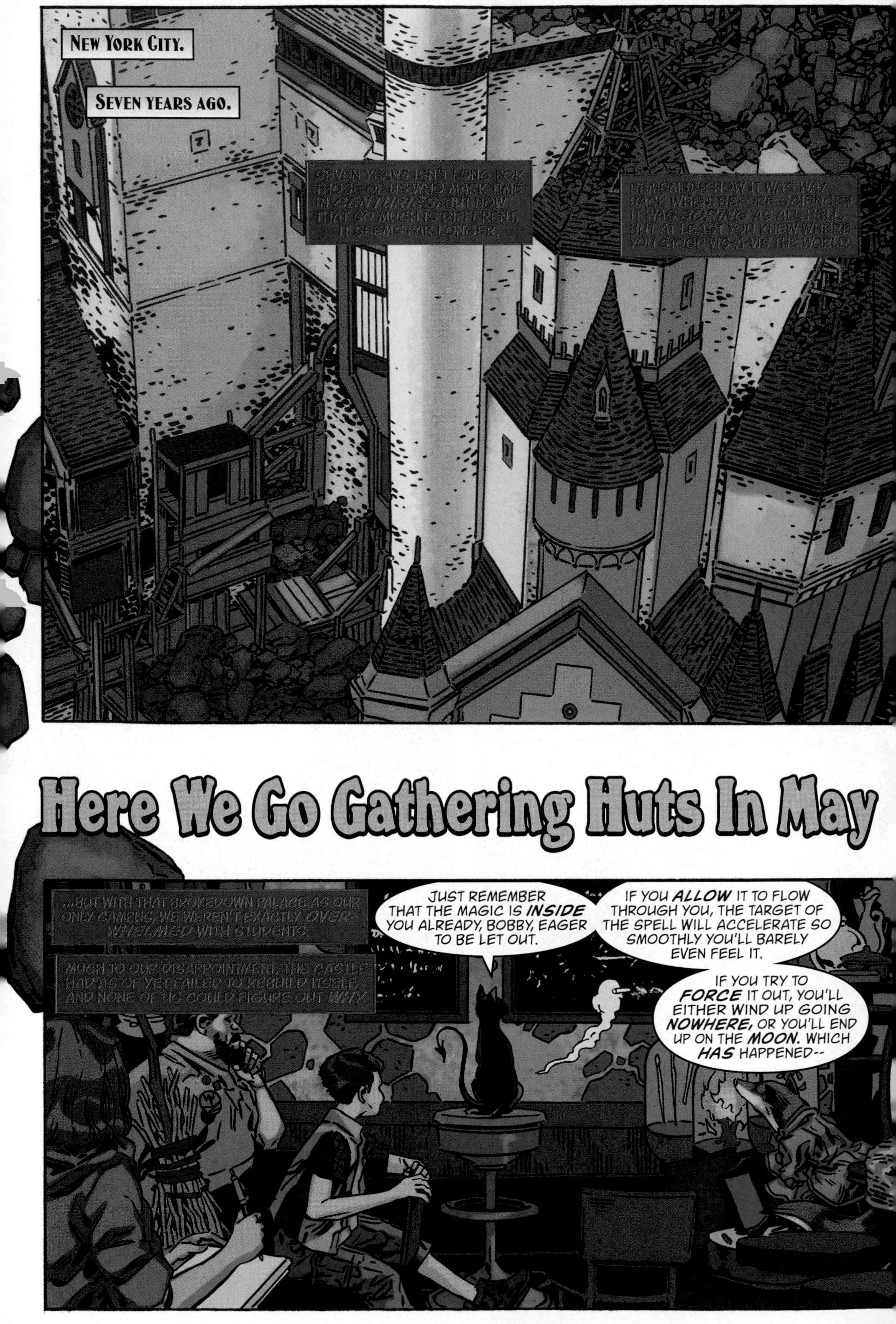
NEW YORK CITY.
SEVEN YEARS AGO.
SEVEN YEARS ISN'T LONG FOR THOSE OF US WHO MARK TIME IN CENTURIES, BUT NOW THAT SO MUCH IS DIFFERENT, IT SEEMS FAR LONGER.
REMEMBER HOW IT WAS WAY BACK WHEN, BEFORE SCIENCE? IT WAS BORING AS ALL HELL, BUT AT LEAST YOU KNEW WHERE YOU STOOD VIS-A-VIS THE WORLD.
Here We Go Gathering Huts In May
...BUT WITH THAT BROKEDOWN PALACE AS OUR ONLY CAMPUS, WE WEREN'T EXACTLY OVER-WHELMED WITH STUDENTS.
MUCH TO OUR DISAPPOINTMENT, THE CASTLE HAD AS OF YET FAILED TO REBUILD ITSELF, AND NONE OF US COULD FIGURE OUT WHY.
JUST REMEMBER THAT THE MAGIC IS INSIDE YOU ALREADY, BOBBY, EAGER TO BE LET OUT.
IF YOU ALLOW IT TO FLOW THROUGH YOU, THE TARGET OF THE SPELL WILL ACCELERATE SO SMOOTHLY YOU'LL BARELY EVEN FEEL IT.
IF YOU TRY TO FORCE IT OUT, YOU'LL EITHER WIND UP GOING NOWHERE, OR YOU'LL END UP ON THE MOON. WHICH HAS HAPPENED--

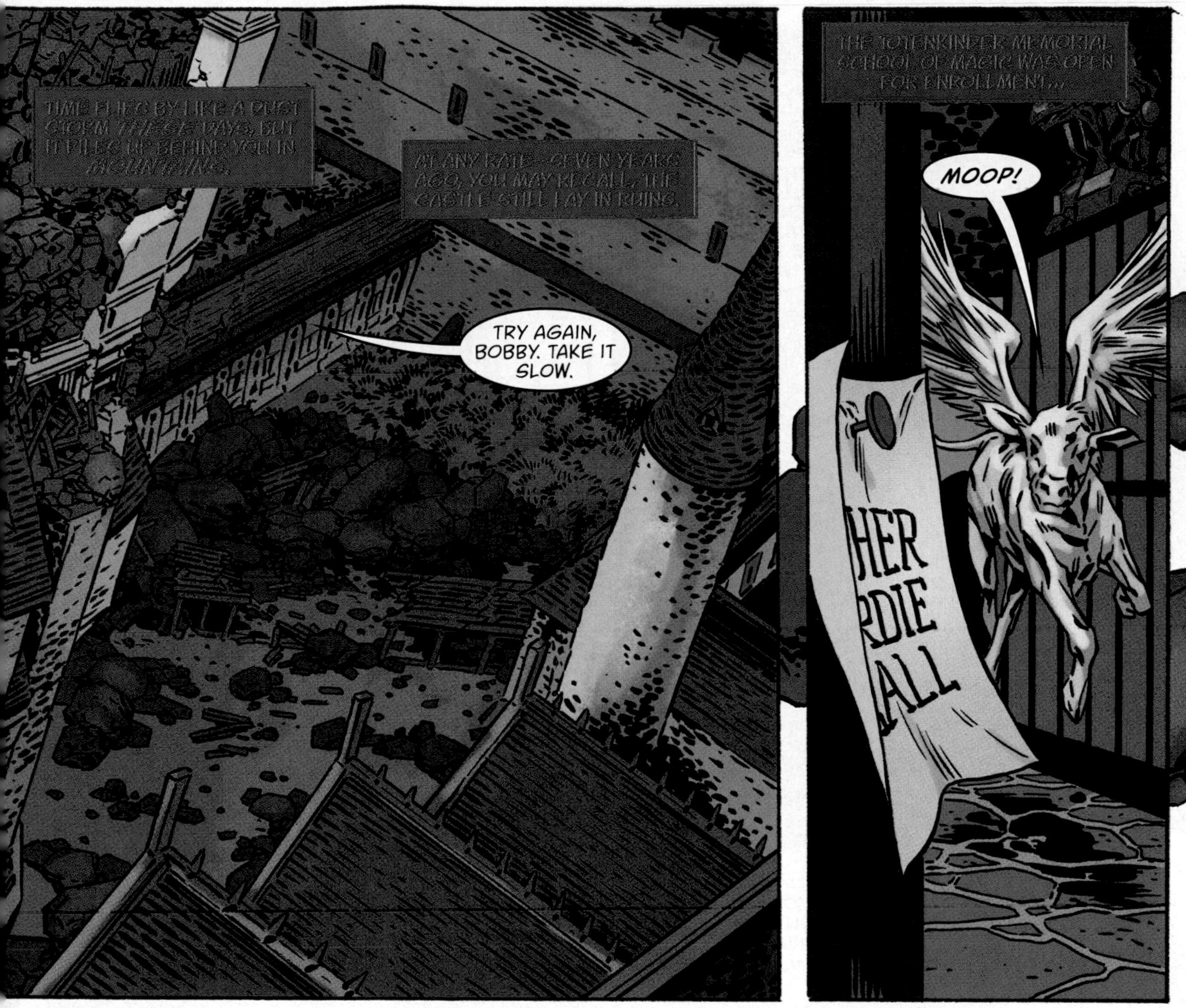
TIME FLIES BY LIKE A DUST STORM THESE DAYS, BUT IT PILES UP BEHIND YOU IN MOUNTAINS.
AT ANY RATE--SEVEN YEARS AGO, YOU MAY RECALL, THE CASTLE STILL LAY IN RUINS.
TRY AGAIN, BOBBY. TAKE IT SLOW.
THE TOTENKINDER MEMORIAL SCHOOL OF MAGIC WAS OPEN FOR ENROLLMENT...
MOOP!
HER
RDIE
ALL

Prologue to The Unsentimental Education

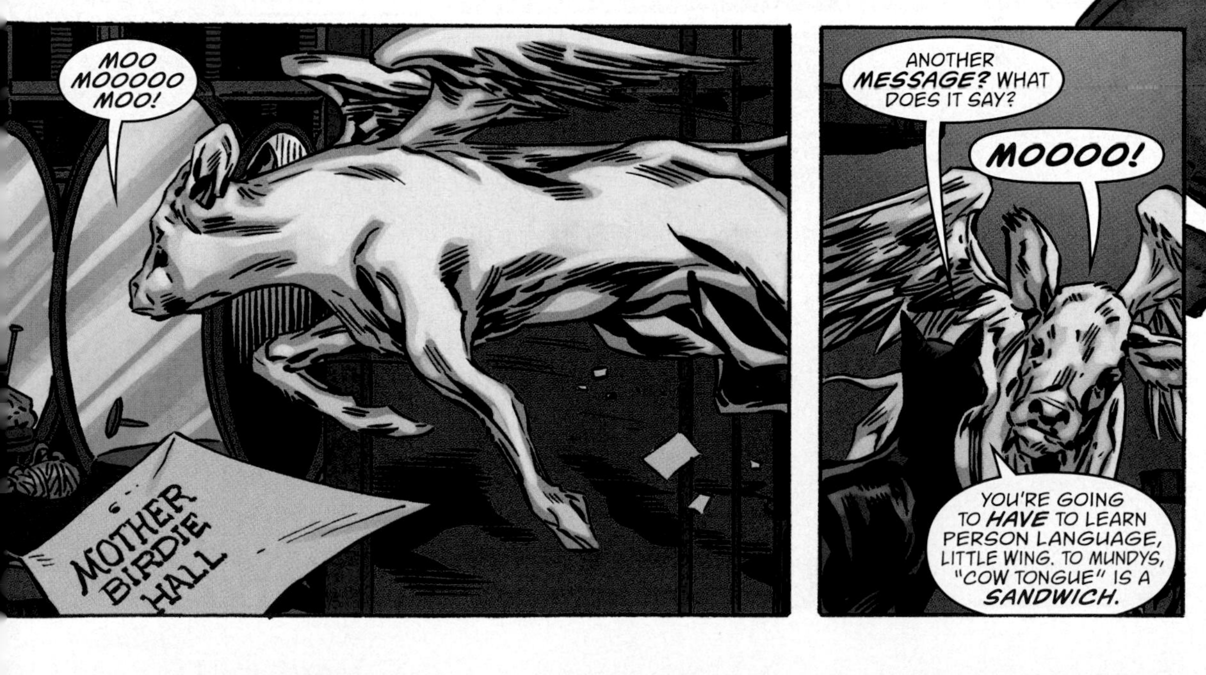
MOO MOOOOO MOO!
MOTHER BIRDIE HALL
ANOTHER MESSAGE? WHAT DOES IT SAY?
MOOOO!
YOU'RE GOING TO HAVE TO LEARN PERSON LANGUAGE, LITTLE WING. TO MUNDYS, "COW TONGUE" IS A SANDWICH.

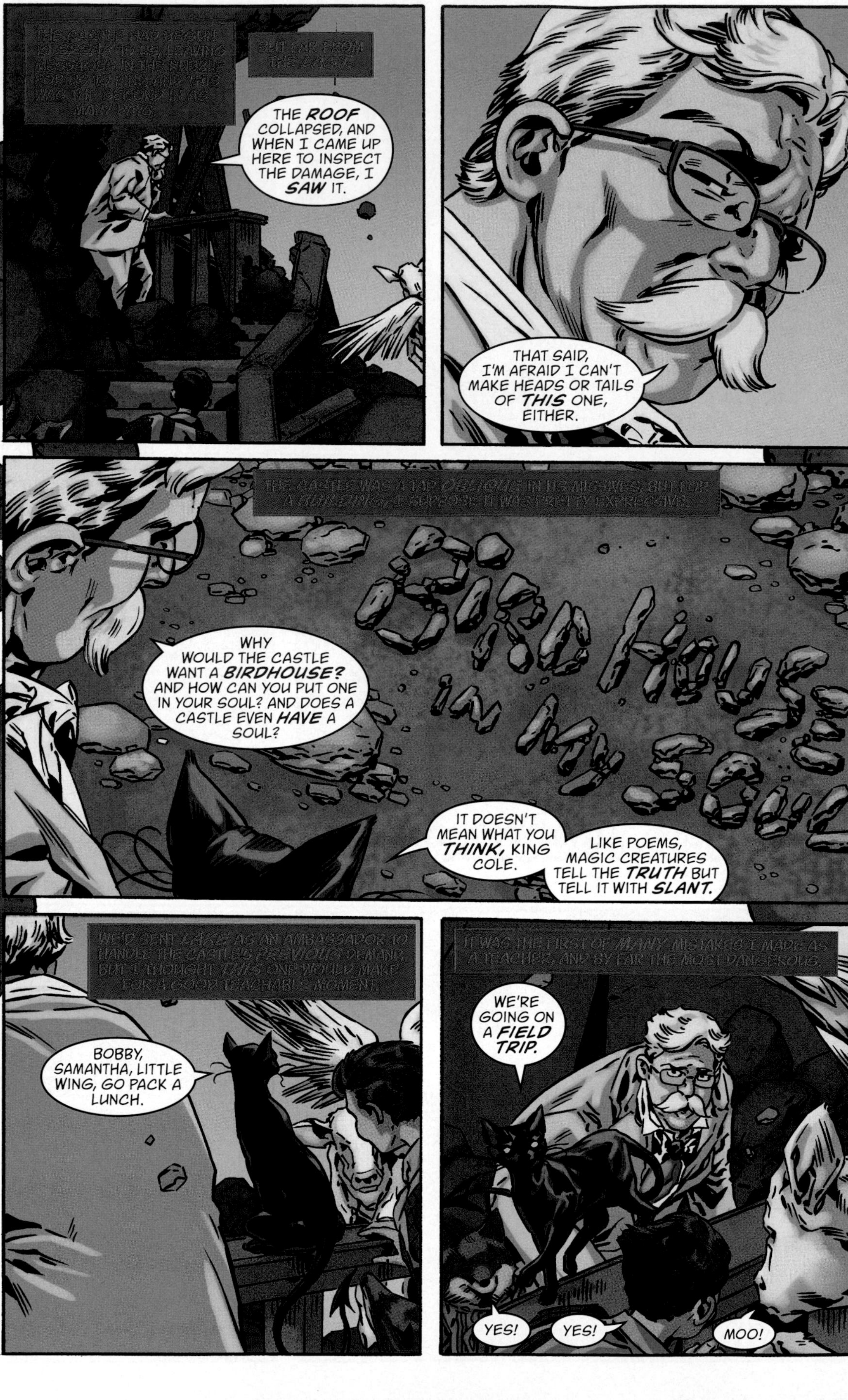
THE CASTLE HAD BEGUN TO SPEAK TO US, LEAVING MESSAGES IN THE RUBBLE FOR US TO FIND, AND THIS WAS THE SECOND IN AS MANY DAYS.
BUT FAR FROM THE LAST.
THE ROOF COLLAPSED, AND WHEN I CAME UP HERE TO INSPECT THE DAMAGE, I SAW IT.
THAT SAID, I'M AFRAID I CAN'T MAKE HEADS OR TAILS OF THIS ONE, EITHER.
THE CASTLE WAS A TAD OBLIQUE IN ITS MISSIVES, BUT FOR A BUILDING, I SUPPOSE IT WAS PRETTY EXPRESSIVE.
BIRD HOUSE IN MY SOUL
WHY WOULD THE CASTLE WANT A BIRDHOUSE? AND HOW CAN YOU PUT ONE IN YOUR SOUL? AND DOES A CASTLE EVEN HAVE A SOUL?
IT DOESN'T MEAN WHAT YOU THINK, KING COLE.
LIKE POEMS, MAGIC CREATURES TELL THE TRUTH BUT TELL IT WITH SLANT.
WE'D SENT LAKE AS AN AMBASSADOR TO HANDLE THE CASTLE'S PREVIOUS DEMAND, BUT I THOUGHT THIS ONE WOULD MAKE FOR A GOOD TEACHABLE MOMENT.
BOBBY, SAMANTHA, LITTLE WING, GO PACK A LUNCH.
IT WAS THE FIRST OF MANY MISTAKES I MADE AS A TEACHER, AND BY FAR THE MOST DANGEROUS.
WE'RE GOING ON A FIELD TRIP.
YES!
YES!
MOO!

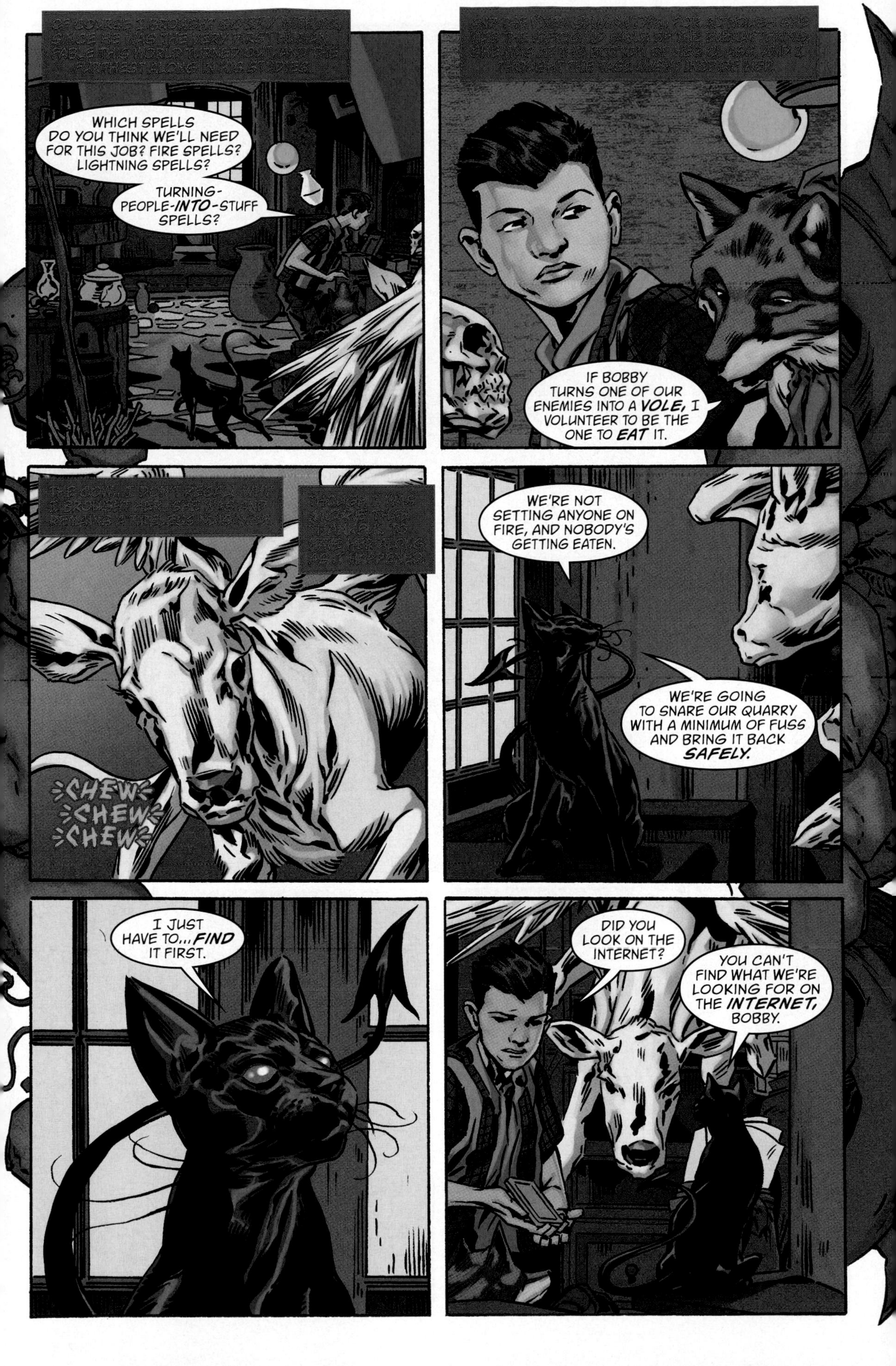
[redacted]
WHICH SPELLS DO YOU THINK WE'LL NEED FOR THIS JOB? FIRE SPELLS? LIGHTNING SPELLS?
TURNING-PEOPLE-INTO-STUFF SPELLS?
[redacted]
IF BOBBY TURNS ONE OF OUR ENEMIES INTO A VOLE, I VOLUNTEER TO BE THE ONE TO EAT IT.
[redacted]
[redacted]
CHEW CHEW CHEW
WE'RE NOT SETTING ANYONE ON FIRE, AND NOBODY'S GETTING EATEN.
WE'RE GOING TO SNARE OUR QUARRY WITH A MINIMUM OF FUSS AND BRING IT BACK SAFELY.
I JUST HAVE TO... FIND IT FIRST.
DID YOU LOOK ON THE INTERNET?
YOU CAN'T FIND WHAT WE'RE LOOKING FOR ON THE INTERNET, BOBBY.

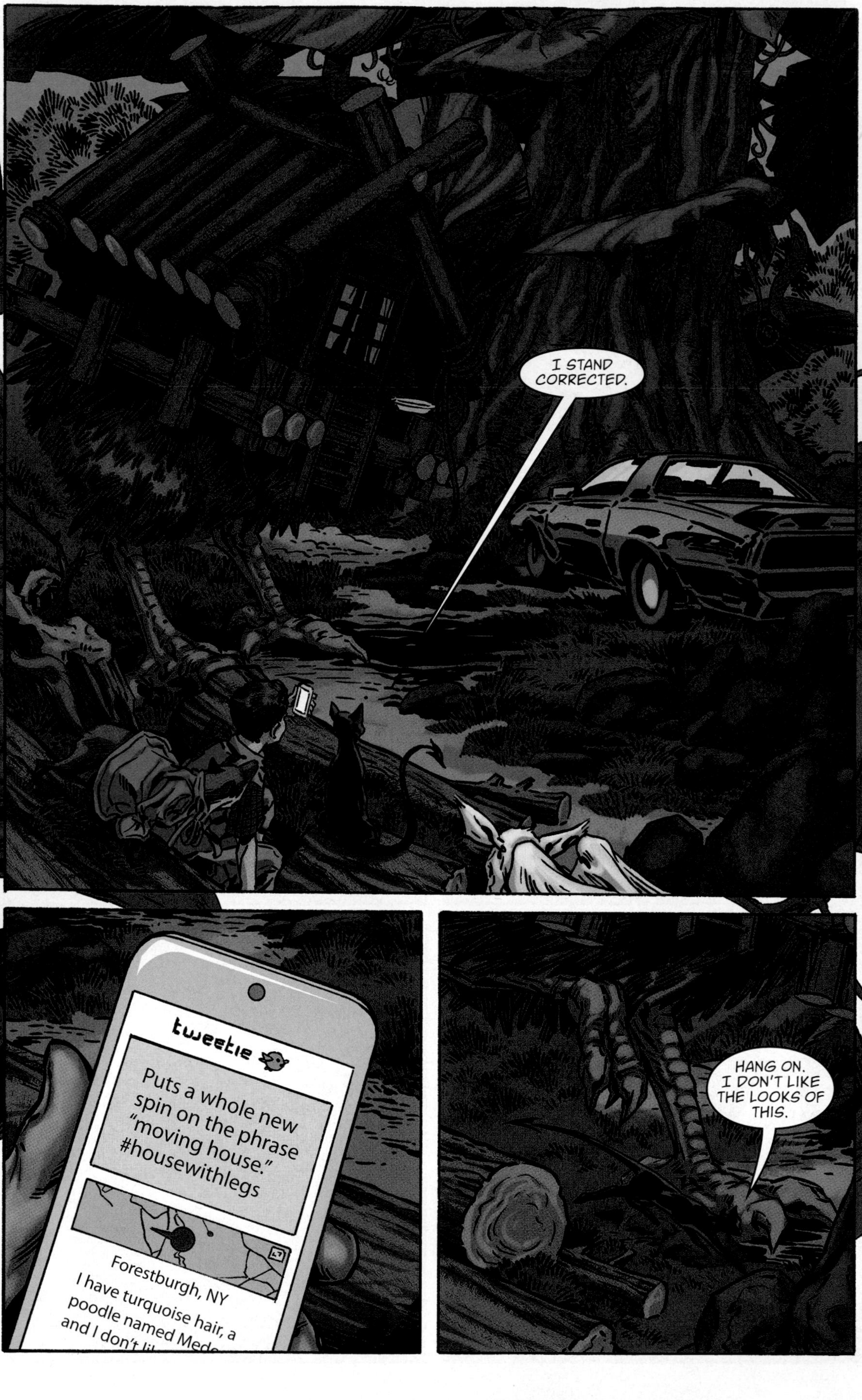
I STAND CORRECTED.
tweetie
Puts a whole new spin on the phrase "moving house." #housewithlegs
Forestburgh, NY
I have turquoise hair, a
HANG ON. I DON'T LIKE THE LOOKS OF THIS.

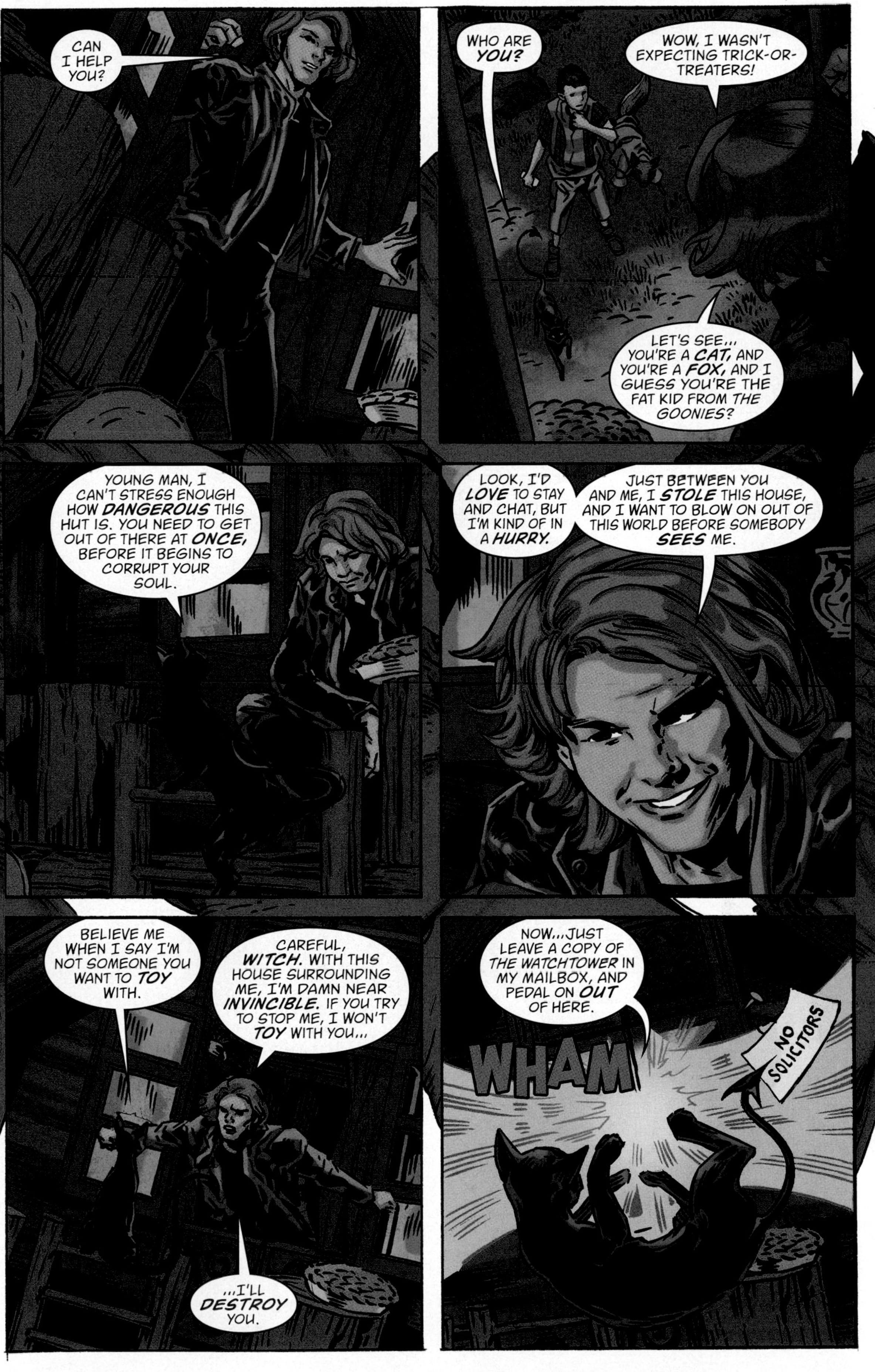
CAN I HELP YOU?
WHO ARE YOU?
WOW, I WASN'T EXPECTING TRICK-OR-TREATERS!
LET'S SEE... YOU'RE A CAT, AND YOU'RE A FOX, AND I GUESS YOU'RE THE FAT KID FROM THE GOONIES?
YOUNG MAN, I CAN'T STRESS ENOUGH HOW DANGEROUS THIS HUT IS. YOU NEED TO GET OUT OF THERE AT ONCE, BEFORE IT BEGINS TO CORRUPT YOUR SOUL.
LOOK, I'D LOVE TO STAY AND CHAT, BUT I'M KIND OF IN A HURRY.
JUST BETWEEN YOU AND ME, I STOLE THIS HOUSE, AND I WANT TO BLOW ON OUT OF THIS WORLD BEFORE SOMEBODY SEES ME.
BELIEVE ME WHEN I SAY I'M NOT SOMEONE YOU WANT TO TOY WITH.
CAREFUL, WITCH. WITH THIS HOUSE SURROUNDING ME, I'M DAMN NEAR INVINCIBLE. IF YOU TRY TO STOP ME, I WON'T TOY WITH YOU...
...I'LL DESTROY YOU.
NOW...JUST LEAVE A COPY OF THE WATCHTOWER IN MY MAILBOX, AND PEDAL ON OUT OF HERE.
WHAM
NO SOLICITORS

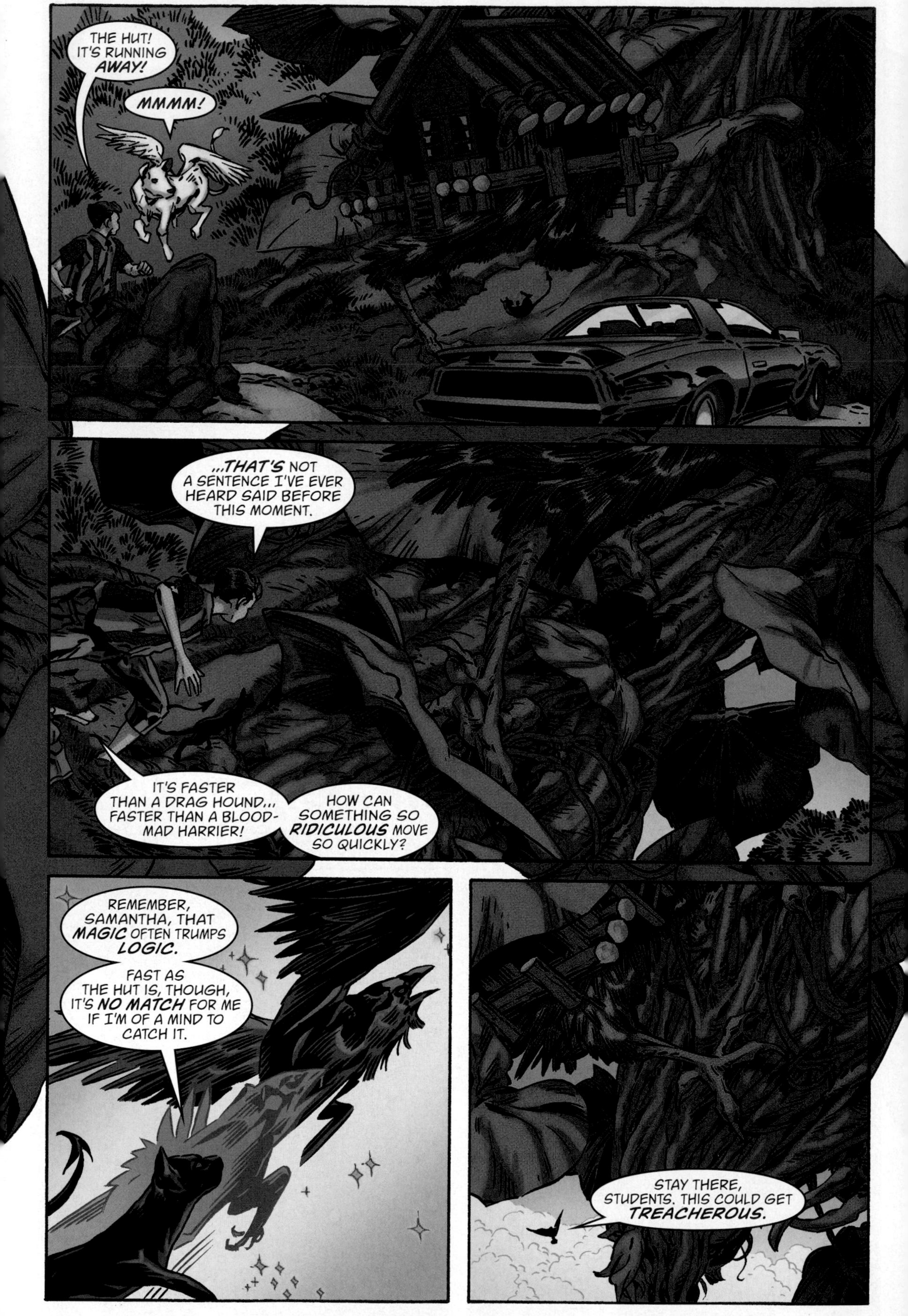
THE HUT! IT'S RUNNING AWAY!
MMMM!
...THAT'S NOT A SENTENCE I'VE EVER HEARD SAID BEFORE THIS MOMENT.
IT'S FASTER THAN A DRAG HOUND... FASTER THAN A BLOOD-MAD HARRIER!
HOW CAN SOMETHING SO RIDICULOUS MOVE SO QUICKLY?
REMEMBER, SAMANTHA, THAT MAGIC OFTEN TRUMPS LOGIC.
FAST AS THE HUT IS, THOUGH, IT'S NO MATCH FOR ME IF I'M OF A MIND TO CATCH IT.
STAY THERE, STUDENTS. THIS COULD GET TREACHEROUS.

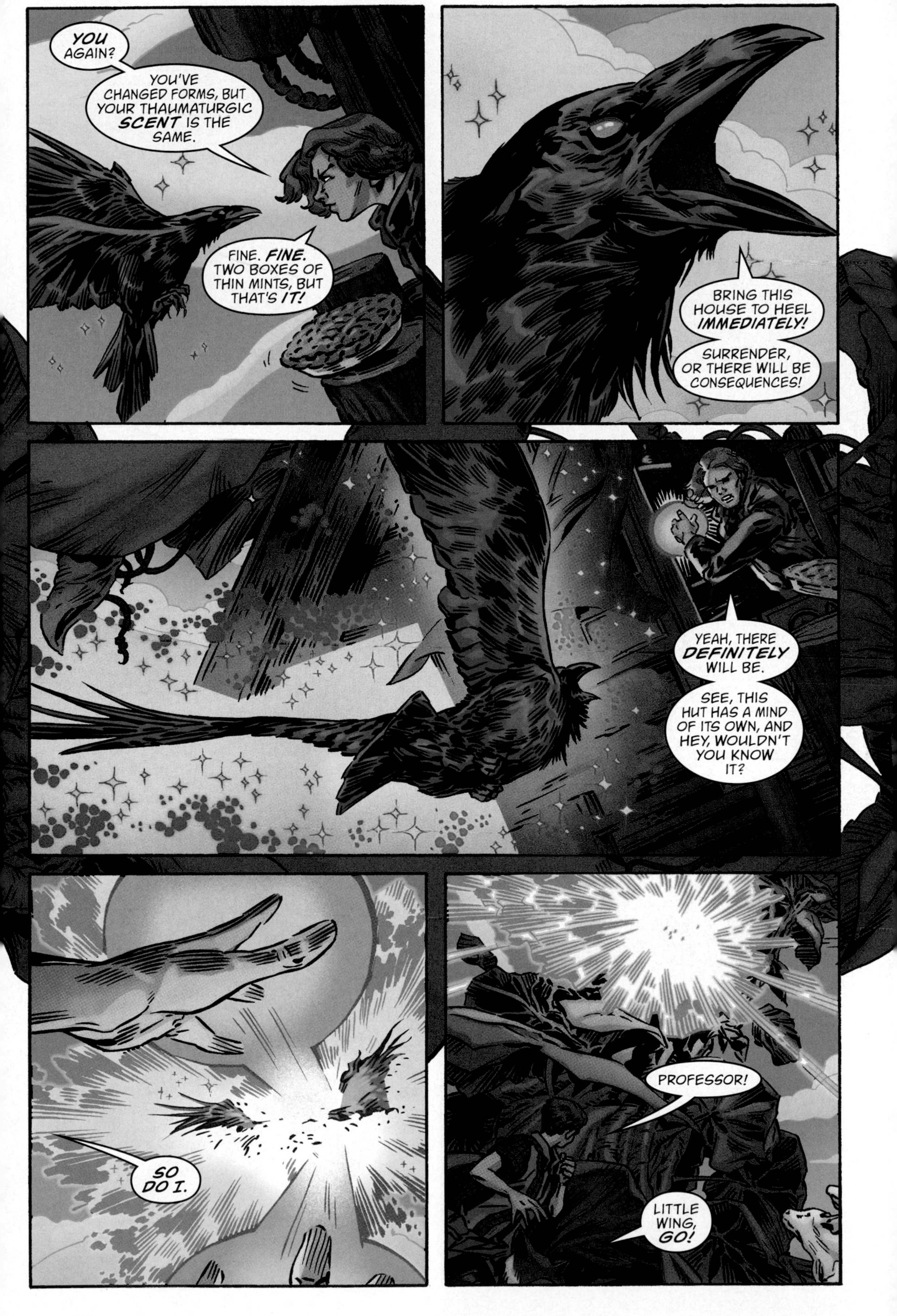
YOU AGAIN?
YOU'VE CHANGED FORMS, BUT YOUR THAUMATURGIC SCENT IS THE SAME.
FINE. FINE. TWO BOXES OF THIN MINTS, BUT THAT'S IT!
BRING THIS HOUSE TO HEEL IMMEDIATELY!
SURRENDER, OR THERE WILL BE CONSEQUENCES!
YEAH, THERE DEFINITELY WILL BE.
SEE, THIS HUT HAS A MIND OF ITS OWN, AND HEY, WOULDN'T YOU KNOW IT?
SO DO I.
PROFESSOR!
LITTLE WING, GO!

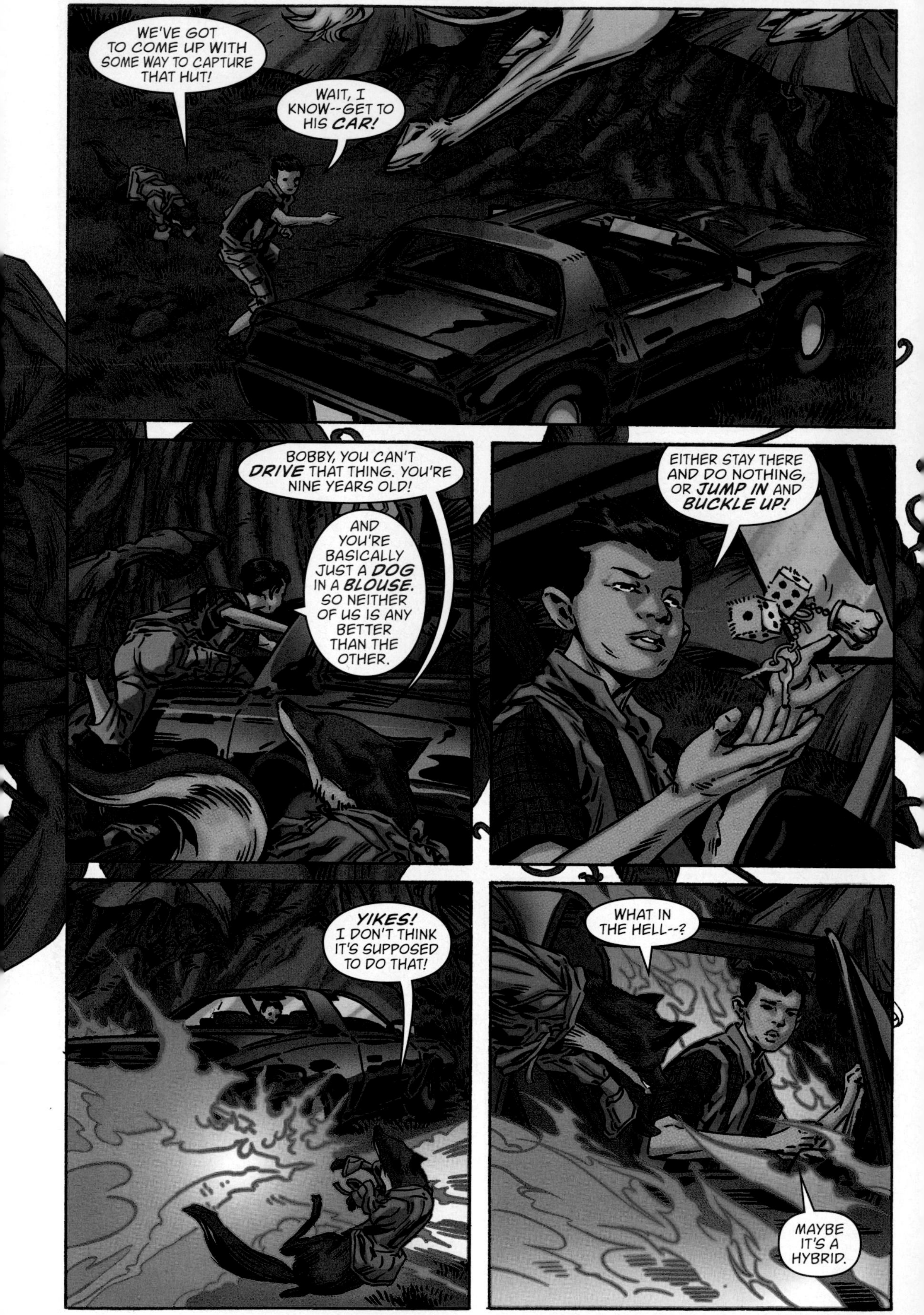
WE'VE GOT TO COME UP WITH SOME WAY TO CAPTURE THAT HUT!
WAIT, I KNOW--GET TO HIS CAR!
BOBBY, YOU CAN'T DRIVE THAT THING. YOU'RE NINE YEARS OLD!
AND YOU'RE BASICALLY JUST A DOG IN A BLOUSE. SO NEITHER OF US IS ANY BETTER THAN THE OTHER.
EITHER STAY THERE AND DO NOTHING, OR JUMP IN AND BUCKLE UP!
YIKES! I DON'T THINK IT'S SUPPOSED TO DO THAT!
WHAT IN THE HELL--?
MAYBE IT'S A HYBRID.

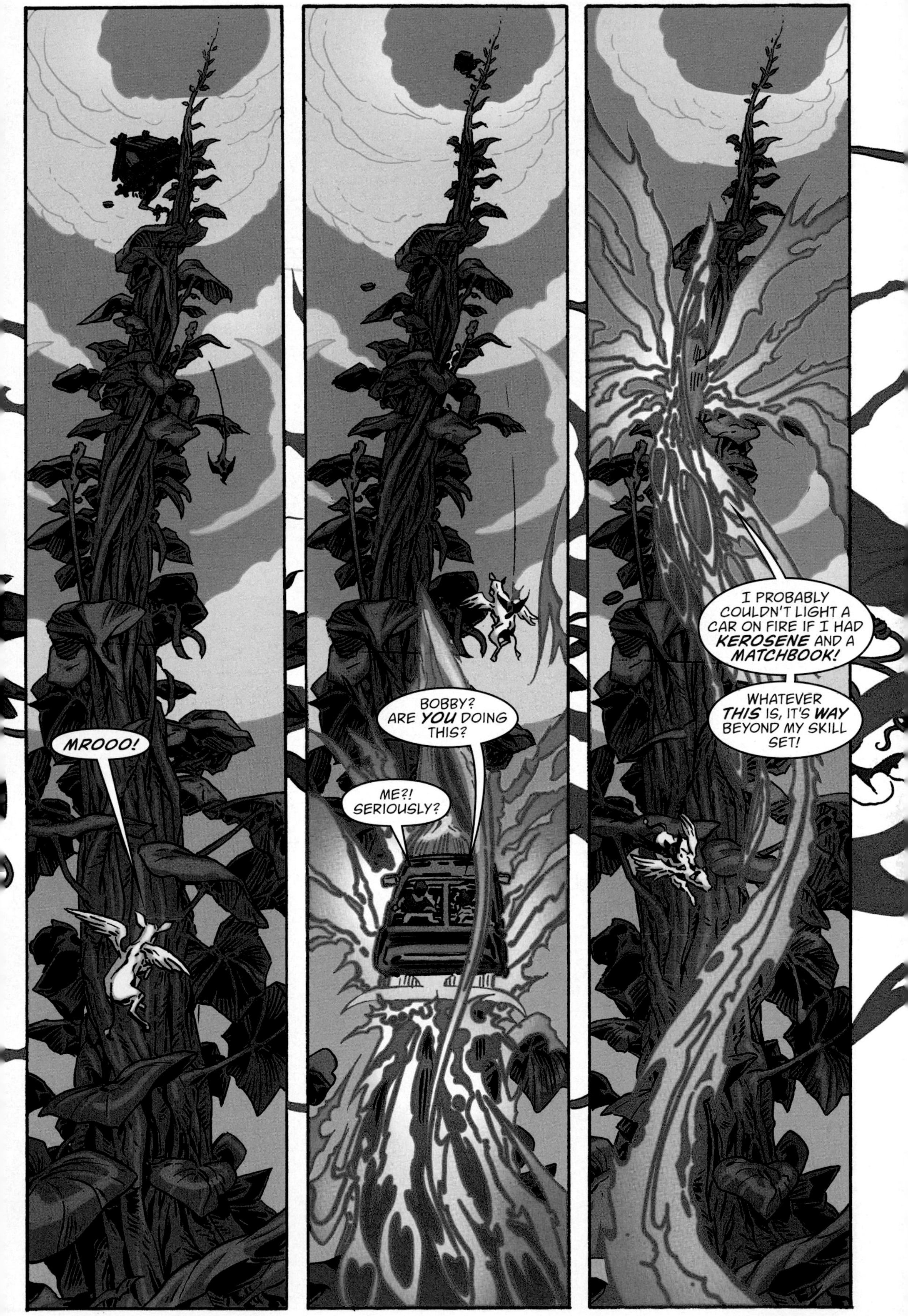
MROOO!
BOBBY? ARE YOU DOING THIS?
ME?! SERIOUSLY?
I PROBABLY COULDN'T LIGHT A CAR ON FIRE IF I HAD KEROSENE AND A MATCHBOOK!
WHATEVER THIS IS, IT'S WAY BEYOND MY SKILL SET!

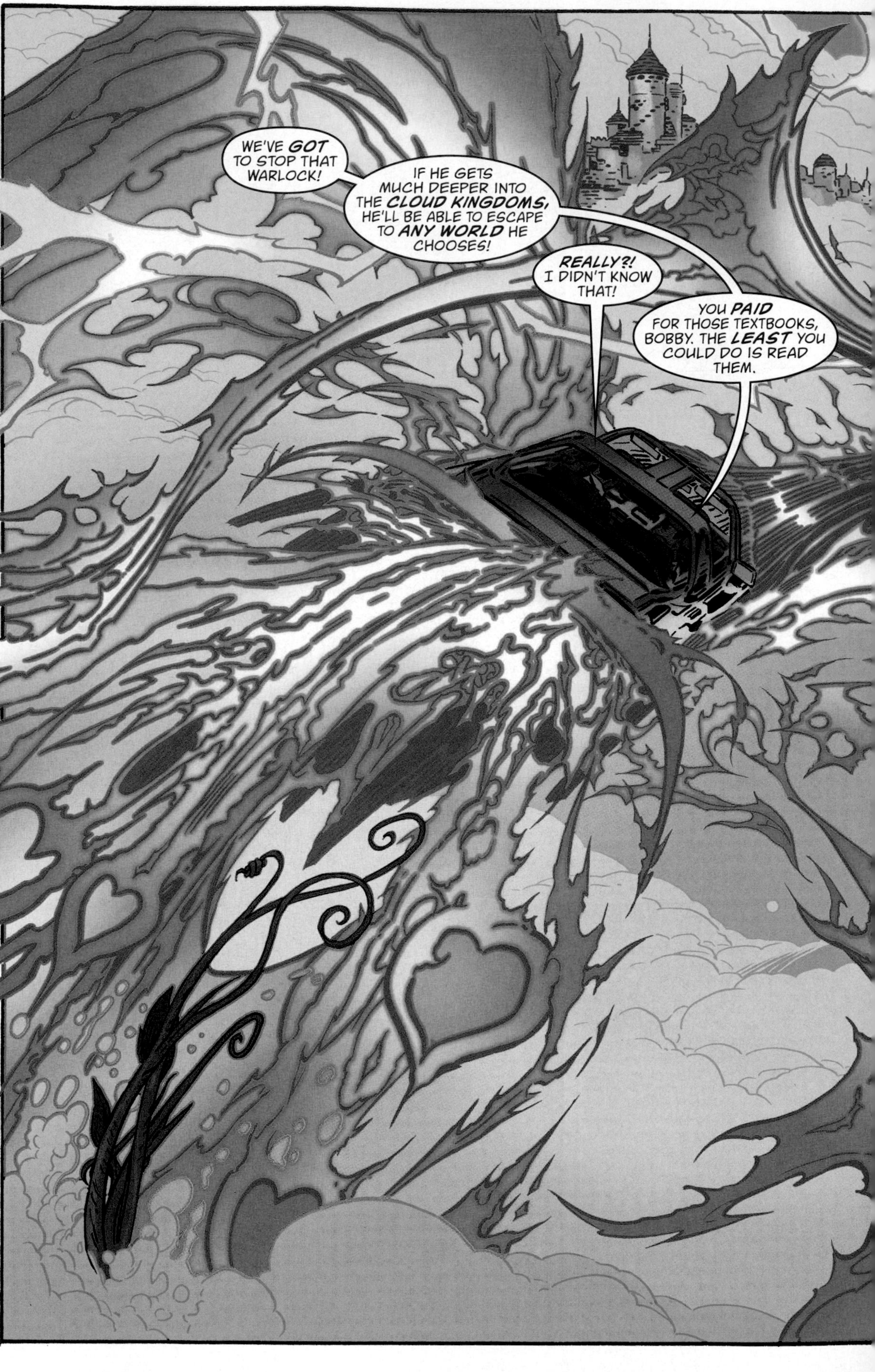
WE'VE GOT TO STOP THAT WARLOCK!
IF HE GETS MUCH DEEPER INTO THE CLOUD KINGDOMS, HE'LL BE ABLE TO ESCAPE TO ANY WORLD HE CHOOSES!
REALLY?! I DIDN'T KNOW THAT!
YOU PAID FOR THOSE TEXTBOOKS, BOBBY. THE LEAST YOU COULD DO IS READ THEM.

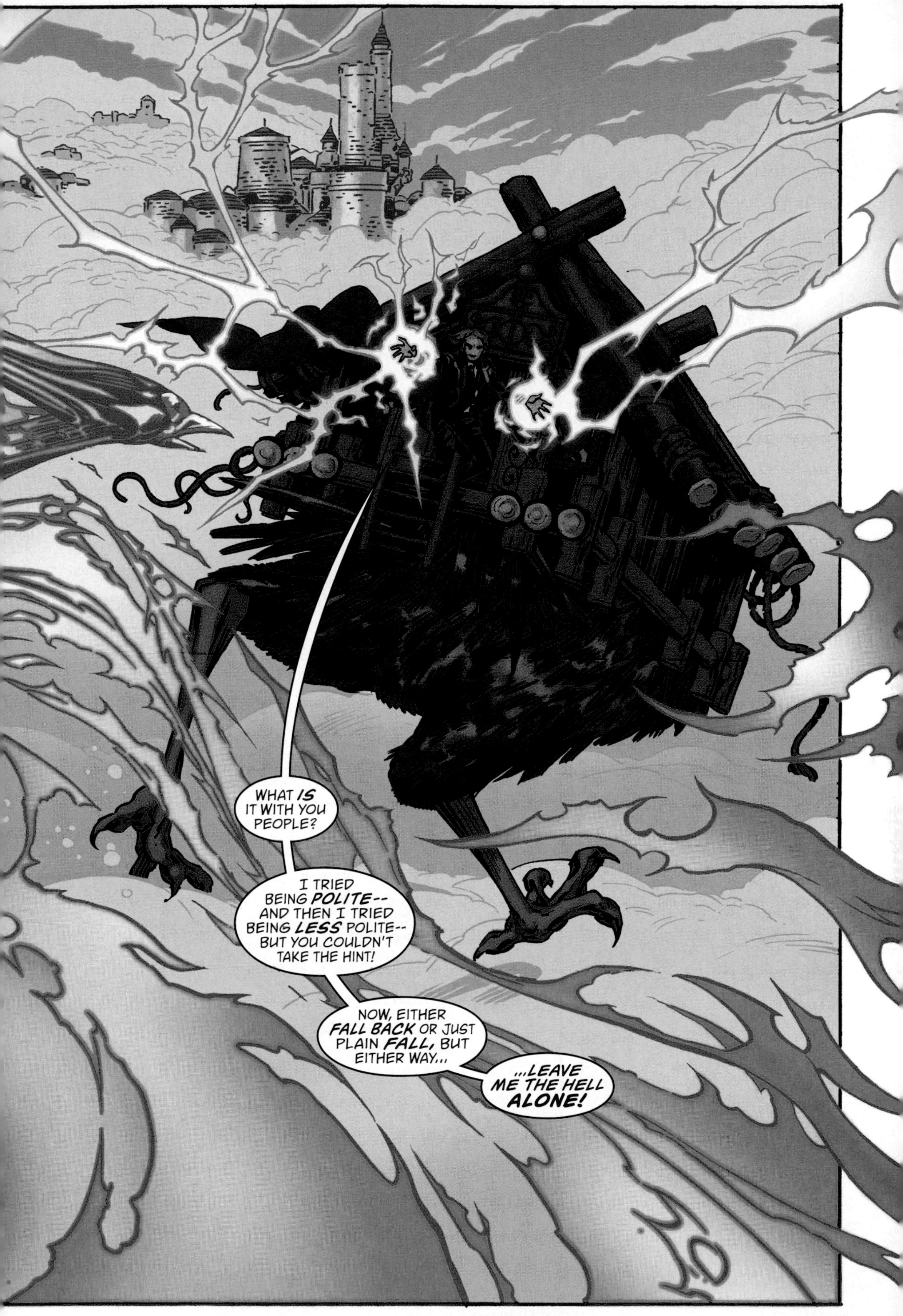
WHAT IS IT WITH YOU PEOPLE?
I TRIED BEING POLITE-- AND THEN I TRIED BEING LESS POLITE-- BUT YOU COULDN'T TAKE THE HINT!
NOW, EITHER FALL BACK OR JUST PLAIN FALL, BUT EITHER WAY...
...LEAVE ME THE HELL ALONE!

BOBBY, GET *DOWN!*

WHOA!

THAT WAS *TOO CLOSE.* WE'RE OUT OF OUR DEPTH HERE.

HE'S WIDENING THE GAP WITH EVERY STEP HE TAKES. THERE'S NO *WAY* WE'LL EVER CATCH HIM.

ON THEIR OWN? NO, LITTLE WING, I DON'T BELIEVE THEY CAN.

BUT, INJURED THOUGH I AM, PERHAPS I CAN *ASSIST* FROM HERE.

WAIT, I KNOW! I'LL CAST THE *ACCELERATION SPELL* WE LEARNED IN CLASS!

I THINK *"LEARNED"* MIGHT BE OVERSELLING IT.

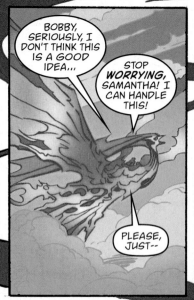

BOBBY, SERIOUSLY, I DON'T THINK THIS IS A GOOD IDEA...

STOP *WORRYING,* SAMANTHA! I CAN HANDLE THIS!

PLEASE, JUST--

FLICKER, BRIGHT WING, QUICK AND FRIGHTENING, HEIGHTENING HASTE LIKE SLICKENED LIGHTNING!

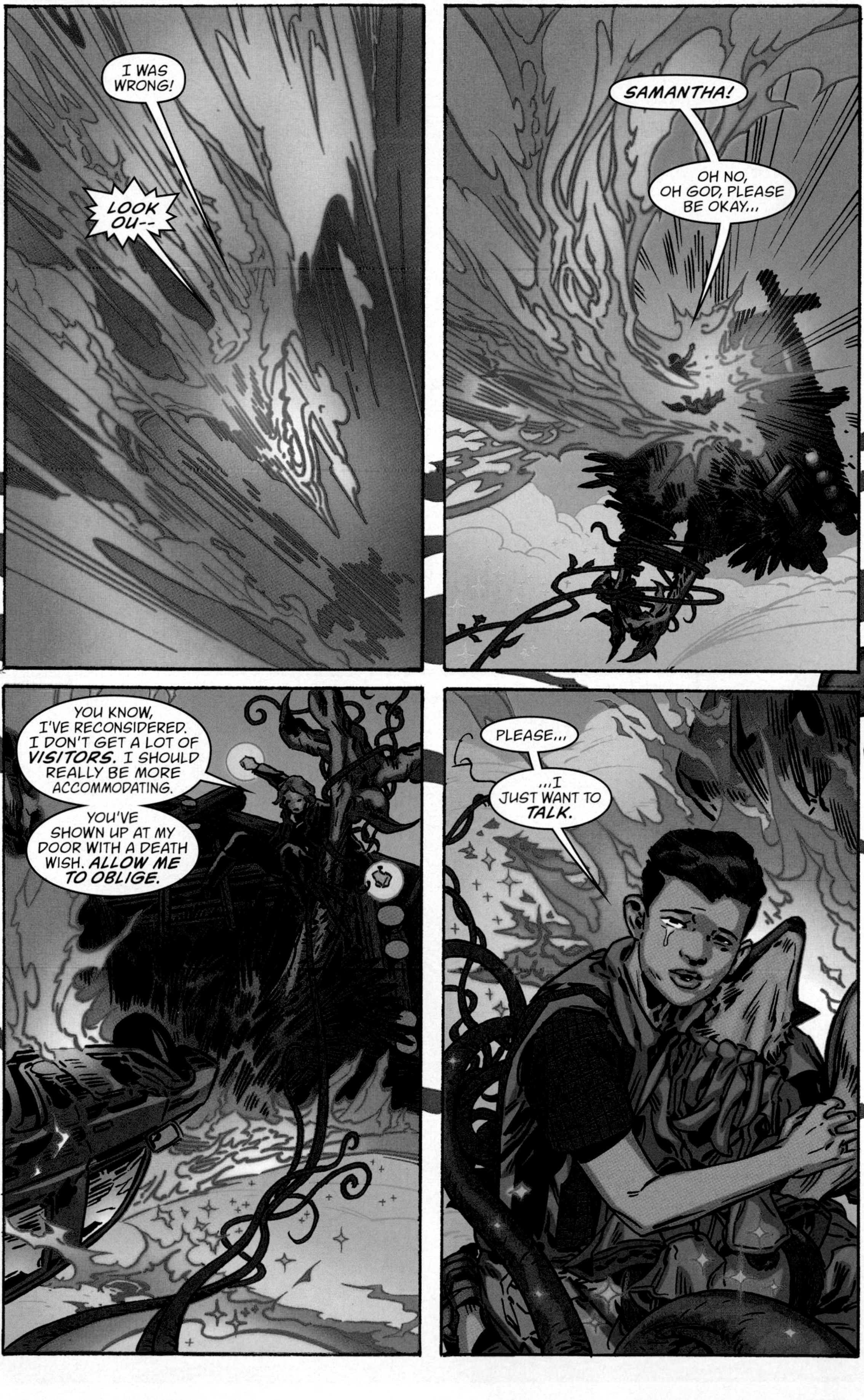
I WAS WRONG!
LOOK OU--
SAMANTHA!
OH NO, OH GOD, PLEASE BE OKAY...
YOU KNOW, I'VE RECONSIDERED. I DON'T GET A LOT OF VISITORS. I SHOULD REALLY BE MORE ACCOMMODATING.
YOU'VE SHOWN UP AT MY DOOR WITH A DEATH WISH. ALLOW ME TO OBLIGE.
PLEASE...
...I JUST WANT TO TALK.

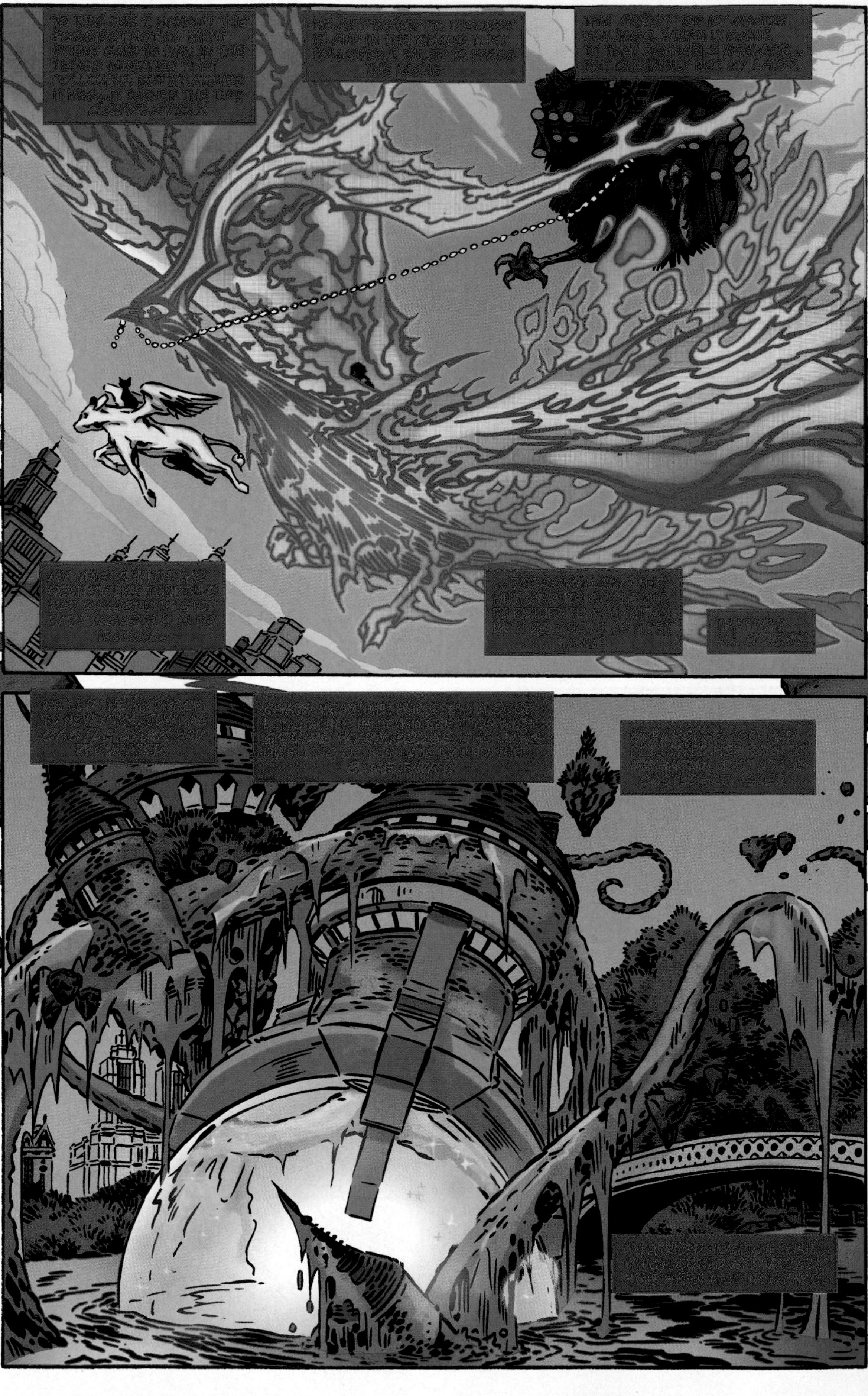
[redacted]
[redacted]
[redacted]
[redacted]
[redacted]
[redacted]
[redacted]
[redacted]
[redacted]
[redacted]

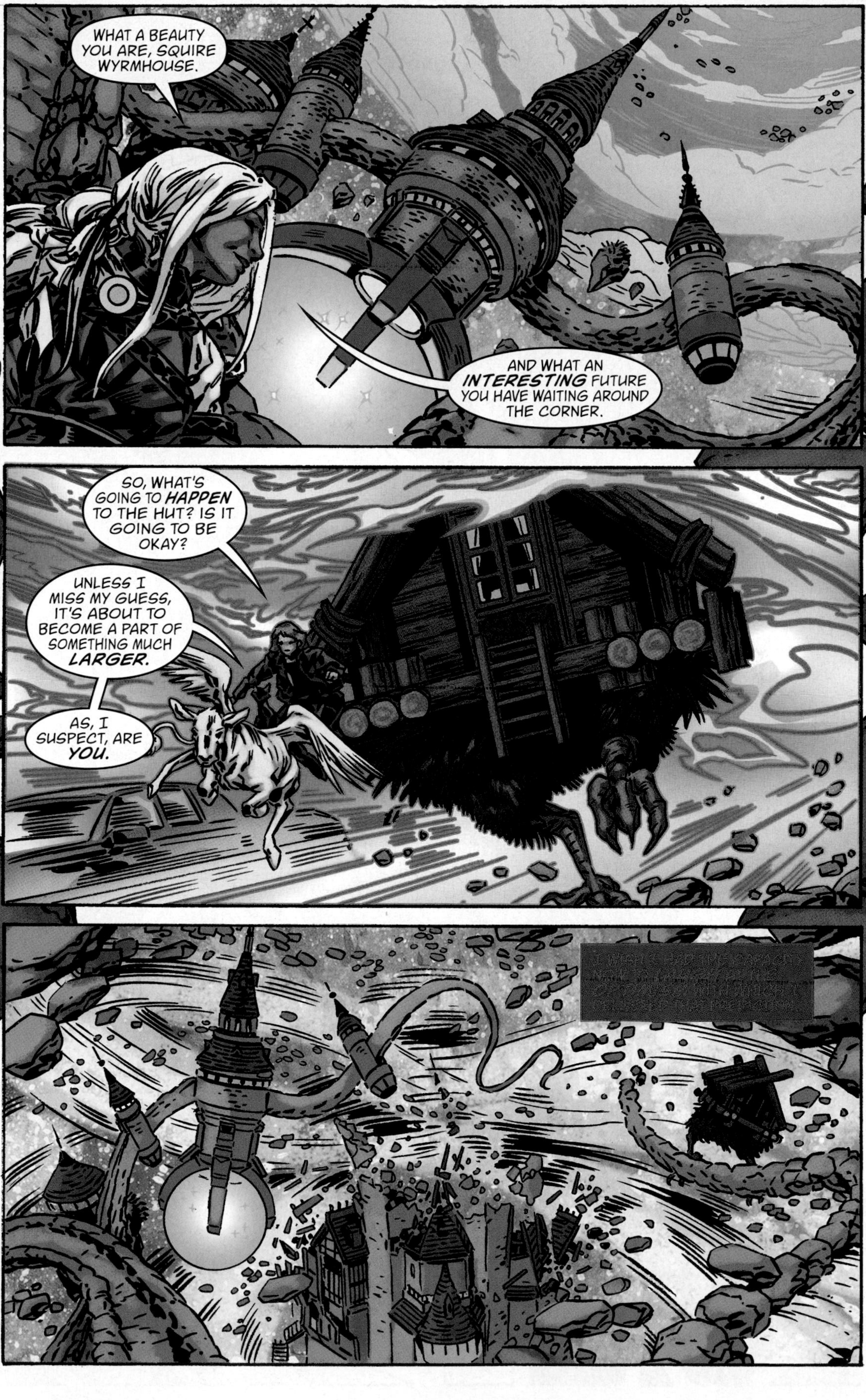
WHAT A BEAUTY YOU ARE, SQUIRE WYRMHOUSE.
AND WHAT AN INTERESTING FUTURE YOU HAVE WAITING AROUND THE CORNER.
SO, WHAT'S GOING TO HAPPEN TO THE HUT? IS IT GOING TO BE OKAY?
UNLESS I MISS MY GUESS, IT'S ABOUT TO BECOME A PART OF SOMETHING MUCH LARGER.
AS, I SUSPECT, ARE YOU.

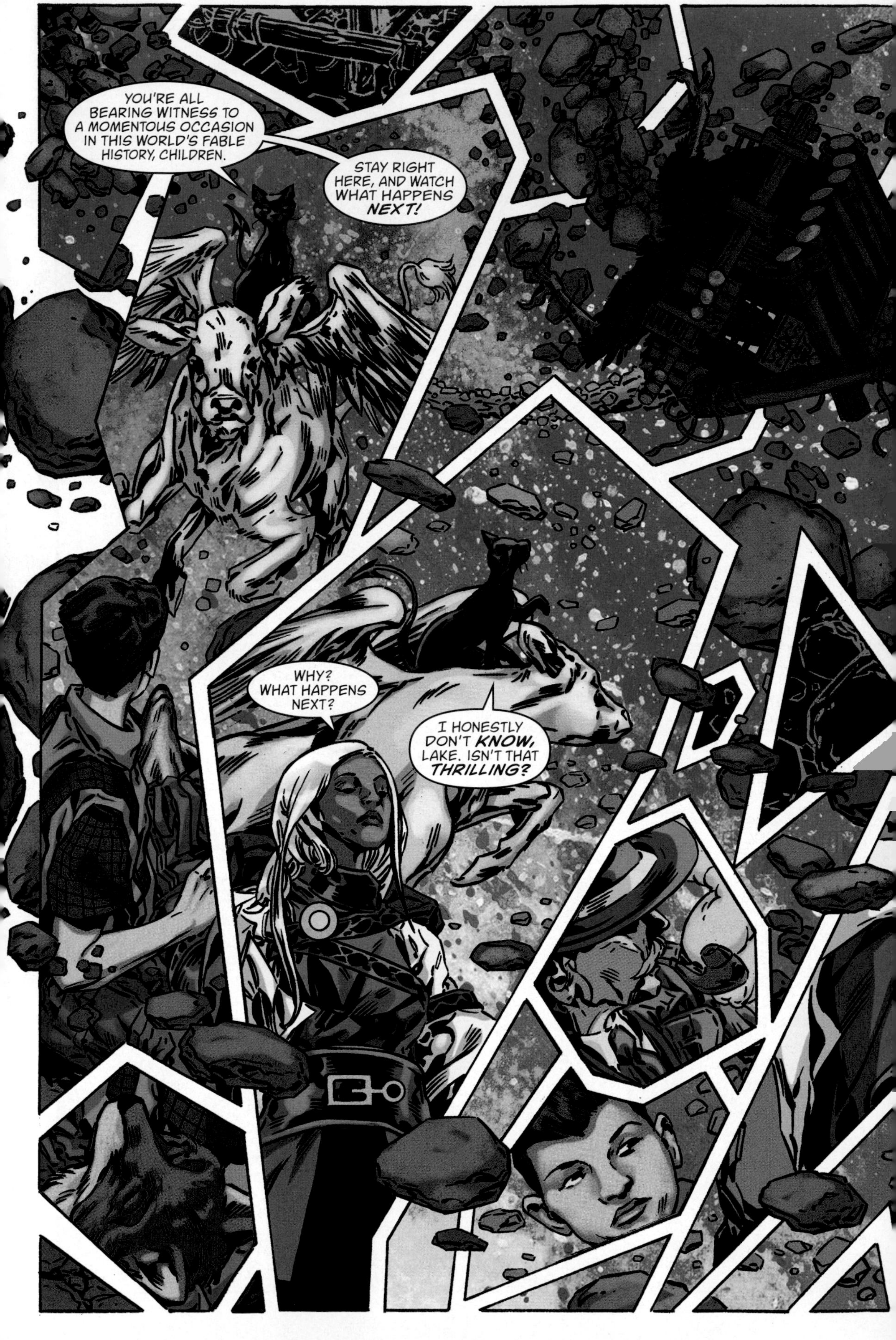
YOU'RE ALL BEARING WITNESS TO A MOMENTOUS OCCASION IN THIS WORLD'S FABLE HISTORY, CHILDREN.
STAY RIGHT HERE, AND WATCH WHAT HAPPENS NEXT!
WHY? WHAT HAPPENS NEXT?
I HONESTLY DON'T KNOW, LAKE. ISN'T THAT THRILLING?

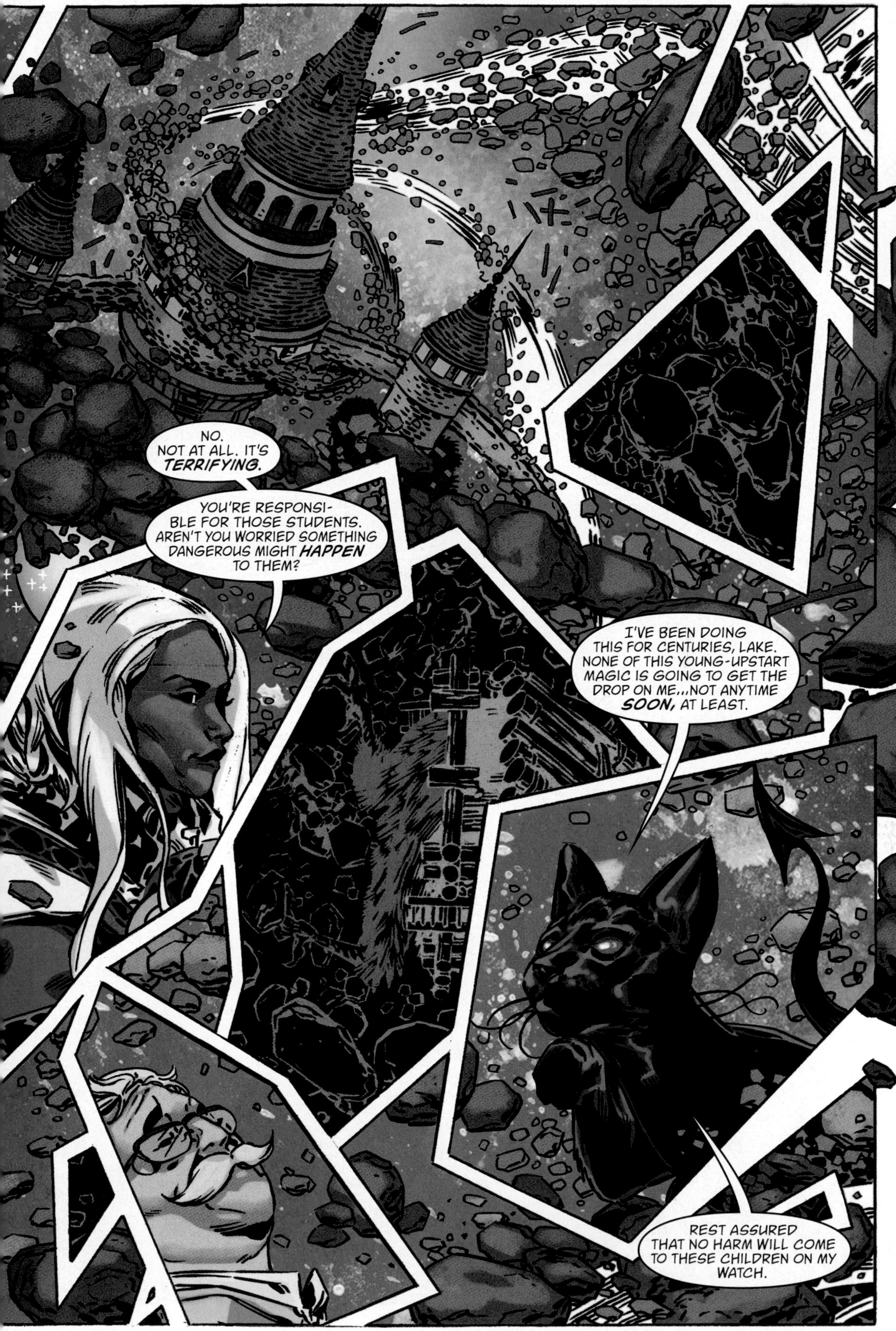
NO. NOT AT ALL. IT'S TERRIFYING.
YOU'RE RESPONSI-BLE FOR THOSE STUDENTS. AREN'T YOU WORRIED SOMETHING DANGEROUS MIGHT HAPPEN TO THEM?
I'VE BEEN DOING THIS FOR CENTURIES, LAKE. NONE OF THIS YOUNG-UPSTART MAGIC IS GOING TO GET THE DROP ON ME...NOT ANYTIME SOON, AT LEAST.
REST ASSURED THAT NO HARM WILL COME TO THESE CHILDREN ON MY WATCH.

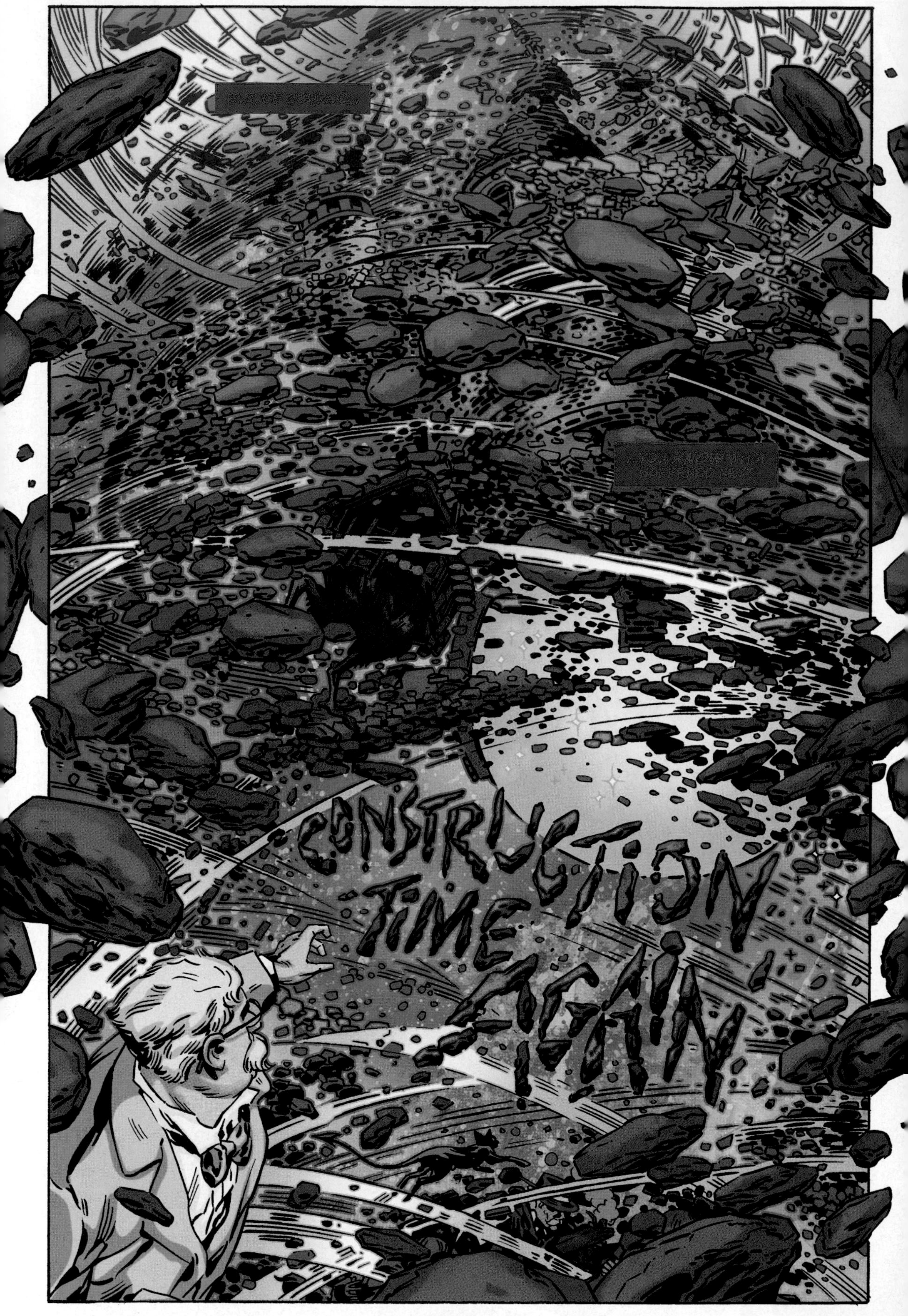
CONSTRUCTION TIME AGAIN

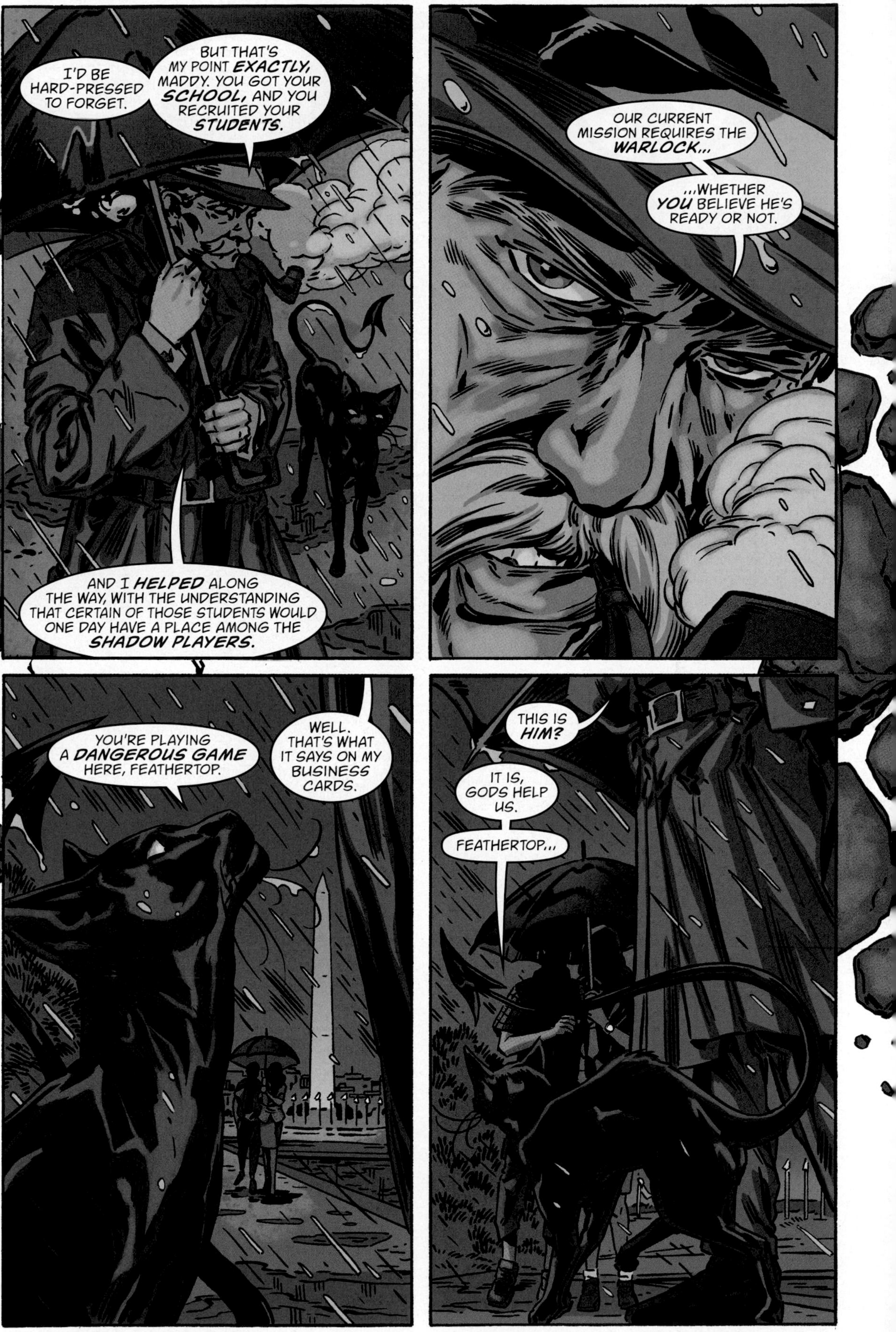
I'D BE HARD-PRESSED TO FORGET.
BUT THAT'S MY POINT EXACTLY, MADDY. YOU GOT YOUR SCHOOL, AND YOU RECRUITED YOUR STUDENTS.
AND I HELPED ALONG THE WAY, WITH THE UNDERSTANDING THAT CERTAIN OF THOSE STUDENTS WOULD ONE DAY HAVE A PLACE AMONG THE SHADOW PLAYERS.
OUR CURRENT MISSION REQUIRES THE WARLOCK...
...WHETHER YOU BELIEVE HE'S READY OR NOT.
YOU'RE PLAYING A DANGEROUS GAME HERE, FEATHERTOP.
WELL. THAT'S WHAT IT SAYS ON MY BUSINESS CARDS.
THIS IS HIM?
IT IS, GODS HELP US.
FEATHERTOP...

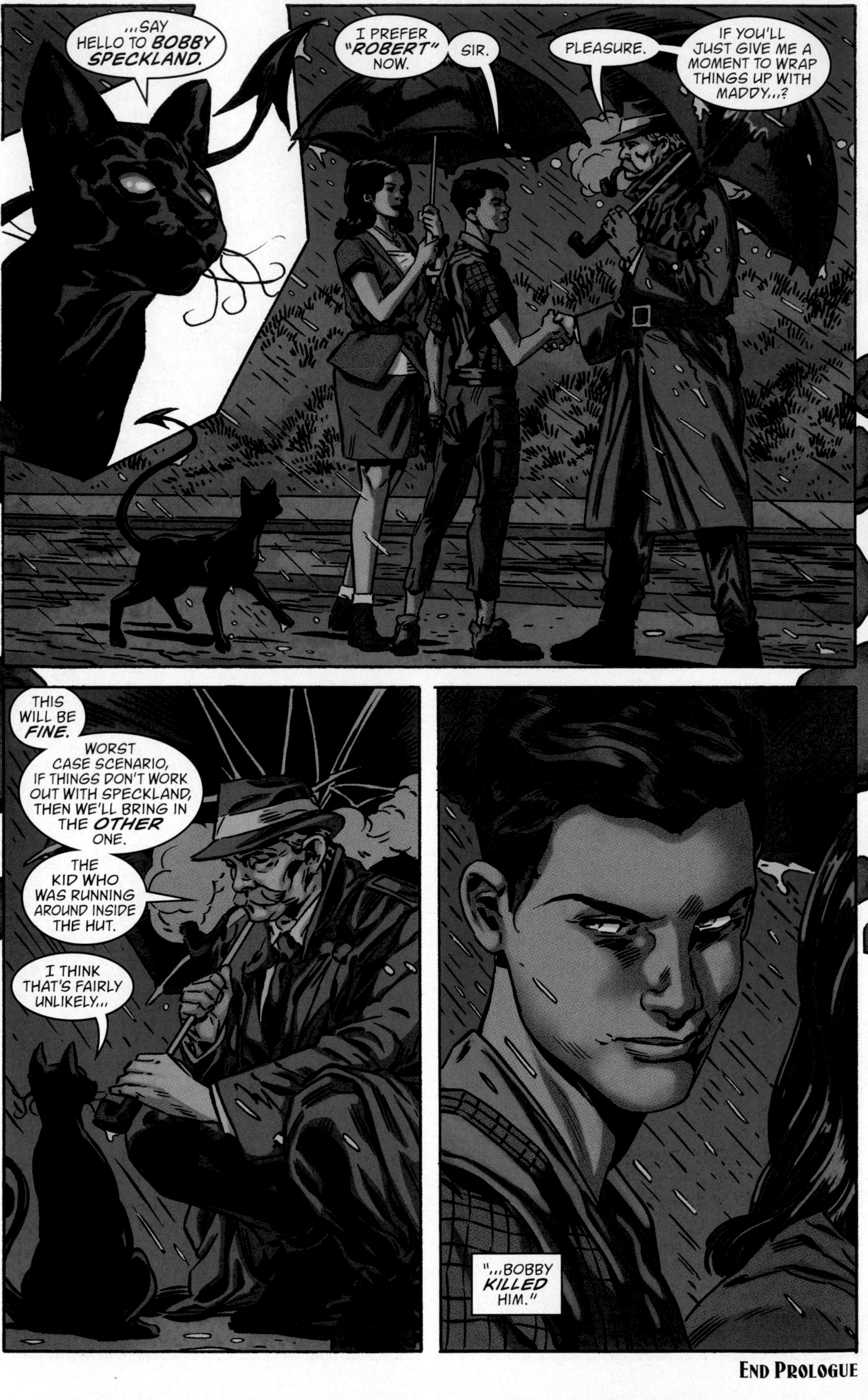
...SAY HELLO TO BOBBY SPECKLAND.
I PREFER "ROBERT" NOW.
SIR.
PLEASURE.
IF YOU'LL JUST GIVE ME A MOMENT TO WRAP THINGS UP WITH MADDY...?
THIS WILL BE FINE.
WORST CASE SCENARIO, IF THINGS DON'T WORK OUT WITH SPECKLAND, THEN WE'LL BRING IN THE OTHER ONE.
THE KID WHO WAS RUNNING AROUND INSIDE THE HUT.
I THINK THAT'S FAIRLY UNLIKELY...
"...BOBBY KILLED HIM."

End Prologue

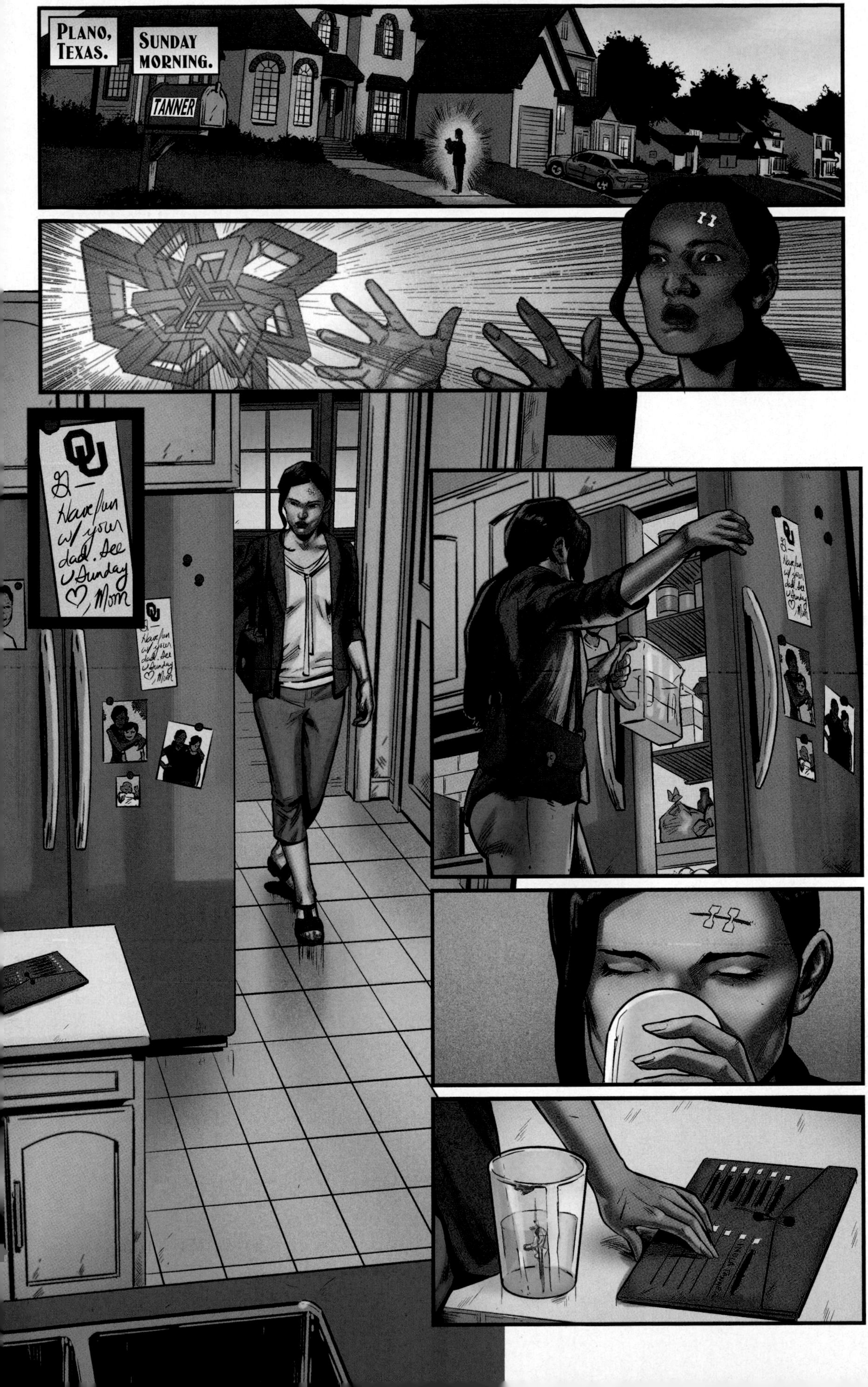
PLANO, TEXAS.
SUNDAY MORNING.
TANNER
OU
G—
Have fun w/ your dad. See u Sunday
♡, Mom

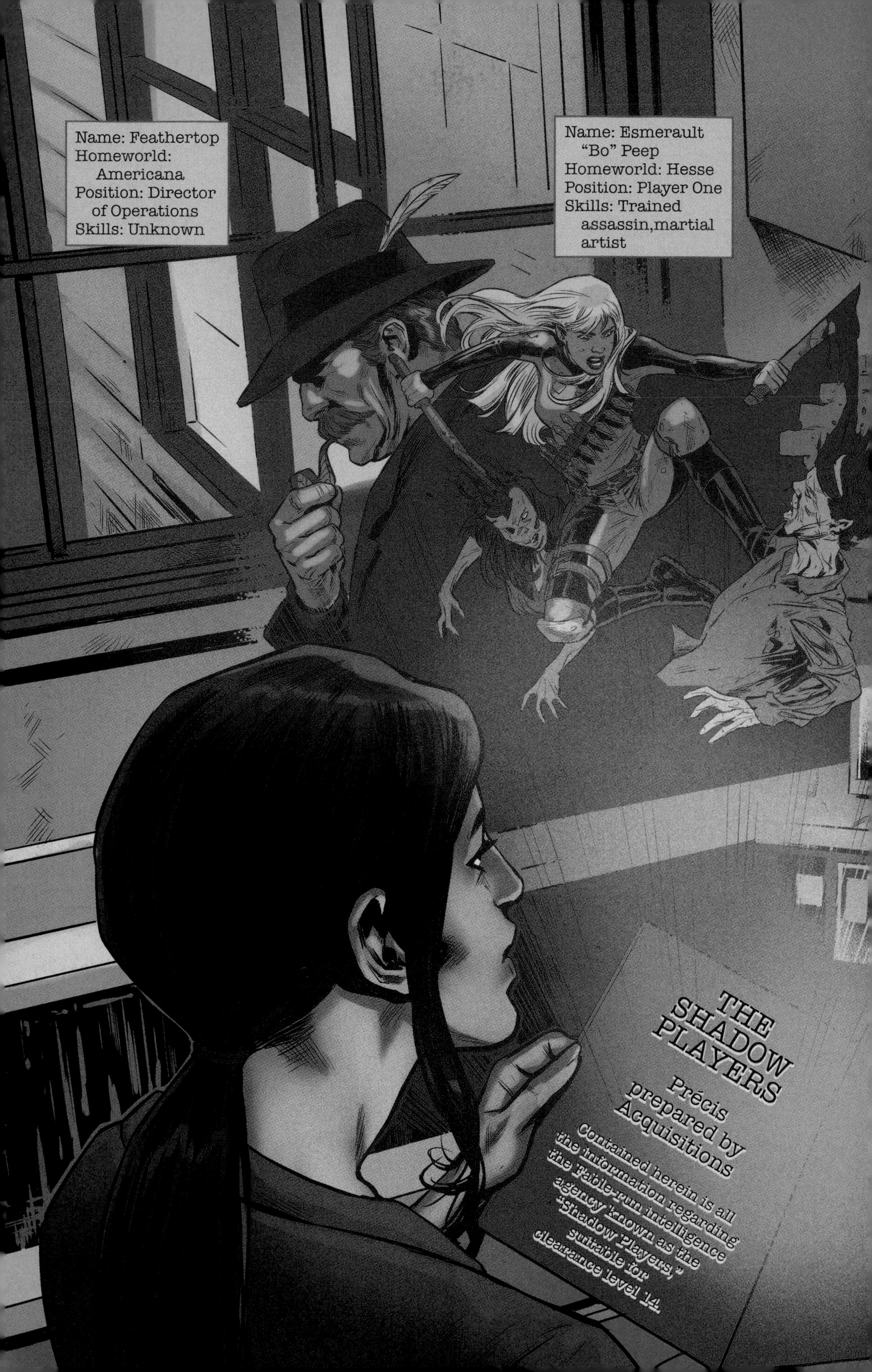
Name: Feathertop
Homeworld: Americana
Position: Director of Operations
Skills: Unknown
Name: Esmerault "Bo" Peep
Homeworld: Hesse
Position: Player One
Skills: Trained assassin,martial artist
THE SHADOW PLAYERS
Précis prepared by Acquisitions
Contained herein is all the information regarding the Fable-run intelligence agency known as the "Shadow Players," suitable for clearance level 14.

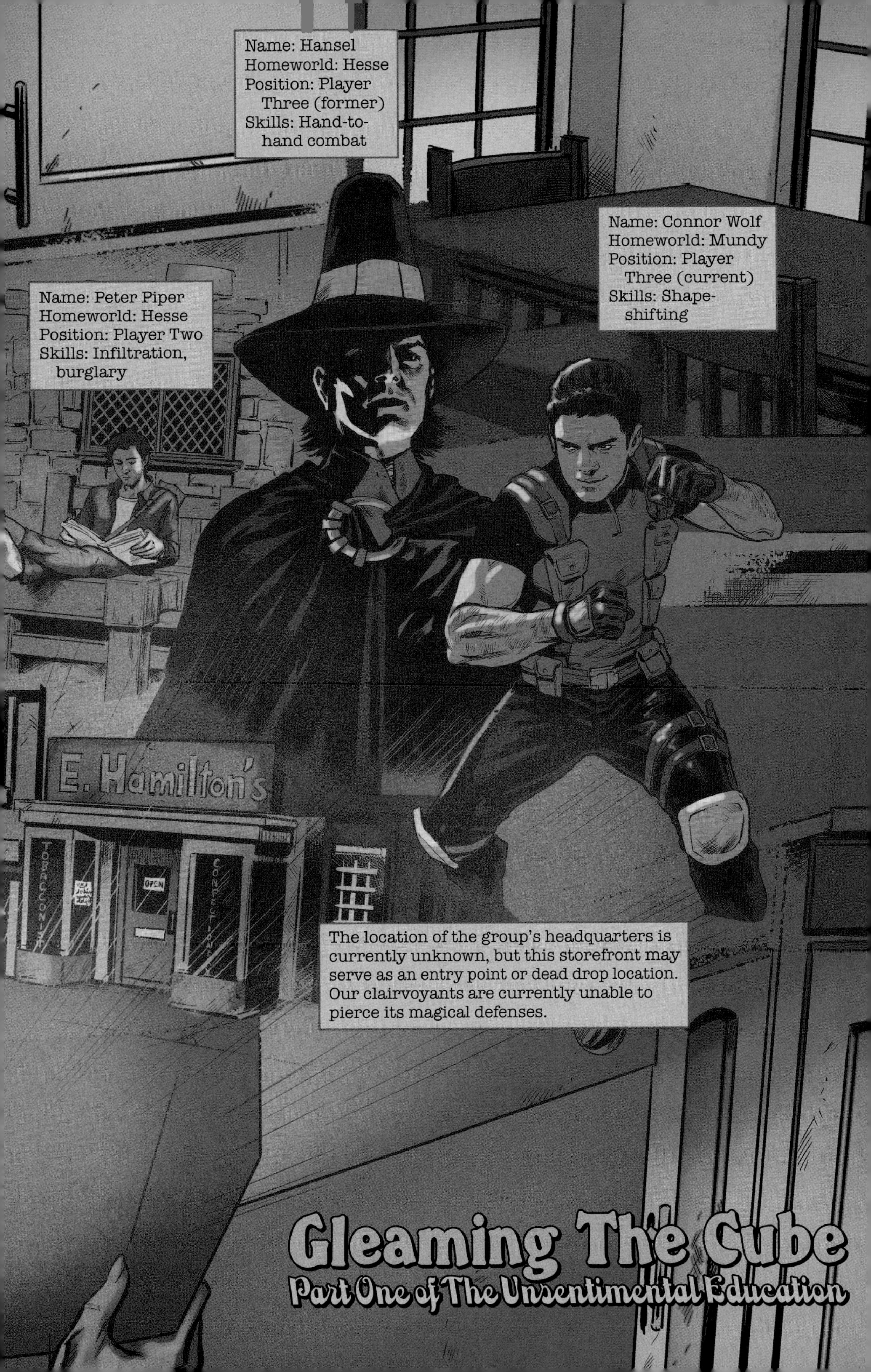
Name: Hansel
Homeworld: Hesse
Position: Player Three (former)
Skills: Hand-to-hand combat
Name: Peter Piper
Homeworld: Hesse
Position: Player Two
Skills: Infiltration, burglary
Name: Connor Wolf
Homeworld: Mundy
Position: Player Three (current)
Skills: Shape-shifting
E. Hamilton's
TOBACCONIST
OPEN
CONFECTIONER
The location of the group's headquarters is currently unknown, but this storefront may serve as an entry point or dead drop location. Our clairvoyants are currently unable to pierce its magical defenses.
Gleaming The Cube
Part One of The Unsentimental Education

MOM? IS THAT YOU?

WHAT ARE YOU *DOING* HERE?

HEY, MOM. NICE TO SEE YOU, TOO.

GARRETT?

WAIT. HAVE YOU BEEN HERE ALL *WEEKEND?*

DID HE AT LEAST *CALL?*

HE SENT ME A TEXT.

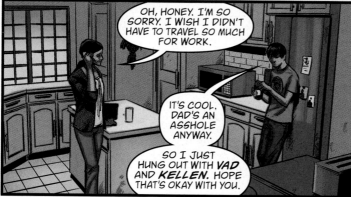

OH, HONEY. I'M SO SORRY. I WISH I DIDN'T HAVE TO TRAVEL SO MUCH FOR WORK.

IT'S COOL, DAD'S AN ASSHOLE ANYWAY.

SO I JUST HUNG OUT WITH *VAD* AND *KELLEN.* HOPE THAT'S OKAY WITH YOU.

OF *COURSE* IT'S OKAY.

HEY, I NEED TO RUN SOME ERRANDS. DO YOU WANT TO COME WITH?

NAH. I'LL PROBABLY JUST CHILL HERE.

YOU FUCKING PIECE OF *SHIT!* HOW *COULD* YOU?

YEAH? WELL, MAYBE HE'D SAY MORE THAN TWO WORDS TO YOU IF YOU ACTUALLY *SHOWED UP* EVERY ONCE IN A WHILE.

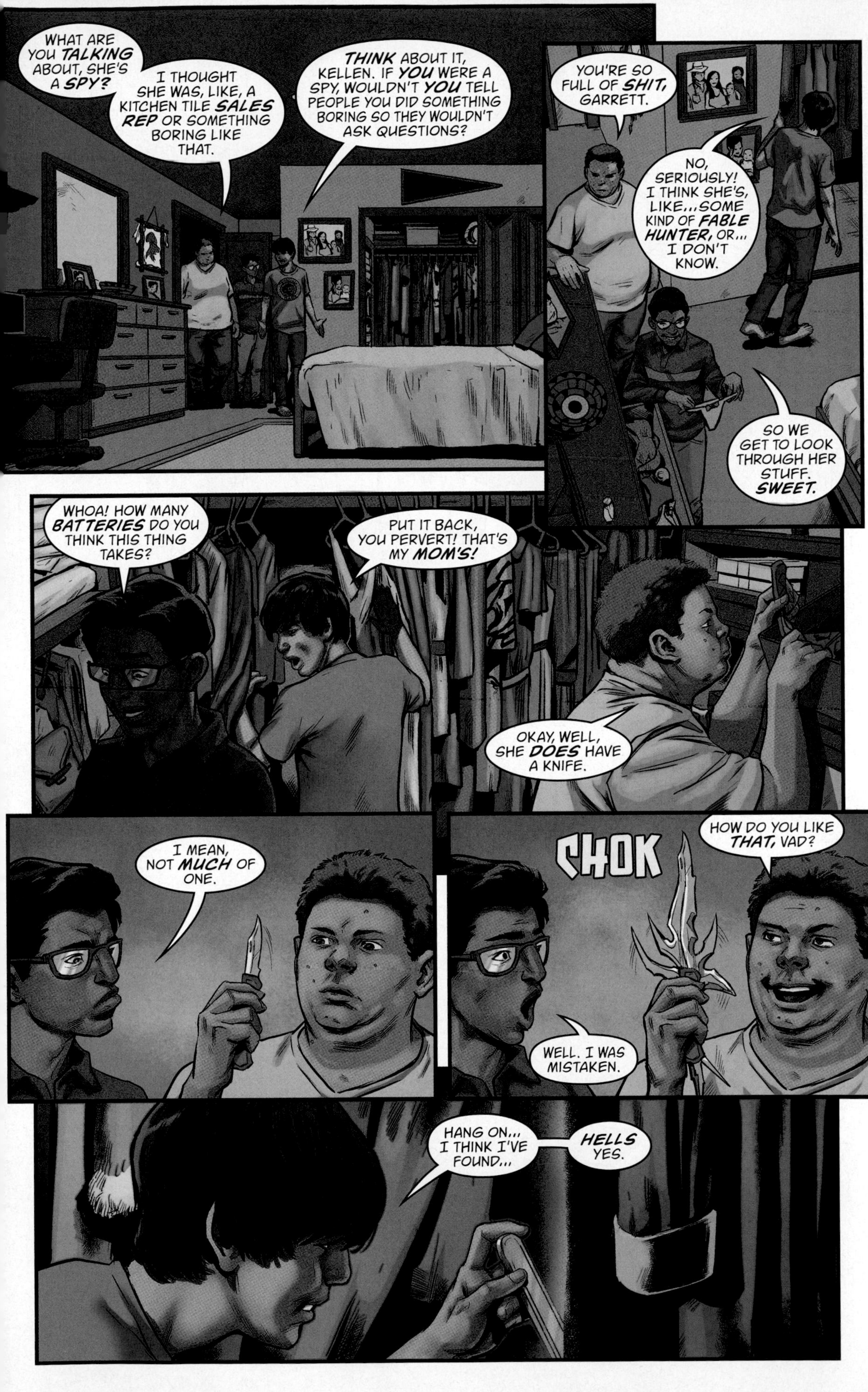
WHAT ARE YOU TALKING ABOUT, SHE'S A SPY?
I THOUGHT SHE WAS, LIKE, A KITCHEN TILE SALES REP OR SOMETHING BORING LIKE THAT.
THINK ABOUT IT, KELLEN. IF YOU WERE A SPY, WOULDN'T YOU TELL PEOPLE YOU DID SOMETHING BORING SO THEY WOULDN'T ASK QUESTIONS?
YOU'RE SO FULL OF SHIT, GARRETT.
NO, SERIOUSLY! I THINK SHE'S, LIKE... SOME KIND OF FABLE HUNTER, OR... I DON'T KNOW.
SO WE GET TO LOOK THROUGH HER STUFF. SWEET.
WHOA! HOW MANY BATTERIES DO YOU THINK THIS THING TAKES?
PUT IT BACK, YOU PERVERT! THAT'S MY MOM'S!
OKAY, WELL, SHE DOES HAVE A KNIFE.
I MEAN, NOT MUCH OF ONE.
CHOK
HOW DO YOU LIKE THAT, VAD?
WELL. I WAS MISTAKEN.
HANG ON... I THINK I'VE FOUND...
HELLS YES.

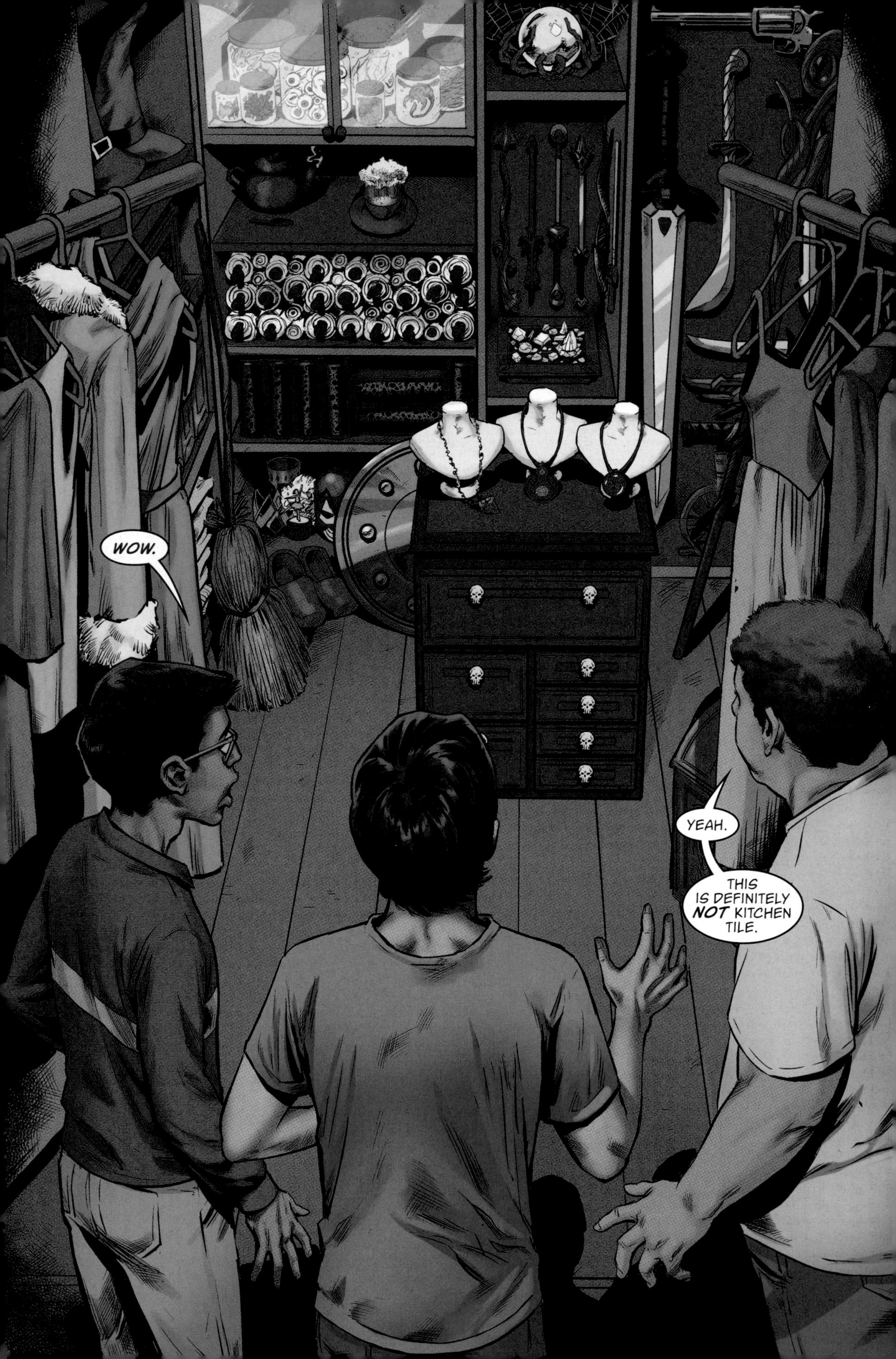
WOW.
YEAH.
THIS IS DEFINITELY **NOT** KITCHEN TILE.

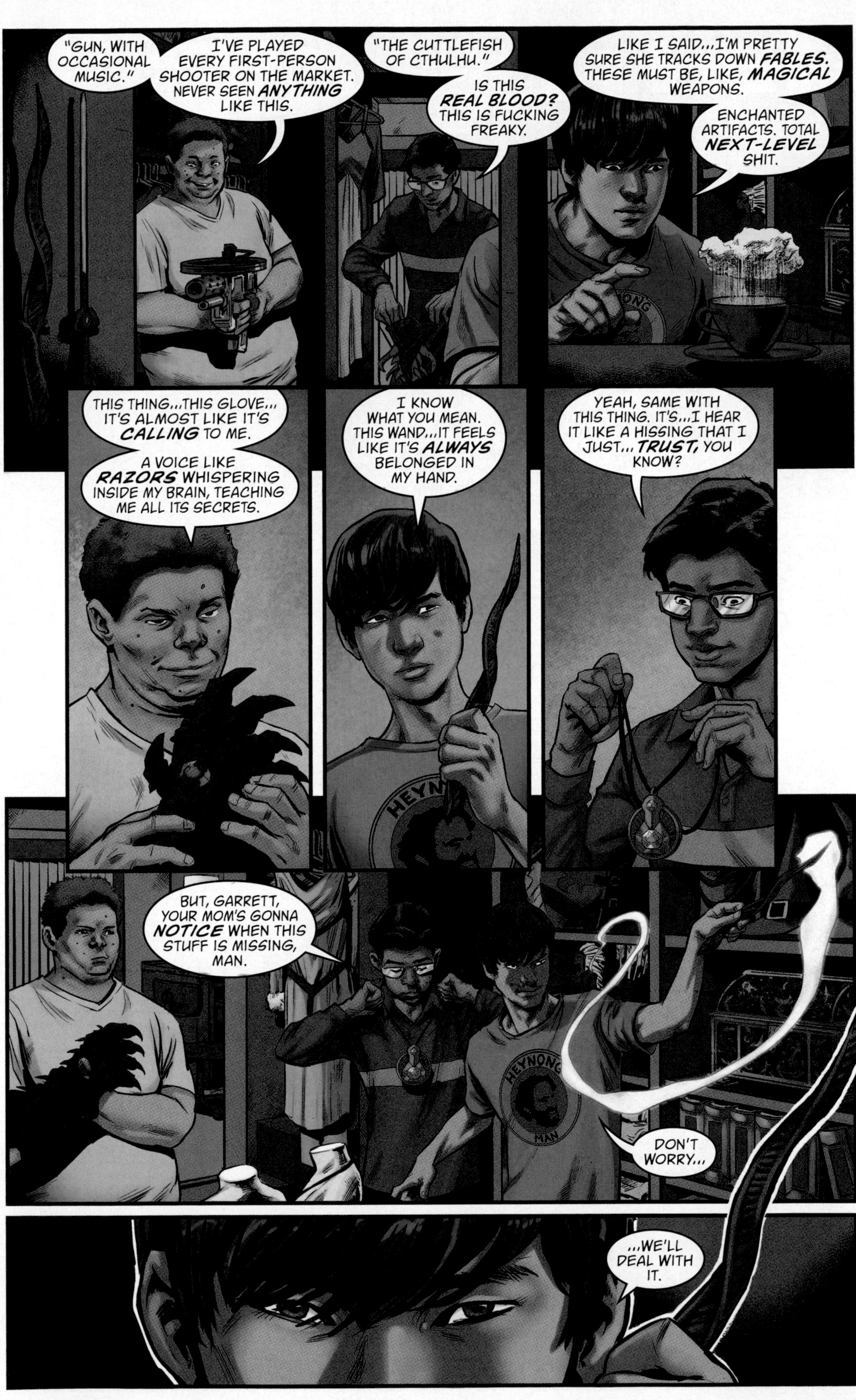
"GUN, WITH OCCASIONAL MUSIC."
I'VE PLAYED EVERY FIRST-PERSON SHOOTER ON THE MARKET. NEVER SEEN ANYTHING LIKE THIS.
"THE CUTTLEFISH OF CTHULHU."
IS THIS REAL BLOOD? THIS IS FUCKING FREAKY.
LIKE I SAID...I'M PRETTY SURE SHE TRACKS DOWN FABLES. THESE MUST BE, LIKE, MAGICAL WEAPONS.
ENCHANTED ARTIFACTS. TOTAL NEXT-LEVEL SHIT.
THIS THING...THIS GLOVE... IT'S ALMOST LIKE IT'S CALLING TO ME.
A VOICE LIKE RAZORS WHISPERING INSIDE MY BRAIN, TEACHING ME ALL ITS SECRETS.
I KNOW WHAT YOU MEAN. THIS WAND...IT FEELS LIKE IT'S ALWAYS BELONGED IN MY HAND.
YEAH, SAME WITH THIS THING. IT'S...I HEAR IT LIKE A HISSING THAT I JUST...TRUST, YOU KNOW?
BUT, GARRETT, YOUR MOM'S GONNA NOTICE WHEN THIS STUFF IS MISSING, MAN.
DON'T WORRY...
...WE'LL DEAL WITH IT.

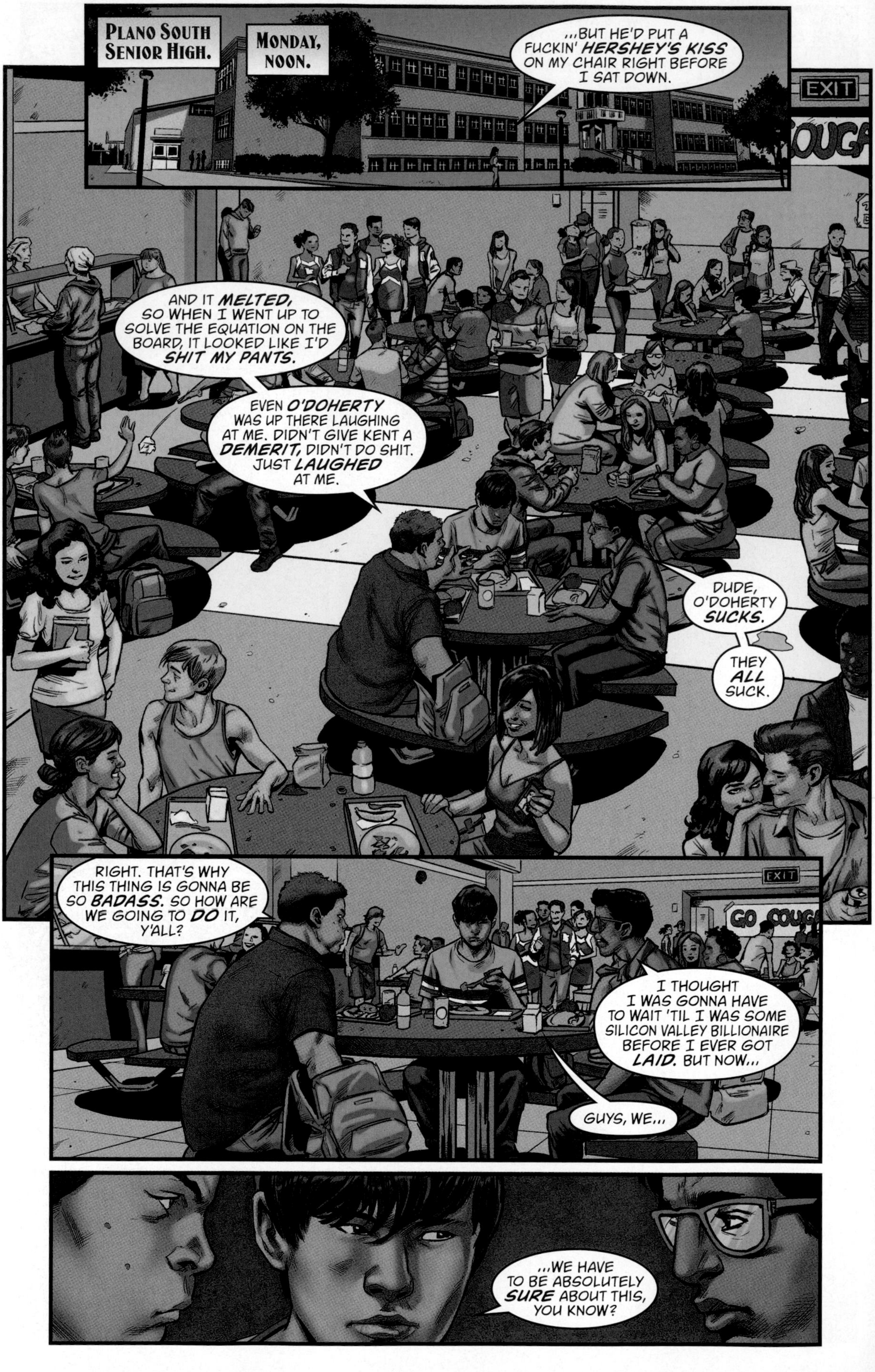

PLANO SOUTH SENIOR HIGH.
MONDAY, NOON.
...BUT HE'D PUT A FUCKIN' HERSHEY'S KISS ON MY CHAIR RIGHT BEFORE I SAT DOWN.
EXIT
AND IT MELTED, SO WHEN I WENT UP TO SOLVE THE EQUATION ON THE BOARD, IT LOOKED LIKE I'D SHIT MY PANTS.
EVEN O'DOHERTY WAS UP THERE LAUGHING AT ME. DIDN'T GIVE KENT A DEMERIT, DIDN'T DO SHIT. JUST LAUGHED AT ME.
DUDE, O'DOHERTY SUCKS.
THEY ALL SUCK.
RIGHT. THAT'S WHY THIS THING IS GONNA BE SO BADASS. SO HOW ARE WE GOING TO DO IT, Y'ALL?
EXIT
GO COUGA
I THOUGHT I WAS GONNA HAVE TO WAIT 'TIL I WAS SOME SILICON VALLEY BILLIONAIRE BEFORE I EVER GOT LAID. BUT NOW...
GUYS, WE...
...WE HAVE TO BE ABSOLUTELY SURE ABOUT THIS, YOU KNOW?

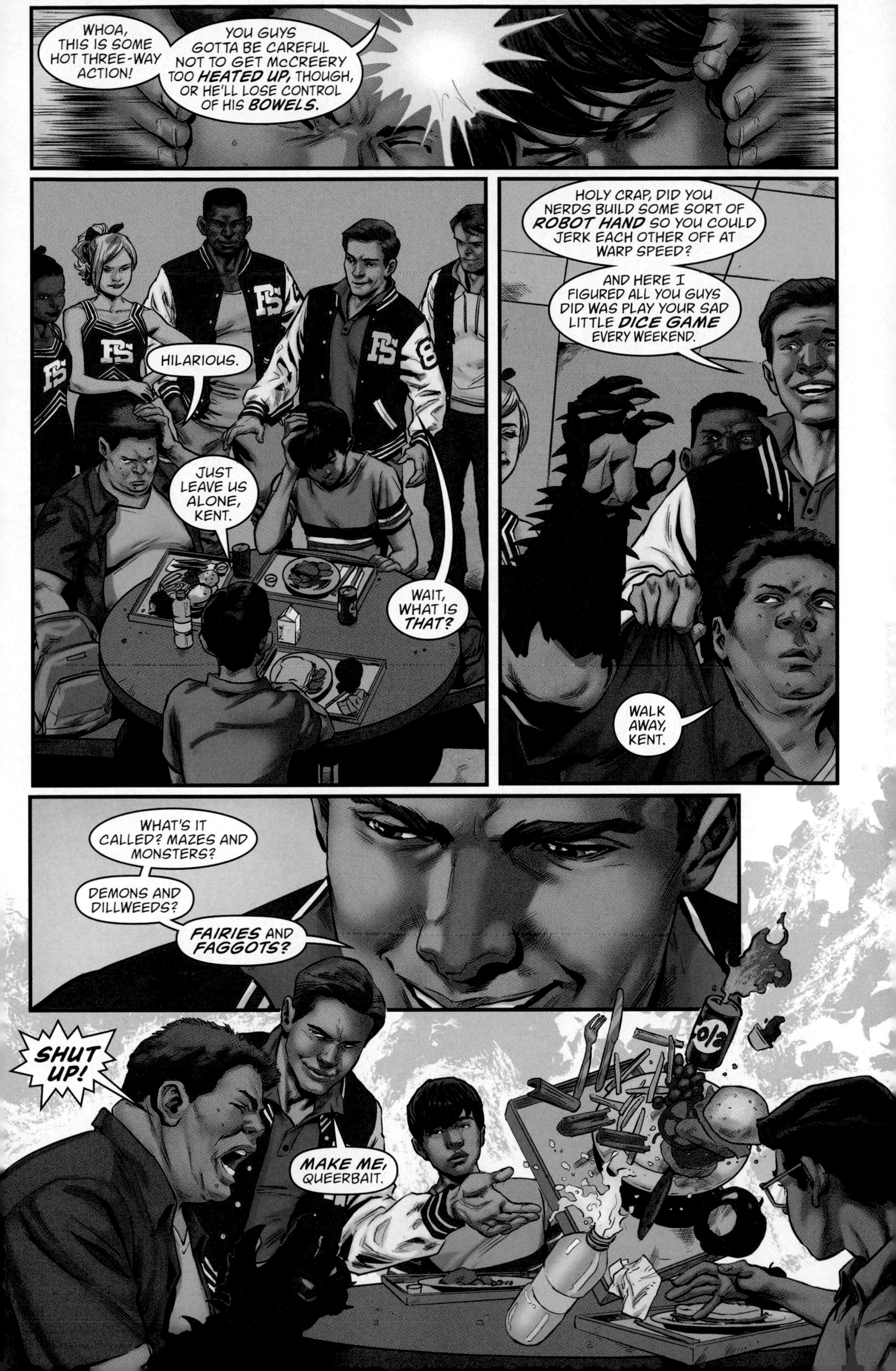
WHOA, THIS IS SOME HOT THREE-WAY ACTION!
YOU GUYS GOTTA BE CAREFUL NOT TO GET McCREERY TOO HEATED UP, THOUGH, OR HE'LL LOSE CONTROL OF HIS BOWELS.
HILARIOUS.
JUST LEAVE US ALONE, KENT.
WAIT, WHAT IS THAT?
HOLY CRAP, DID YOU NERDS BUILD SOME SORT OF ROBOT HAND SO YOU COULD JERK EACH OTHER OFF AT WARP SPEED?
AND HERE I FIGURED ALL YOU GUYS DID WAS PLAY YOUR SAD LITTLE DICE GAME EVERY WEEKEND.
WALK AWAY, KENT.
WHAT'S IT CALLED? MAZES AND MONSTERS?
DEMONS AND DILLWEEDS?
FAIRIES AND FAGGOTS?
SHUT UP!
MAKE ME, QUEERBAIT.

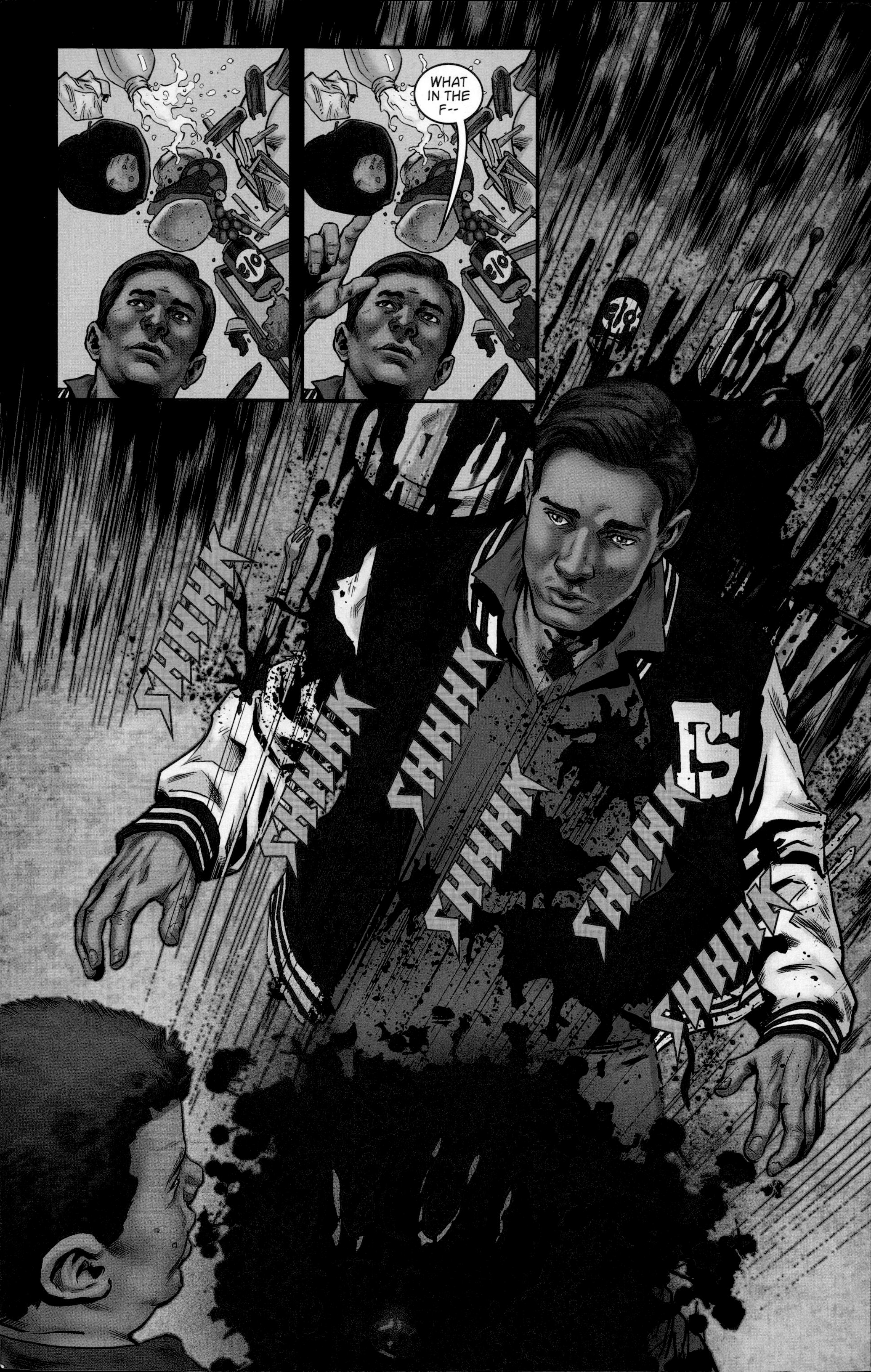
WHAT IN THE F--
SHHHK
SHHHK
SHHHK
SHHHK
SHHHK
SHHHK
SHHHK

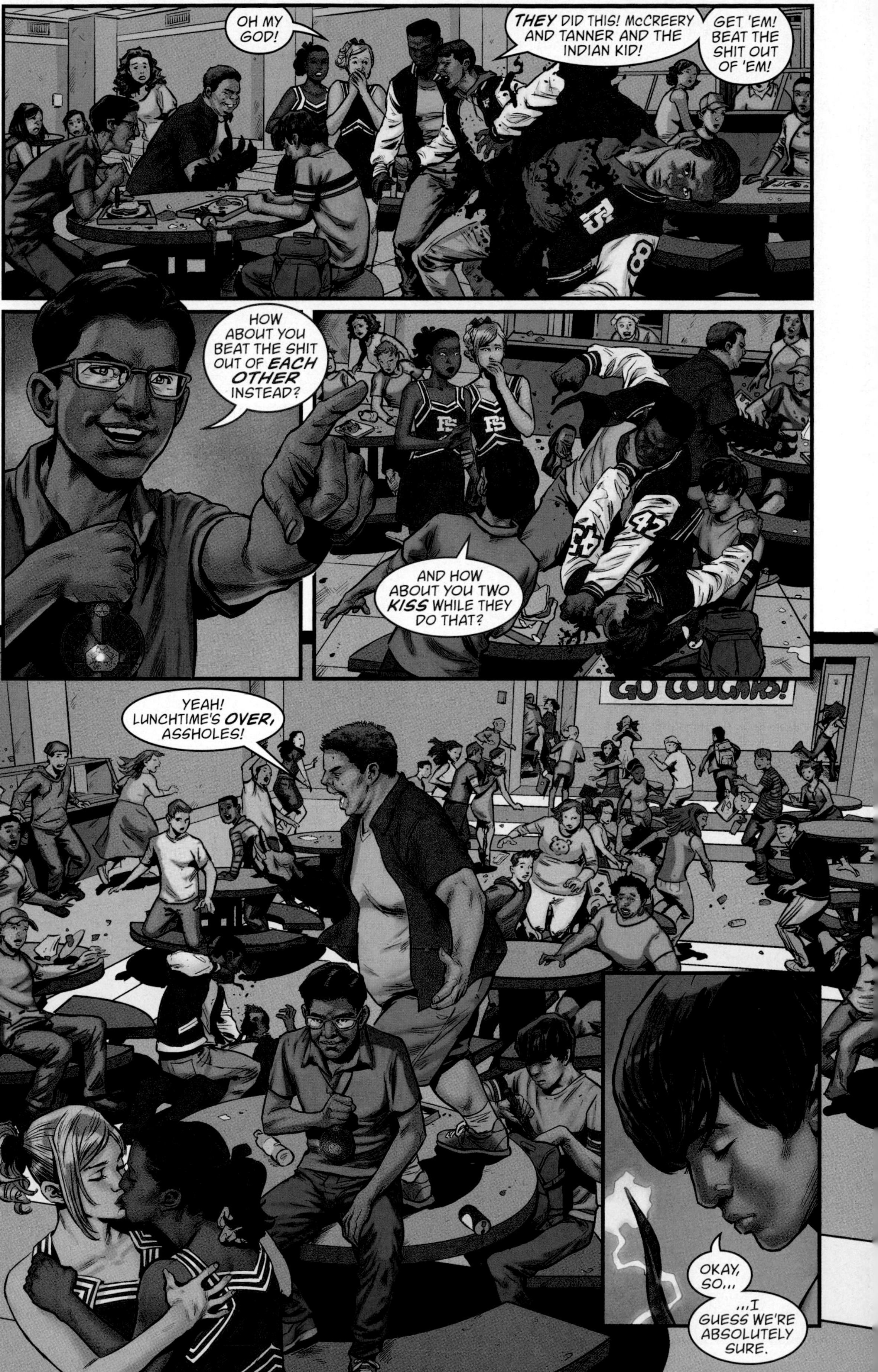
OH MY GOD!
THEY DID THIS! McCREERY AND TANNER AND THE INDIAN KID!
GET 'EM! BEAT THE SHIT OUT OF 'EM!
HOW ABOUT YOU BEAT THE SHIT OUT OF EACH OTHER INSTEAD?
AND HOW ABOUT YOU TWO KISS WHILE THEY DO THAT?
GO COUGARS!
YEAH! LUNCHTIME'S OVER, ASSHOLES!
OKAY, SO...
...I GUESS WE'RE ABSOLUTELY SURE.

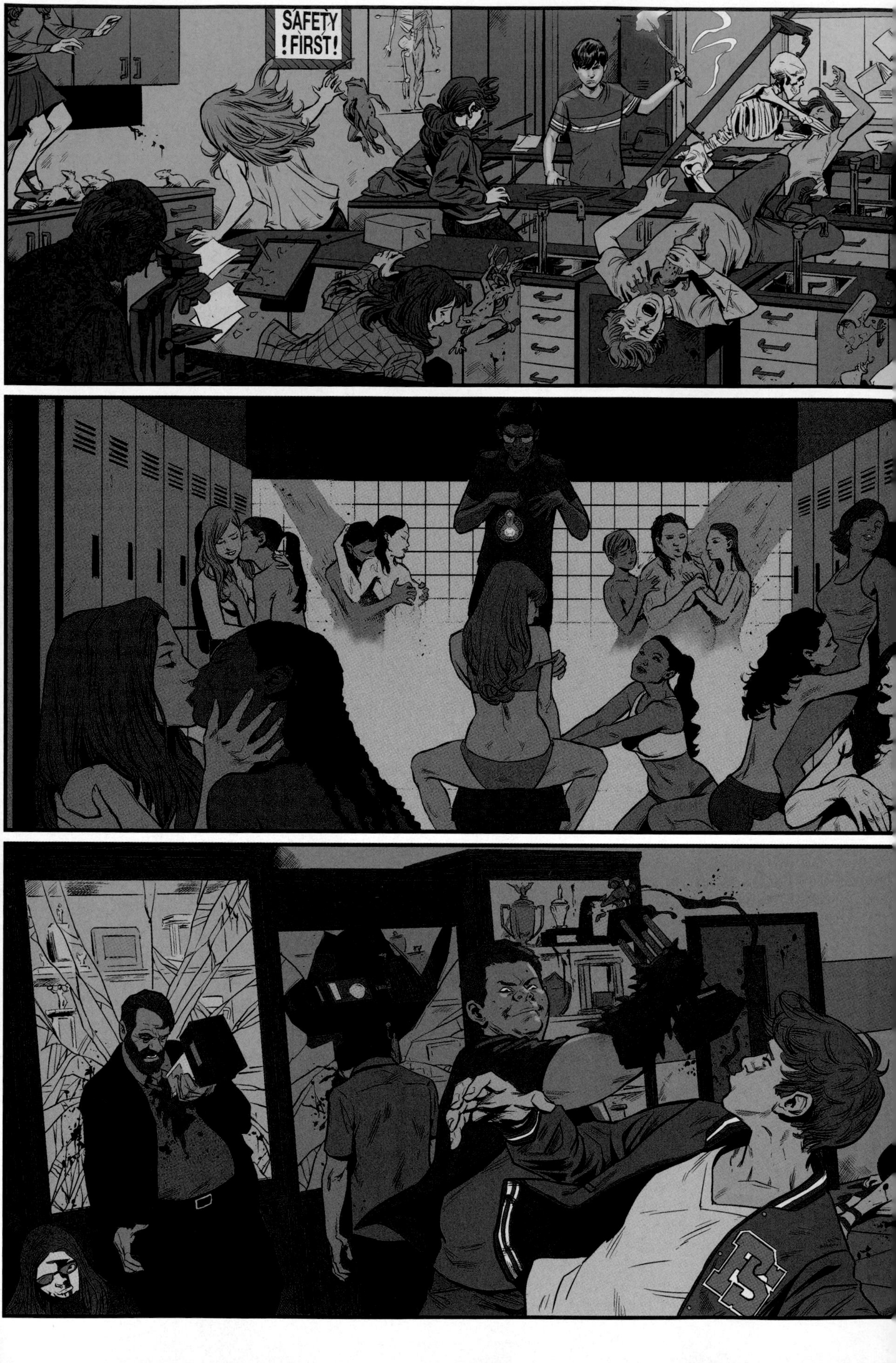
SAFETY
! FIRST !

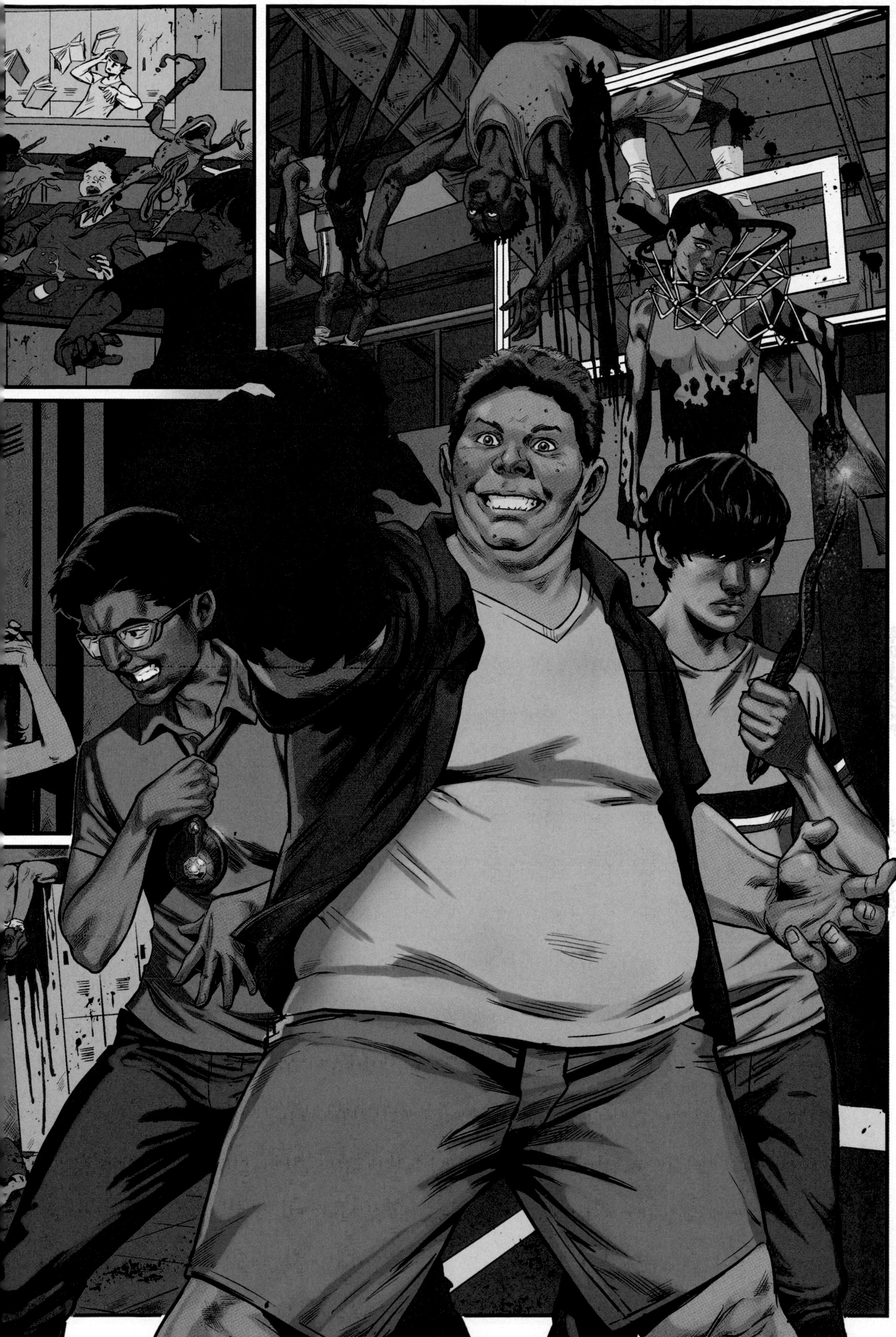

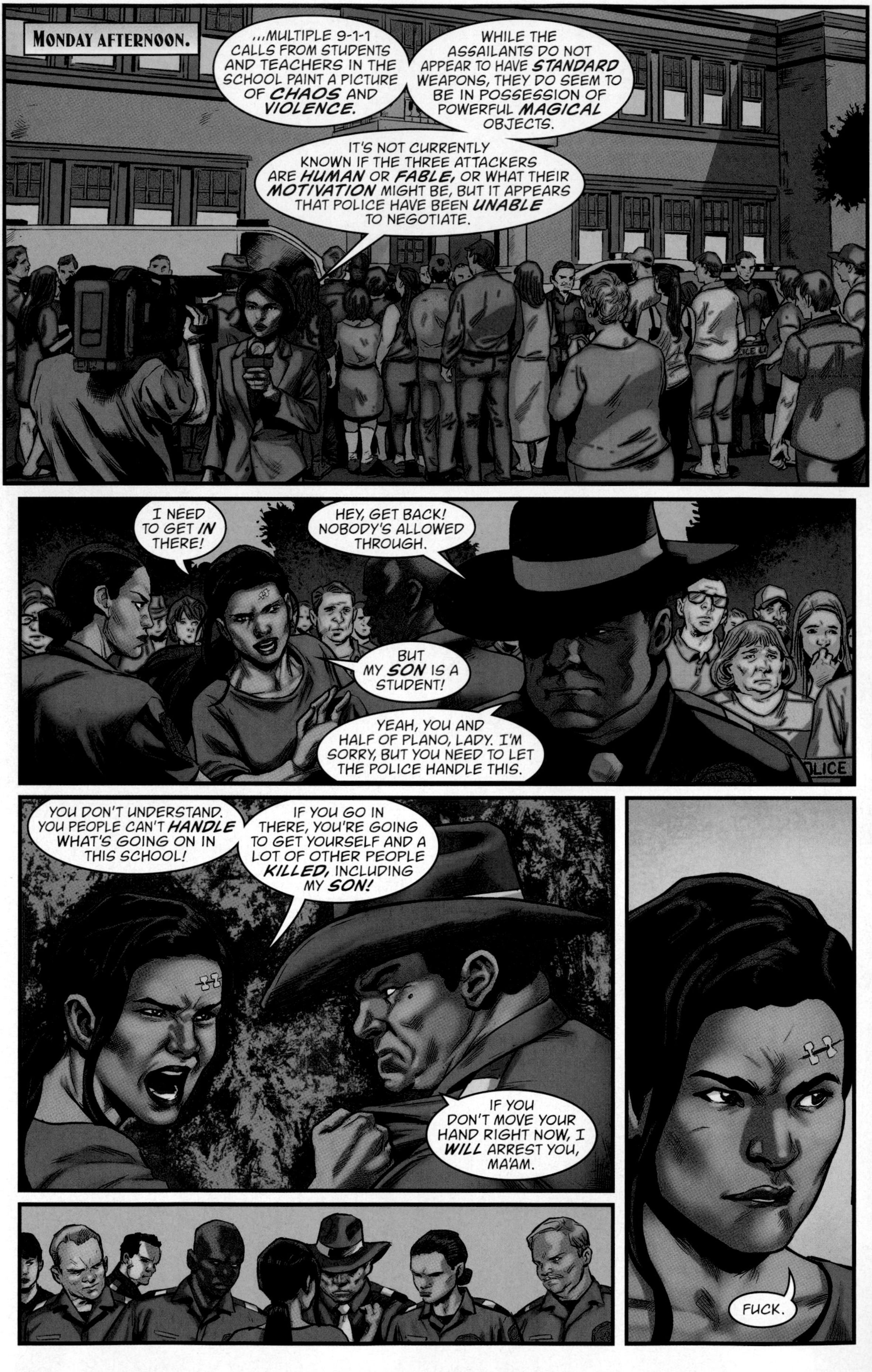
MONDAY AFTERNOON.
...MULTIPLE 9-1-1 CALLS FROM STUDENTS AND TEACHERS IN THE SCHOOL PAINT A PICTURE OF CHAOS AND VIOLENCE.
WHILE THE ASSAILANTS DO NOT APPEAR TO HAVE STANDARD WEAPONS, THEY DO SEEM TO BE IN POSSESSION OF POWERFUL MAGICAL OBJECTS.
IT'S NOT CURRENTLY KNOWN IF THE THREE ATTACKERS ARE HUMAN OR FABLE, OR WHAT THEIR MOTIVATION MIGHT BE, BUT IT APPEARS THAT POLICE HAVE BEEN UNABLE TO NEGOTIATE.
I NEED TO GET IN THERE!
HEY, GET BACK! NOBODY'S ALLOWED THROUGH.
BUT MY SON IS A STUDENT!
YEAH, YOU AND HALF OF PLANO, LADY. I'M SORRY, BUT YOU NEED TO LET THE POLICE HANDLE THIS.
POLICE
YOU DON'T UNDERSTAND. YOU PEOPLE CAN'T HANDLE WHAT'S GOING ON IN THIS SCHOOL!
IF YOU GO IN THERE, YOU'RE GOING TO GET YOURSELF AND A LOT OF OTHER PEOPLE KILLED, INCLUDING MY SON!
IF YOU DON'T MOVE YOUR HAND RIGHT NOW, I WILL ARREST YOU, MA'AM.
FUCK.

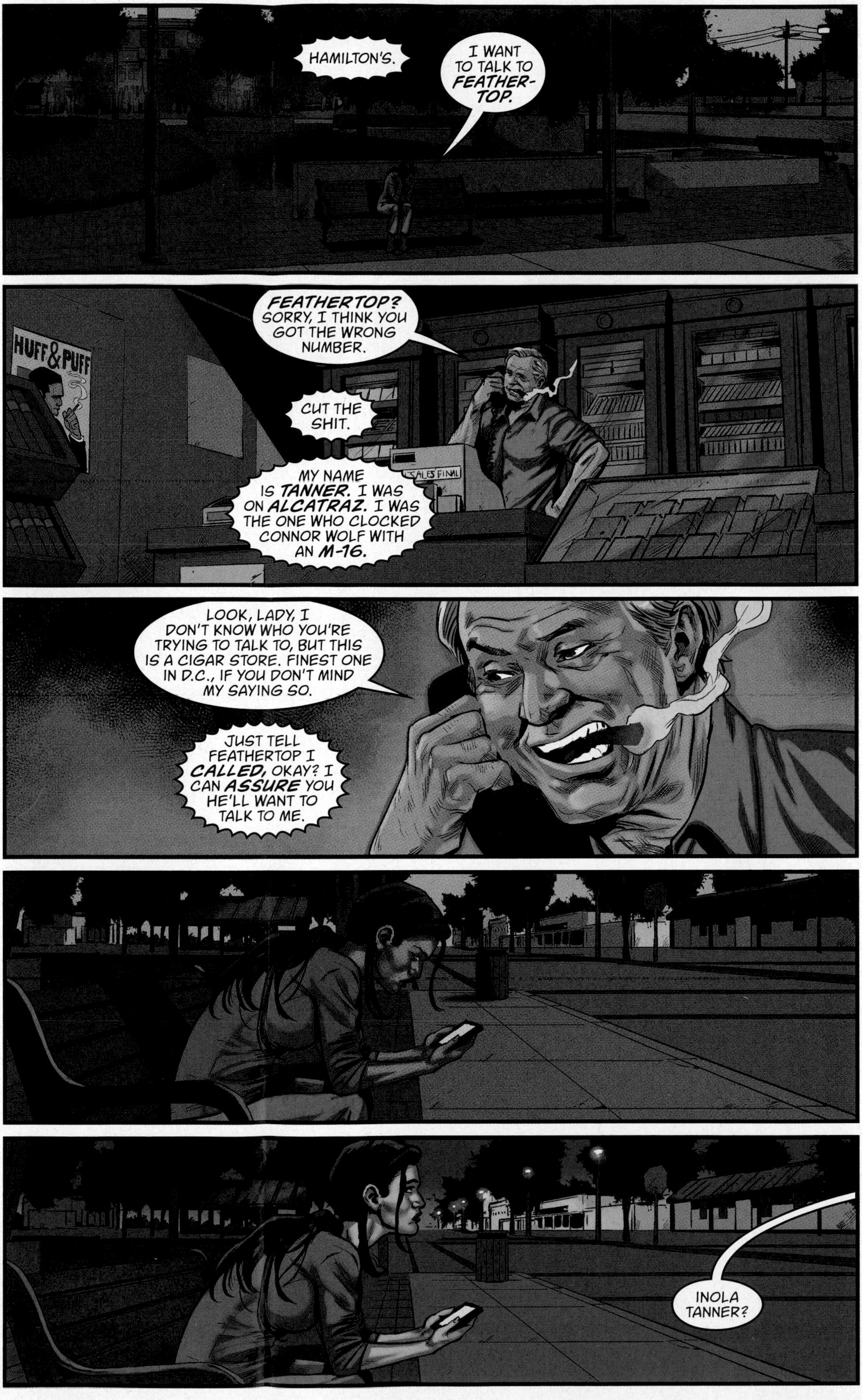
HAMILTON'S.
I WANT TO TALK TO FEATHER-TOP.
HUFF & PUFF
FEATHERTOP? SORRY, I THINK YOU GOT THE WRONG NUMBER.
CUT THE SHIT.
MY NAME IS TANNER. I WAS ON ALCATRAZ. I WAS THE ONE WHO CLOCKED CONNOR WOLF WITH AN M-16.
LOOK, LADY, I DON'T KNOW WHO YOU'RE TRYING TO TALK TO, BUT THIS IS A CIGAR STORE. FINEST ONE IN D.C., IF YOU DON'T MIND MY SAYING SO.
JUST TELL FEATHERTOP I CALLED, OKAY? I CAN ASSURE YOU HE'LL WANT TO TALK TO ME.
INOLA TANNER?

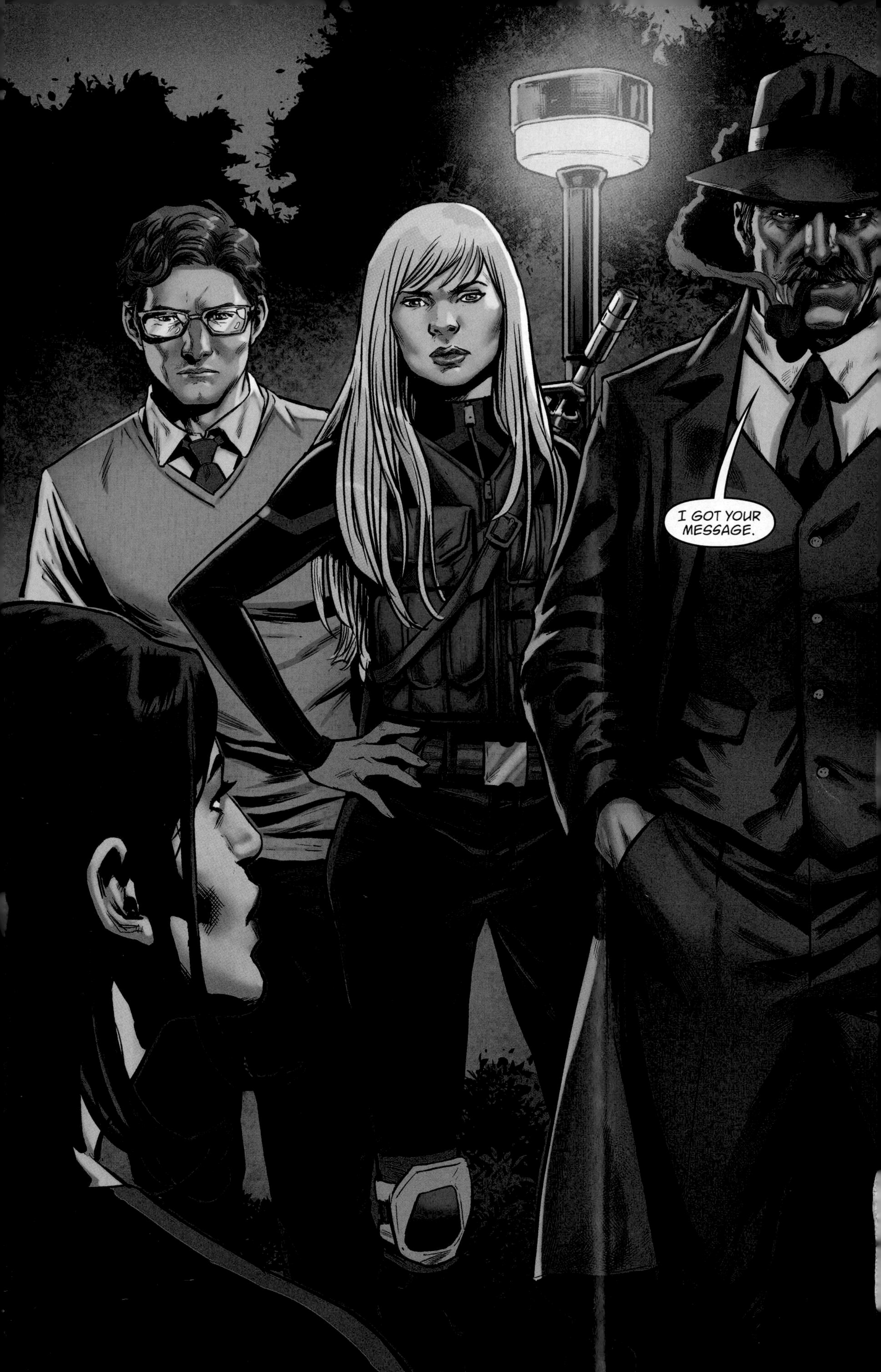
I GOT YOUR MESSAGE.

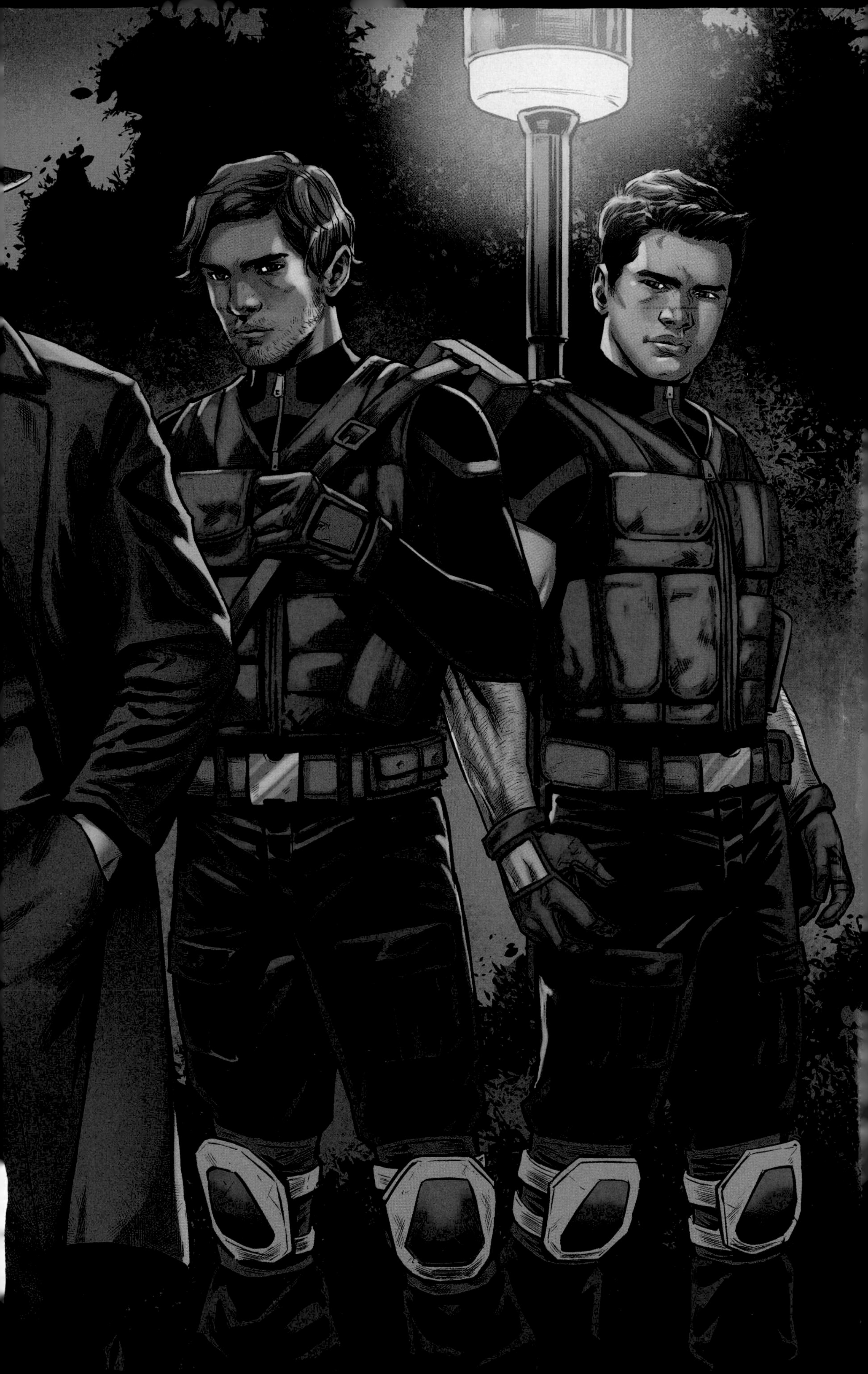

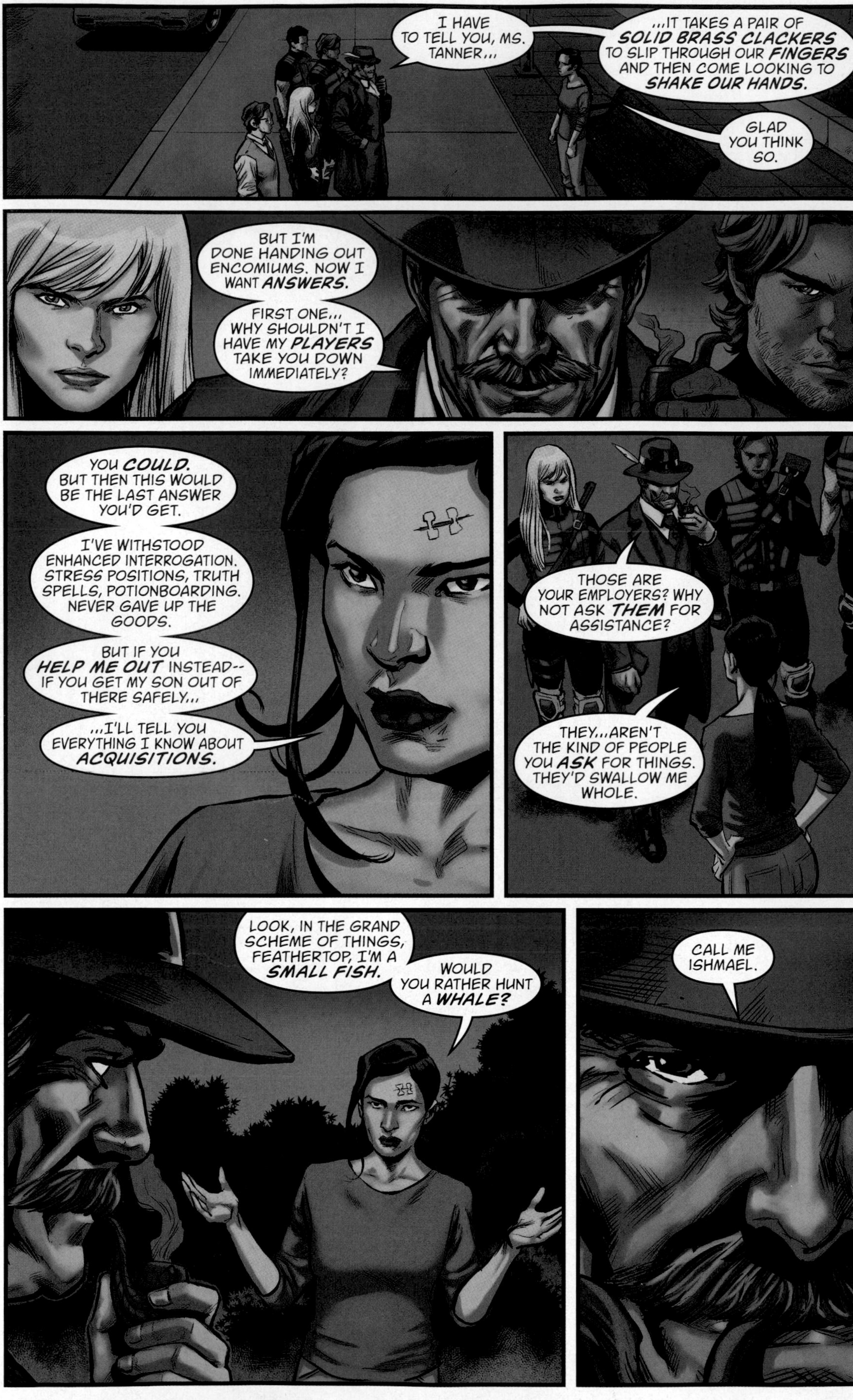
I HAVE TO TELL YOU, MS. TANNER...
...IT TAKES A PAIR OF SOLID BRASS CLACKERS TO SLIP THROUGH OUR FINGERS AND THEN COME LOOKING TO SHAKE OUR HANDS.
GLAD YOU THINK SO.
BUT I'M DONE HANDING OUT ENCOMIUMS. NOW I WANT ANSWERS.
FIRST ONE... WHY SHOULDN'T I HAVE MY PLAYERS TAKE YOU DOWN IMMEDIATELY?
YOU COULD. BUT THEN THIS WOULD BE THE LAST ANSWER YOU'D GET.
I'VE WITHSTOOD ENHANCED INTERROGATION. STRESS POSITIONS, TRUTH SPELLS, POTIONBOARDING. NEVER GAVE UP THE GOODS.
BUT IF YOU HELP ME OUT INSTEAD-- IF YOU GET MY SON OUT OF THERE SAFELY...
...I'LL TELL YOU EVERYTHING I KNOW ABOUT ACQUISITIONS.
THOSE ARE YOUR EMPLOYERS? WHY NOT ASK THEM FOR ASSISTANCE?
THEY...AREN'T THE KIND OF PEOPLE YOU ASK FOR THINGS. THEY'D SWALLOW ME WHOLE.
LOOK, IN THE GRAND SCHEME OF THINGS, FEATHERTOP, I'M A SMALL FISH.
WOULD YOU RATHER HUNT A WHALE?
CALL ME ISHMAEL.

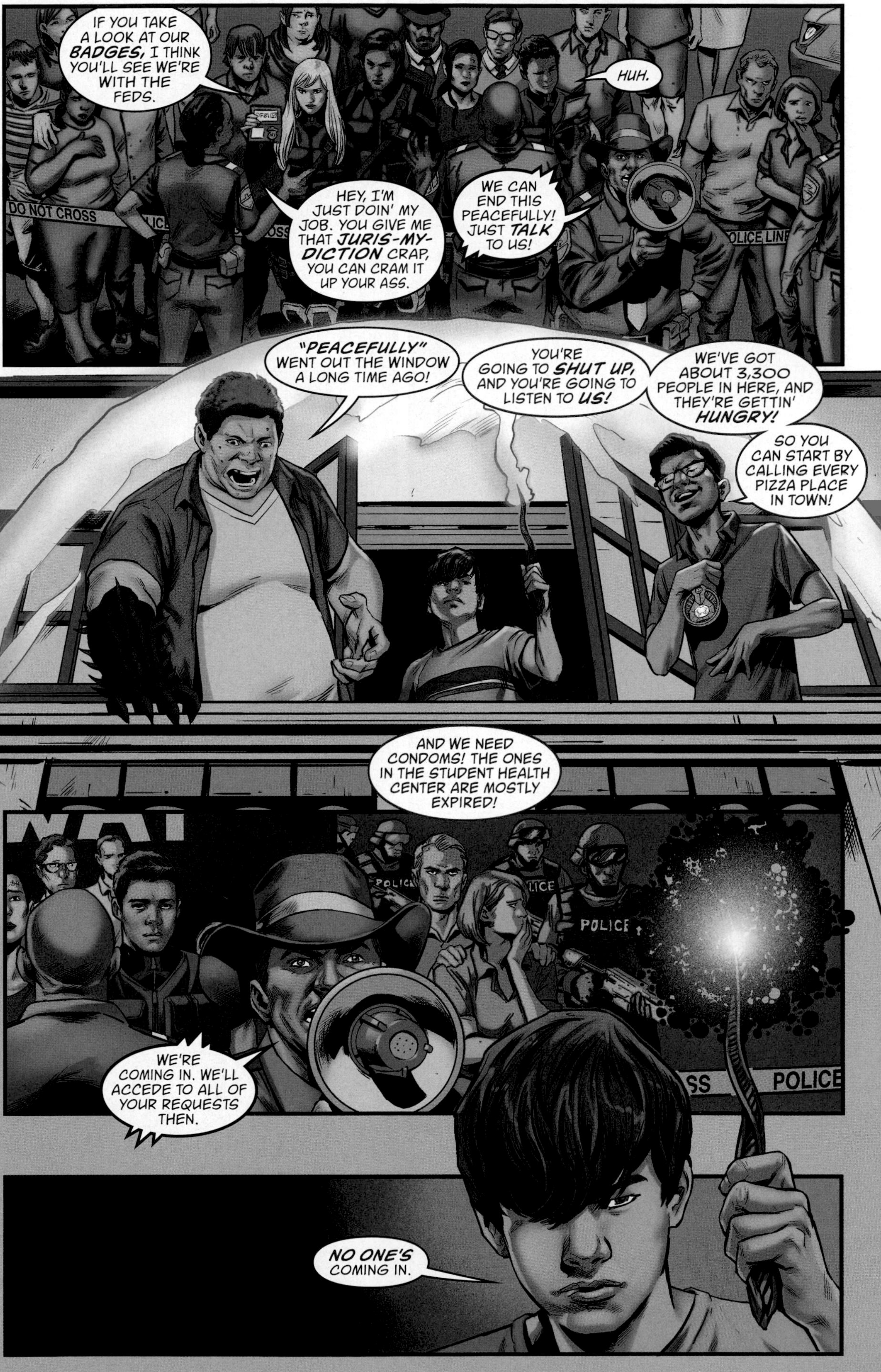

IF YOU TAKE A LOOK AT OUR BADGES, I THINK YOU'LL SEE WE'RE WITH THE FEDS.
HUH.
HEY, I'M JUST DOIN' MY JOB. YOU GIVE ME THAT JURIS-MY-DICTION CRAP, YOU CAN CRAM IT UP YOUR ASS.
WE CAN END THIS PEACEFULLY! JUST TALK TO US!
DO NOT CROSS
POLICE LINE
"PEACEFULLY" WENT OUT THE WINDOW A LONG TIME AGO!
YOU'RE GOING TO SHUT UP, AND YOU'RE GOING TO LISTEN TO US!
WE'VE GOT ABOUT 3,300 PEOPLE IN HERE, AND THEY'RE GETTIN' HUNGRY!
SO YOU CAN START BY CALLING EVERY PIZZA PLACE IN TOWN!
AND WE NEED CONDOMS! THE ONES IN THE STUDENT HEALTH CENTER ARE MOSTLY EXPIRED!
POLICE
POLICE
WE'RE COMING IN. WE'LL ACCEDE TO ALL OF YOUR REQUESTS THEN.
NO ONE'S COMING IN.

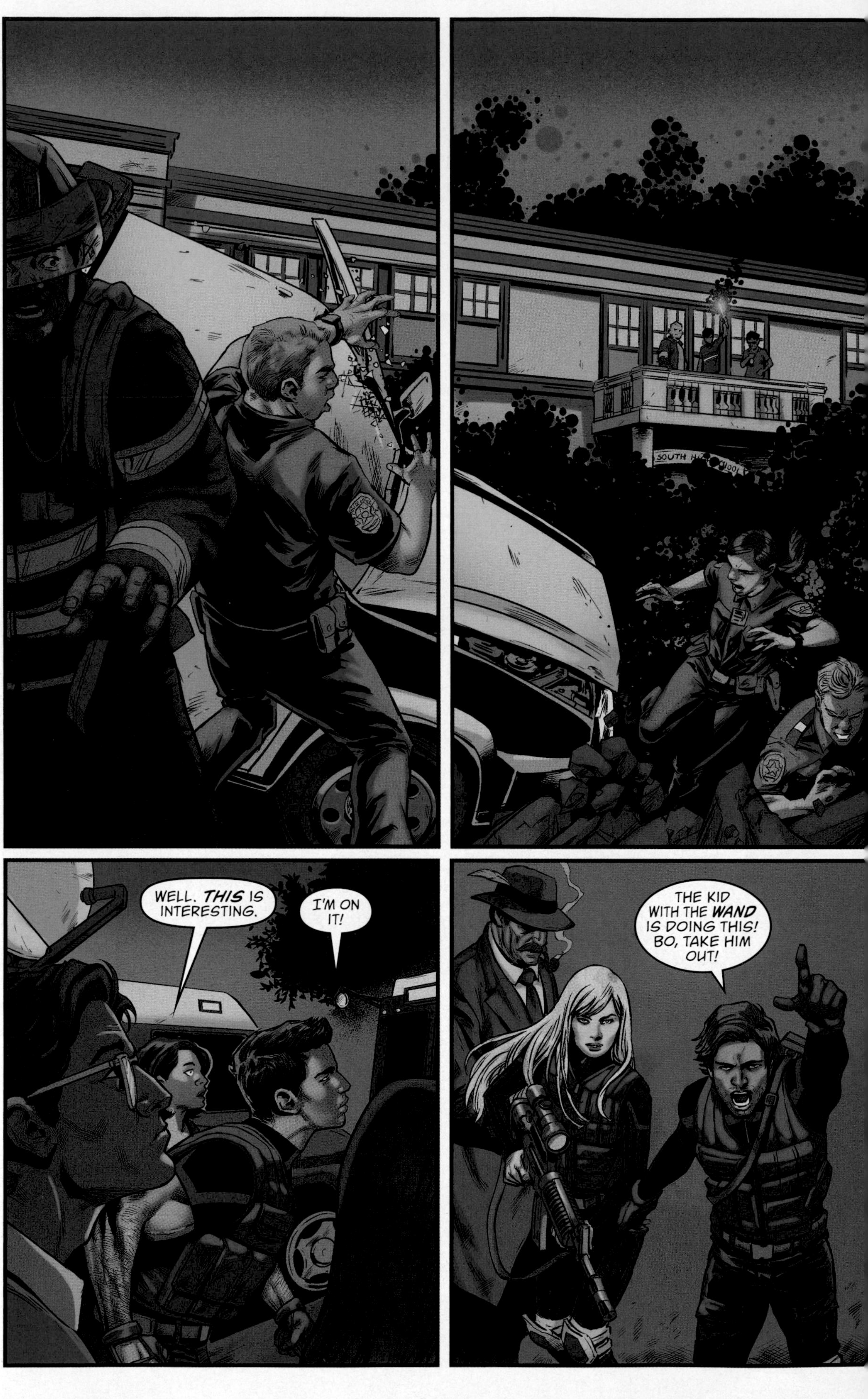
WELL. THIS IS INTERESTING.
I'M ON IT!
THE KID WITH THE WAND IS DOING THIS! BO, TAKE HIM OUT!

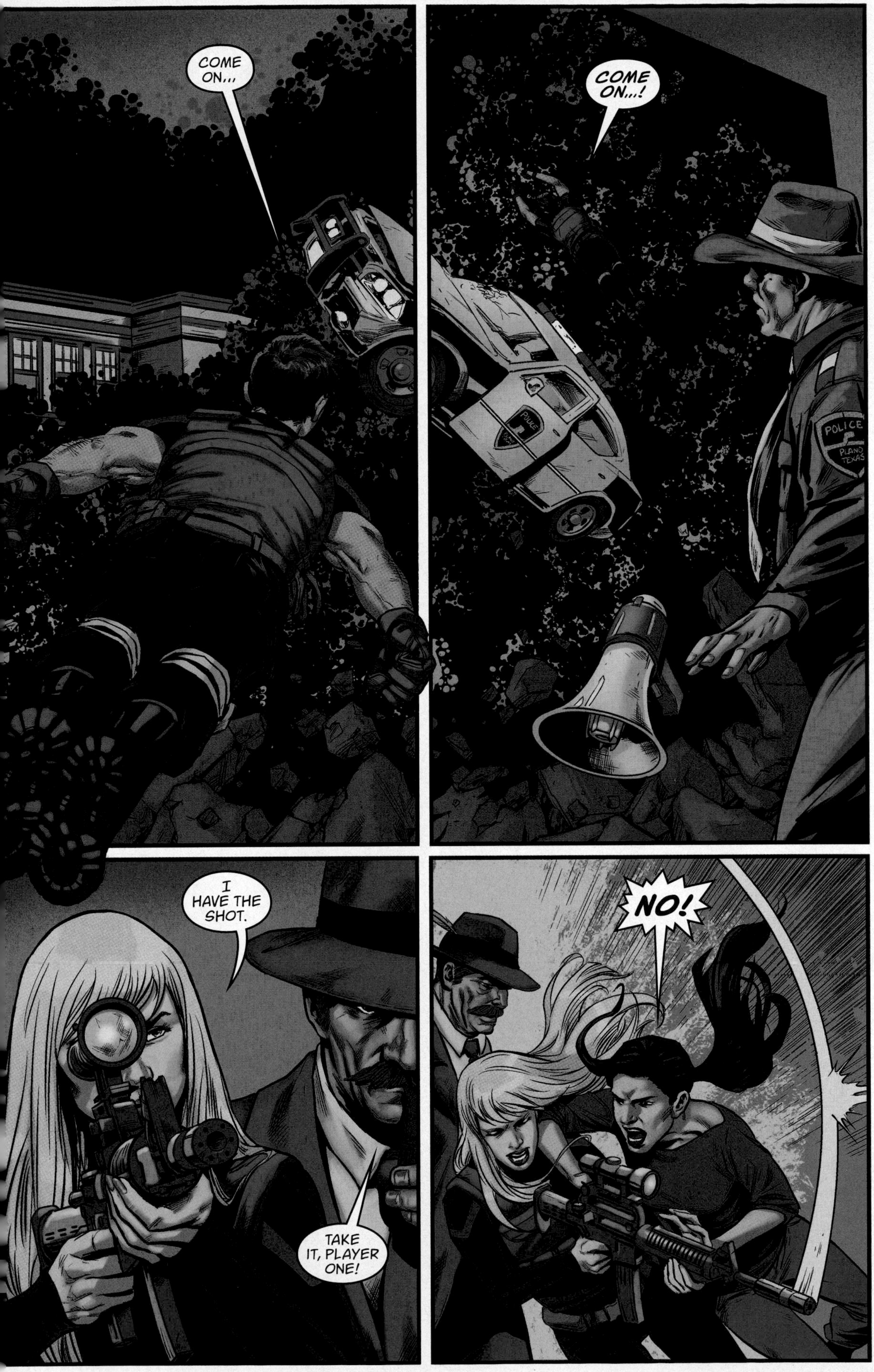
COME ON...
COME ON...!
POLICE
PLANO TEXAS
I HAVE THE SHOT.
TAKE IT, PLAYER ONE!
NO!

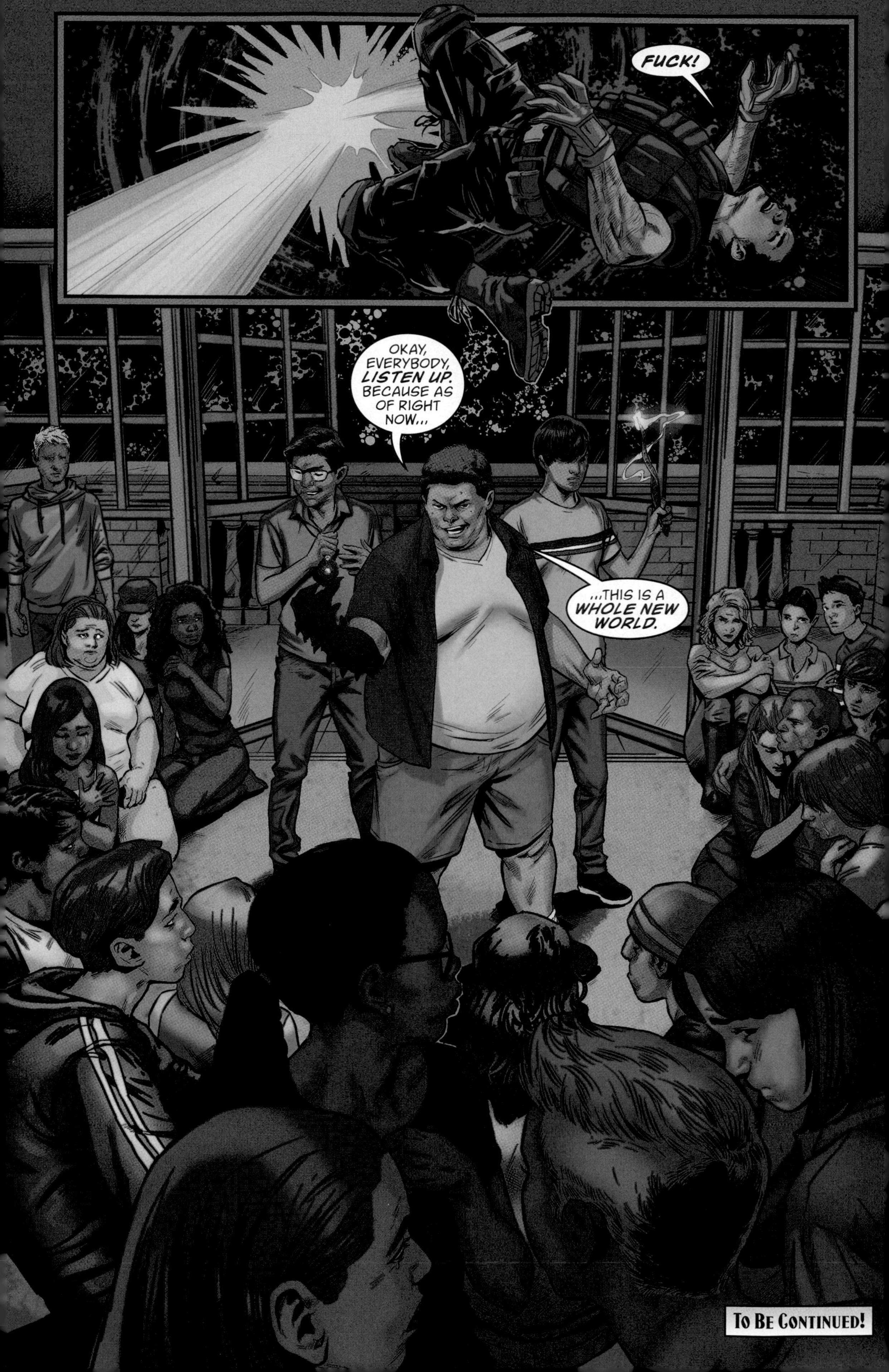
FUCK!
OKAY, EVERYBODY, LISTEN UP. BECAUSE AS OF RIGHT NOW...
...THIS IS A WHOLE NEW WORLD.
TO BE CONTINUED!

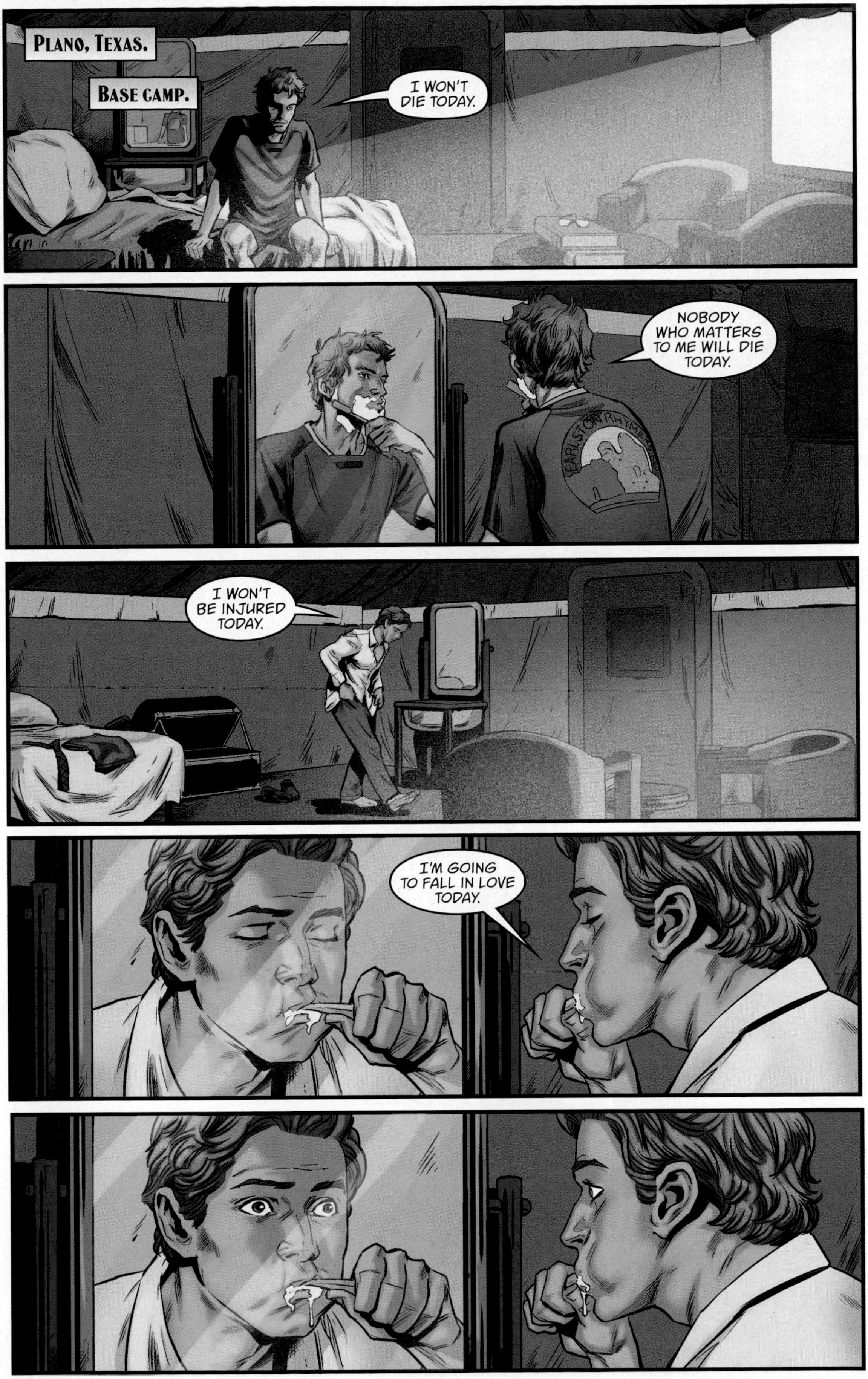
Plano, Texas.
Base camp.
I WON'T DIE TODAY.
NOBODY WHO MATTERS TO ME WILL DIE TODAY.
I WON'T BE INJURED TODAY.
I'M GOING TO FALL IN LOVE TODAY.

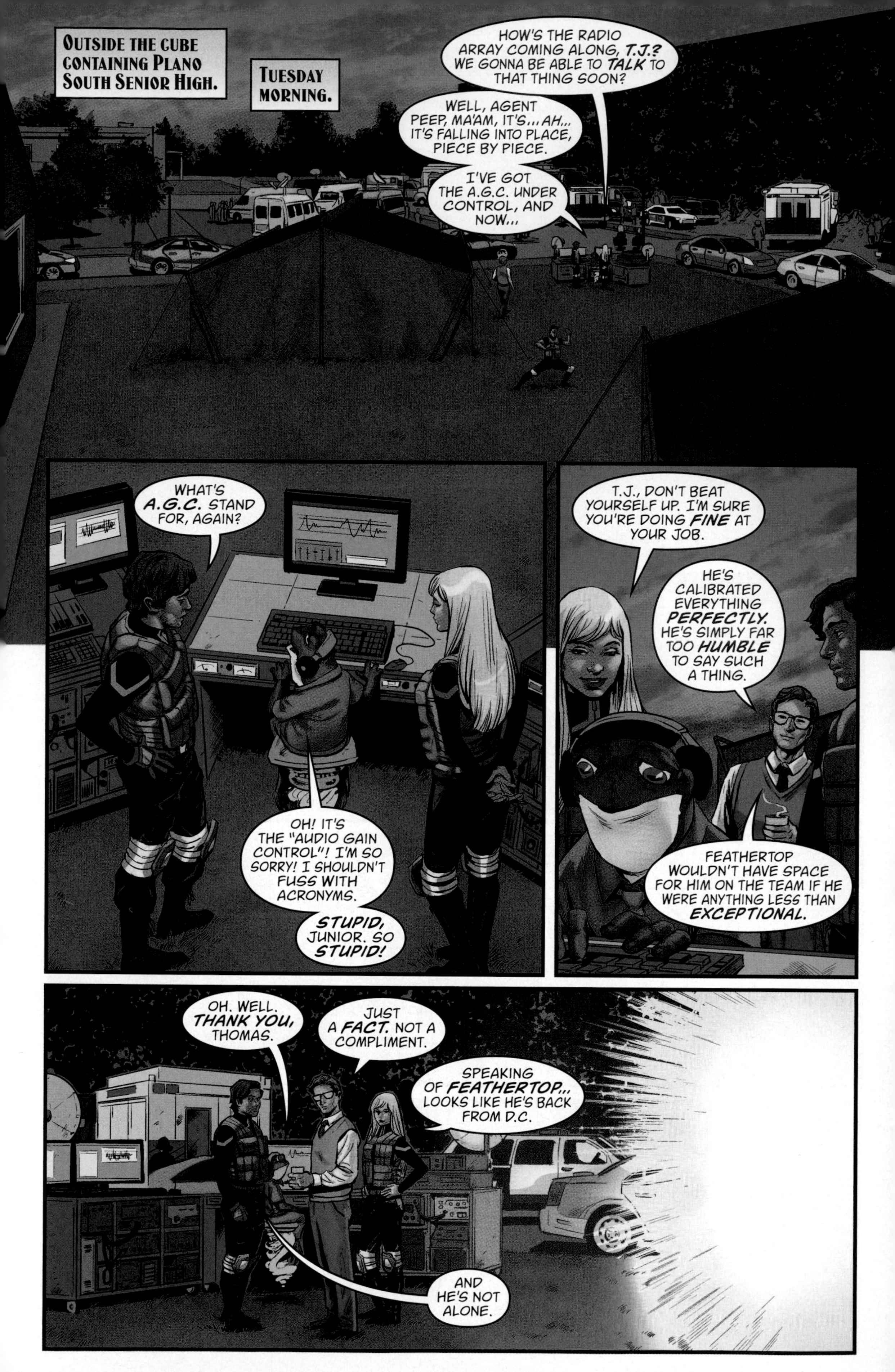

OUTSIDE THE CUBE CONTAINING PLANO SOUTH SENIOR HIGH.
TUESDAY MORNING.
HOW'S THE RADIO ARRAY COMING ALONG, T.J.? WE GONNA BE ABLE TO TALK TO THAT THING SOON?
WELL, AGENT PEEP, MA'AM, IT'S... AH... IT'S FALLING INTO PLACE, PIECE BY PIECE.
I'VE GOT THE A.G.C. UNDER CONTROL, AND NOW...
WHAT'S A.G.C. STAND FOR, AGAIN?
OH! IT'S THE "AUDIO GAIN CONTROL"! I'M SO SORRY! I SHOULDN'T FUSS WITH ACRONYMS.
STUPID, JUNIOR. SO STUPID!
T.J., DON'T BEAT YOURSELF UP. I'M SURE YOU'RE DOING FINE AT YOUR JOB.
HE'S CALIBRATED EVERYTHING PERFECTLY. HE'S SIMPLY FAR TOO HUMBLE TO SAY SUCH A THING.
FEATHERTOP WOULDN'T HAVE SPACE FOR HIM ON THE TEAM IF HE WERE ANYTHING LESS THAN EXCEPTIONAL.
OH. WELL. THANK YOU, THOMAS.
JUST A FACT. NOT A COMPLIMENT.
SPEAKING OF FEATHERTOP... LOOKS LIKE HE'S BACK FROM D.C.
AND HE'S NOT ALONE.

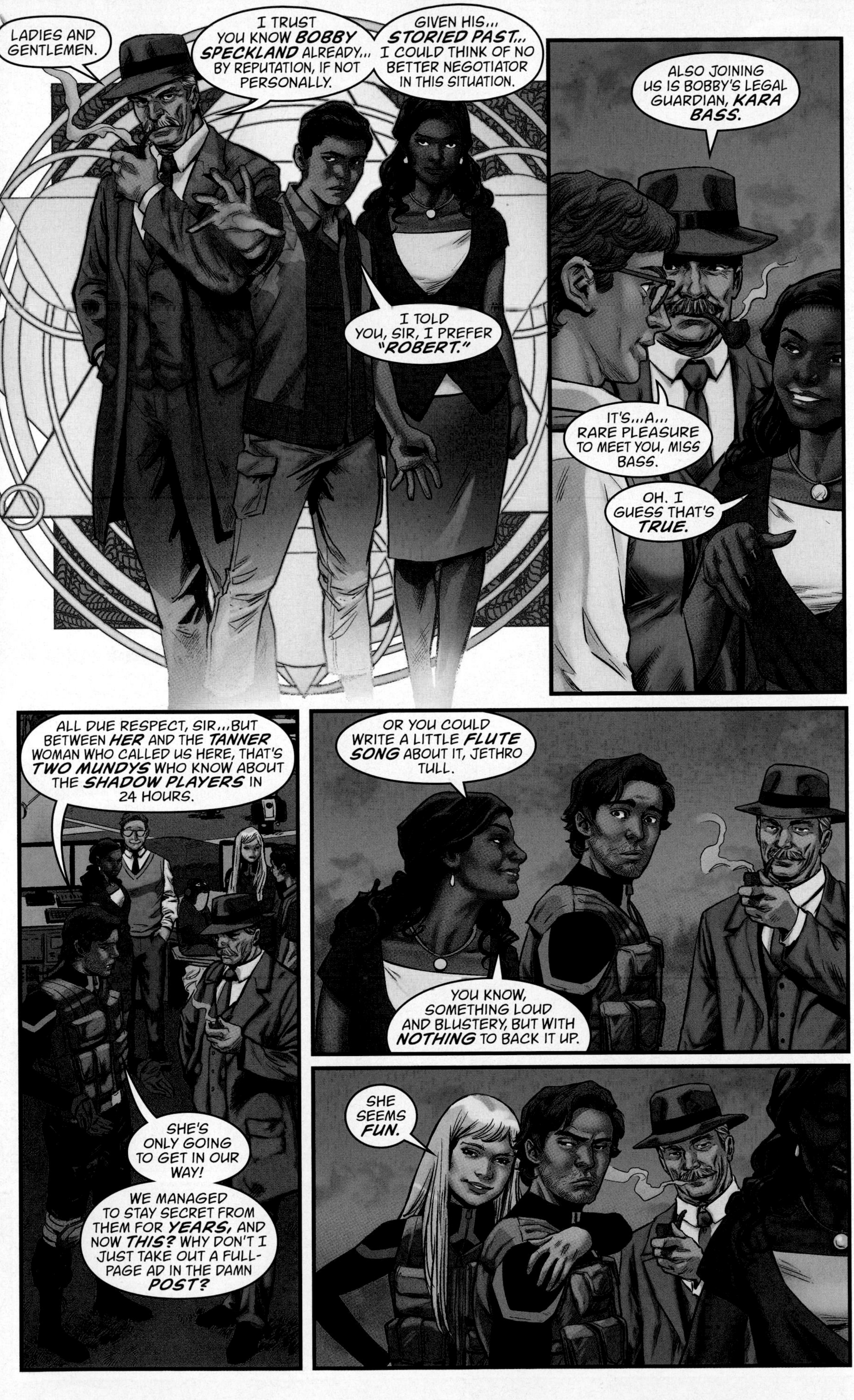
LADIES AND GENTLEMEN.
I TRUST YOU KNOW BOBBY SPECKLAND ALREADY... BY REPUTATION, IF NOT PERSONALLY.
GIVEN HIS... STORIED PAST... I COULD THINK OF NO BETTER NEGOTIATOR IN THIS SITUATION.
I TOLD YOU, SIR, I PREFER "ROBERT."
ALSO JOINING US IS BOBBY'S LEGAL GUARDIAN, KARA BASS.
IT'S...A... RARE PLEASURE TO MEET YOU, MISS BASS.
OH. I GUESS THAT'S TRUE.
ALL DUE RESPECT, SIR...BUT BETWEEN HER AND THE TANNER WOMAN WHO CALLED US HERE, THAT'S TWO MUNDYS WHO KNOW ABOUT THE SHADOW PLAYERS IN 24 HOURS.
SHE'S ONLY GOING TO GET IN OUR WAY!
WE MANAGED TO STAY SECRET FROM THEM FOR YEARS, AND NOW THIS? WHY DON'T I JUST TAKE OUT A FULL-PAGE AD IN THE DAMN POST?
OR YOU COULD WRITE A LITTLE FLUTE SONG ABOUT IT, JETHRO TULL.
YOU KNOW, SOMETHING LOUD AND BLUSTERY, BUT WITH NOTHING TO BACK IT UP.
SHE SEEMS FUN.

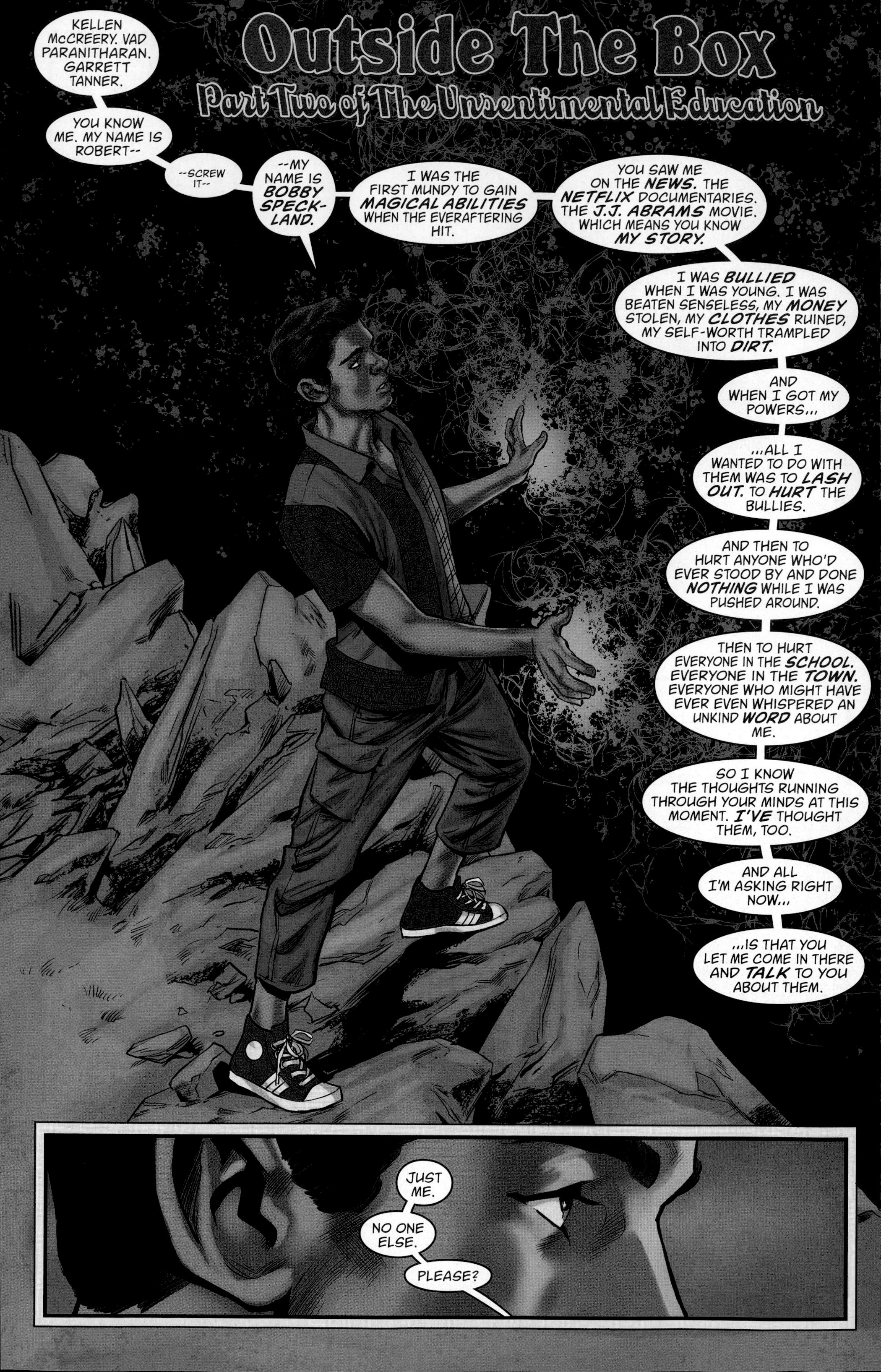
Outside The Box
Part Two of The Unsentimental Education
KELLEN McCREERY. VAD PARANITHARAN. GARRETT TANNER.
YOU KNOW ME. MY NAME IS ROBERT--
--SCREW IT--
--MY NAME IS BOBBY SPECKLAND.
I WAS THE FIRST MUNDY TO GAIN MAGICAL ABILITIES WHEN THE EVERAFTERING HIT.
YOU SAW ME ON THE NEWS. THE NETFLIX DOCUMENTARIES. THE J.J. ABRAMS MOVIE. WHICH MEANS YOU KNOW MY STORY.
I WAS BULLIED WHEN I WAS YOUNG. I WAS BEATEN SENSELESS, MY MONEY STOLEN, MY CLOTHES RUINED, MY SELF-WORTH TRAMPLED INTO DIRT.
AND WHEN I GOT MY POWERS...
...ALL I WANTED TO DO WITH THEM WAS TO LASH OUT. TO HURT THE BULLIES.
AND THEN TO HURT ANYONE WHO'D EVER STOOD BY AND DONE NOTHING WHILE I WAS PUSHED AROUND.
THEN TO HURT EVERYONE IN THE SCHOOL. EVERYONE IN THE TOWN. EVERYONE WHO MIGHT HAVE EVER EVEN WHISPERED AN UNKIND WORD ABOUT ME.
SO I KNOW THE THOUGHTS RUNNING THROUGH YOUR MINDS AT THIS MOMENT. I'VE THOUGHT THEM, TOO.
AND ALL I'M ASKING RIGHT NOW...
...IS THAT YOU LET ME COME IN THERE AND TALK TO YOU ABOUT THEM.
JUST ME.
NO ONE ELSE.
PLEASE?

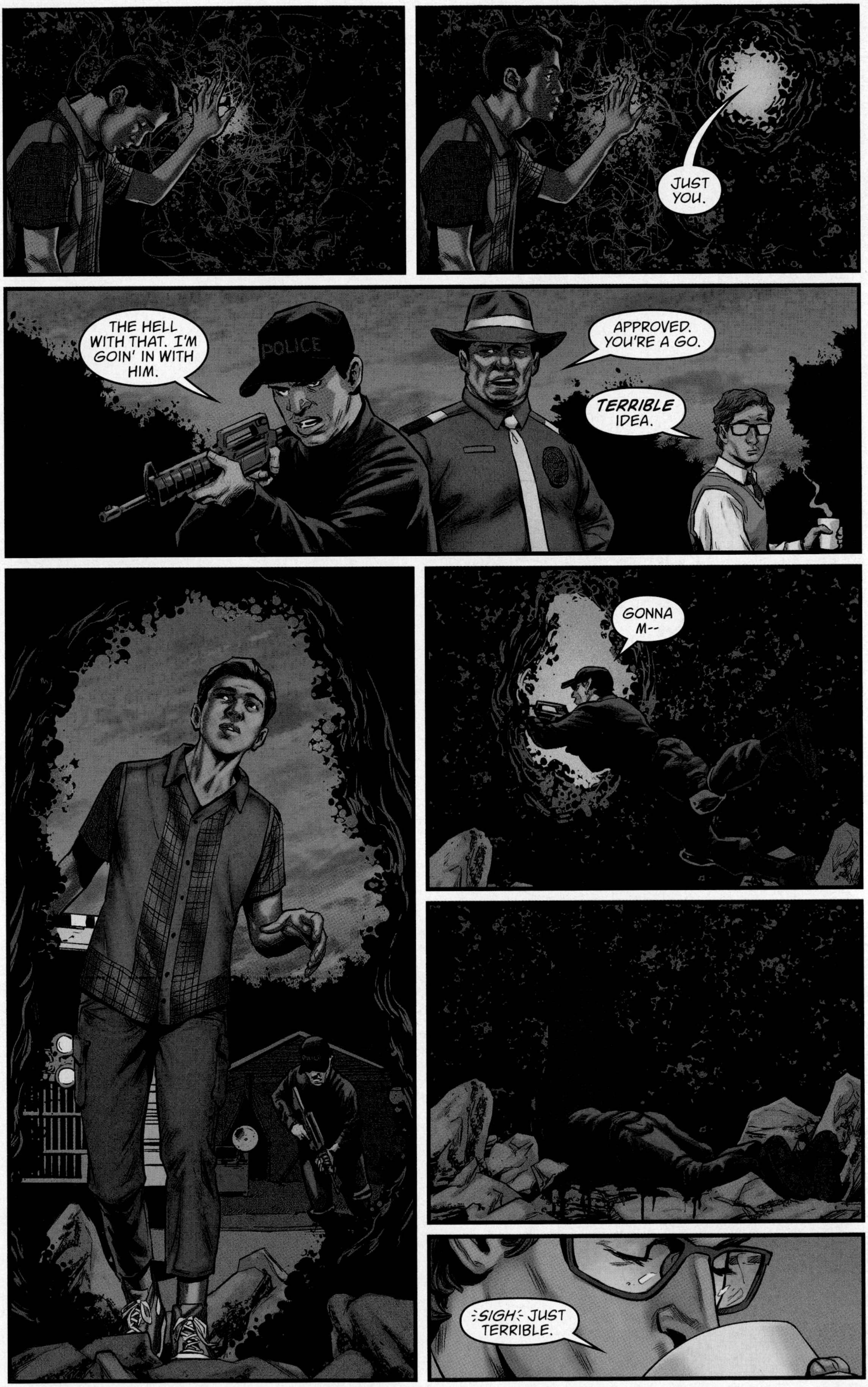
JUST YOU.
THE HELL WITH THAT. I'M GOIN' IN WITH HIM.
APPROVED. YOU'RE A GO.
TERRIBLE IDEA.
POLICE
GONNA M--
SIGH JUST TERRIBLE.

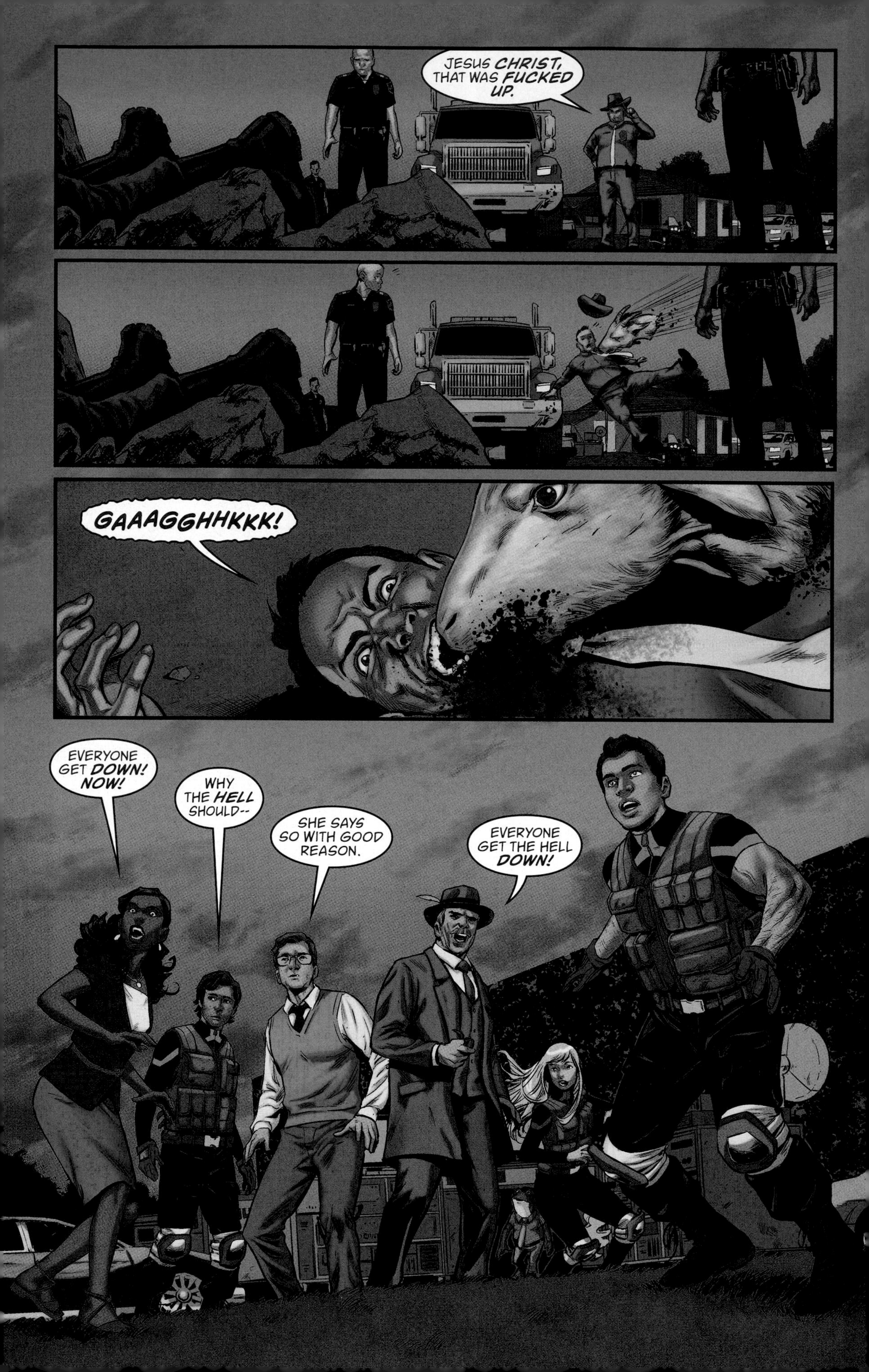
JESUS CHRIST, THAT WAS FUCKED UP.
GAAAGGHHKKK!
EVERYONE GET DOWN! NOW!
WHY THE HELL SHOULD--
SHE SAYS SO WITH GOOD REASON.
EVERYONE GET THE HELL DOWN!

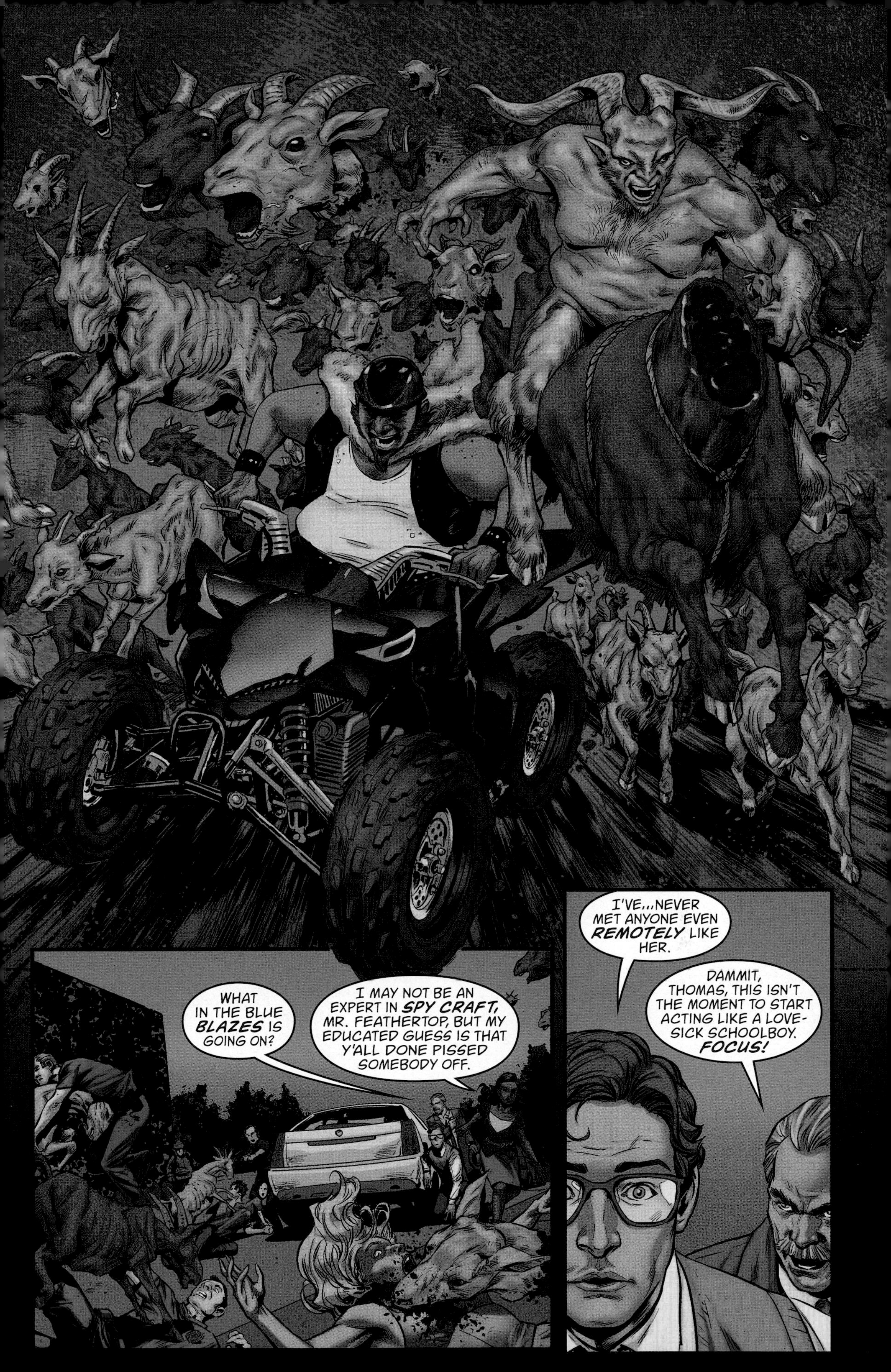
WHAT IN THE BLUE *BLAZES* IS GOING ON?
I MAY NOT BE AN EXPERT IN *SPY CRAFT,* MR. FEATHERTOP, BUT MY EDUCATED GUESS IS THAT Y'ALL DONE PISSED SOMEBODY OFF.
I'VE...NEVER MET ANYONE EVEN *REMOTELY* LIKE HER.
DAMMIT, THOMAS, THIS ISN'T THE MOMENT TO START ACTING LIKE A LOVE-SICK SCHOOLBOY. *FOCUS!*

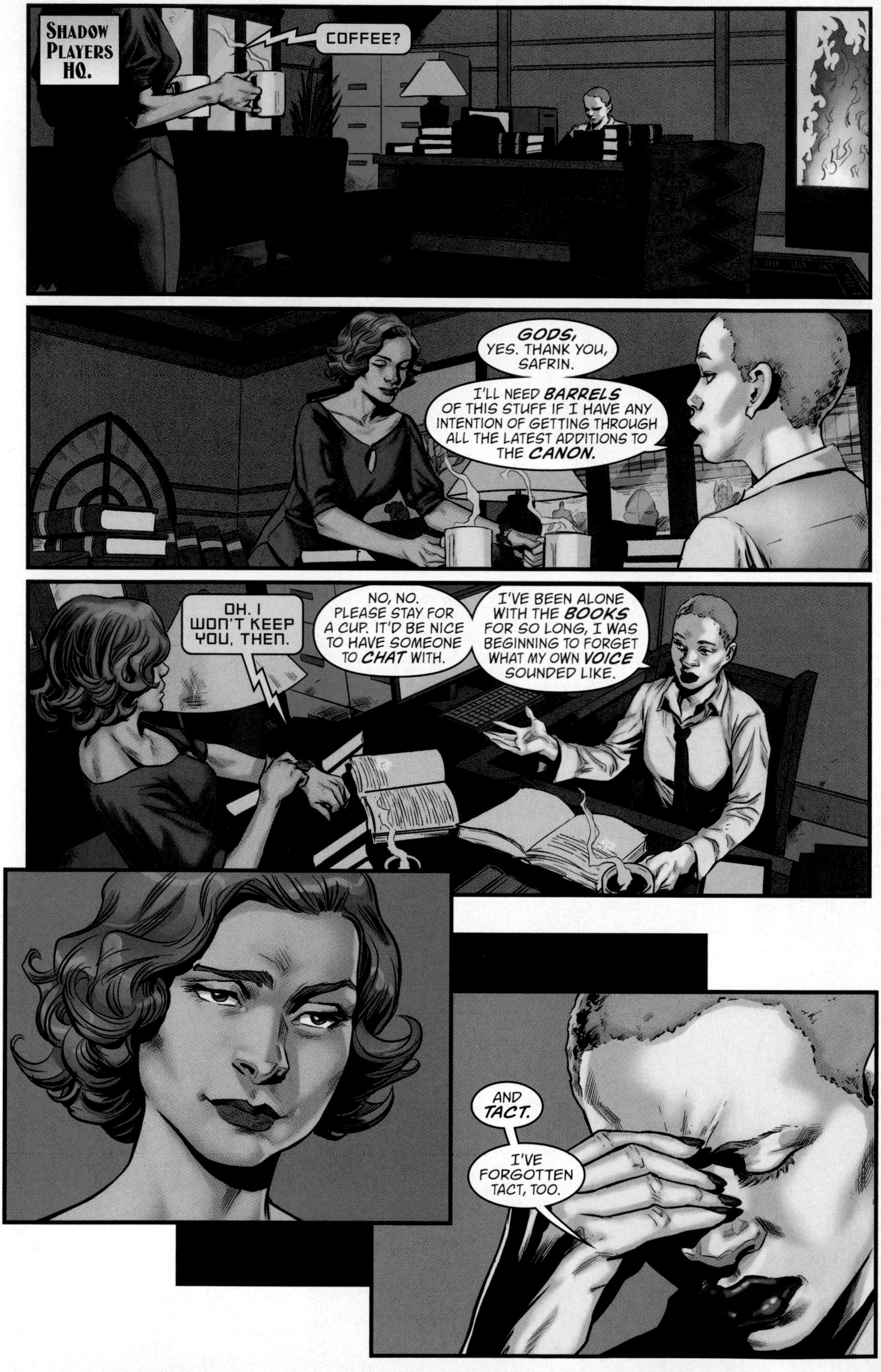
SHADOW PLAYERS HQ.
COFFEE?
GODS, YES. THANK YOU, SAFRIN.
I'LL NEED BARRELS OF THIS STUFF IF I HAVE ANY INTENTION OF GETTING THROUGH ALL THE LATEST ADDITIONS TO THE CANON.
OH. I WON'T KEEP YOU, THEN.
NO, NO. PLEASE STAY FOR A CUP. IT'D BE NICE TO HAVE SOMEONE TO CHAT WITH.
I'VE BEEN ALONE WITH THE BOOKS FOR SO LONG, I WAS BEGINNING TO FORGET WHAT MY OWN VOICE SOUNDED LIKE.
AND TACT.
I'VE FORGOTTEN TACT, TOO.

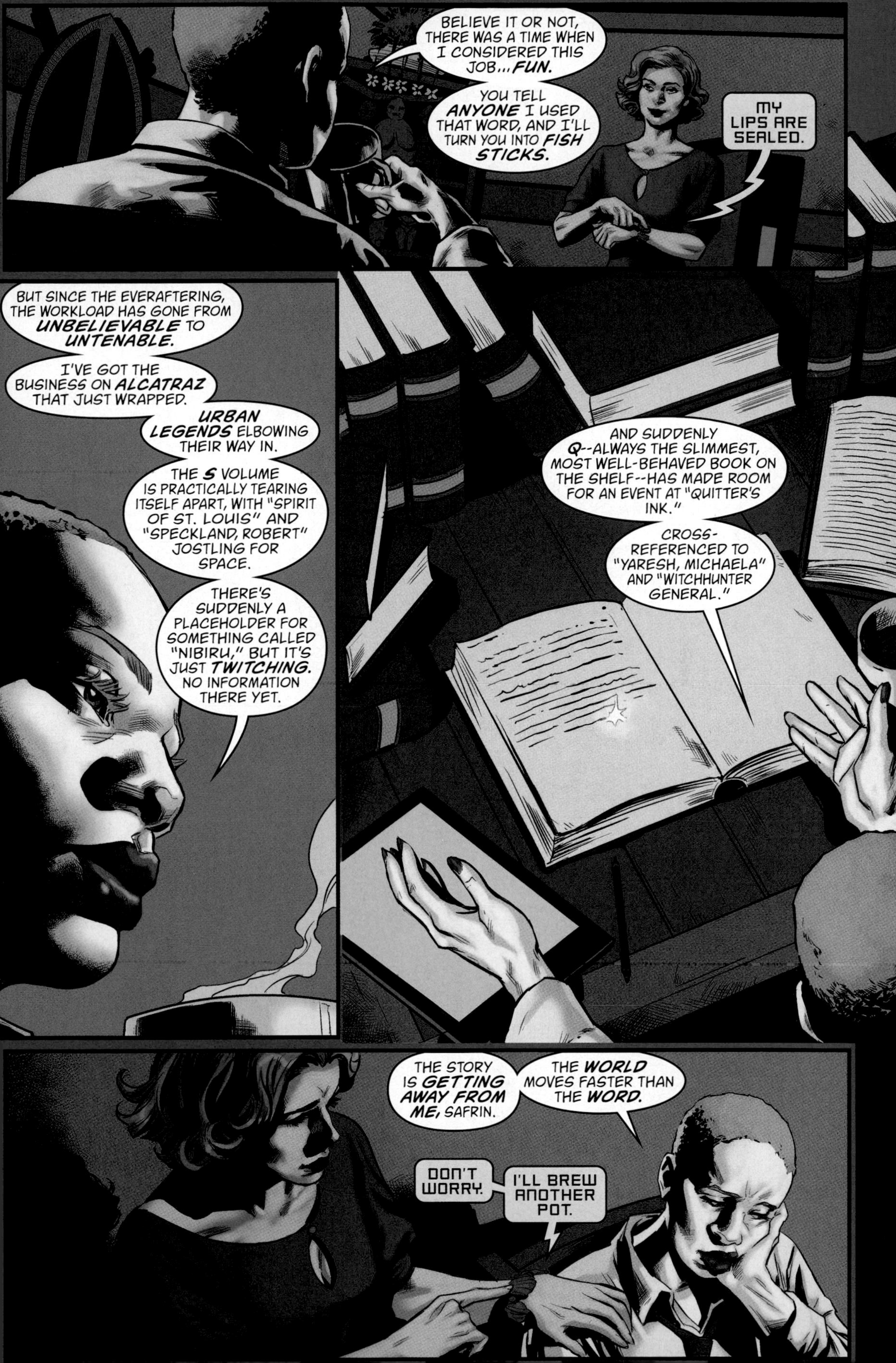
BELIEVE IT OR NOT, THERE WAS A TIME WHEN I CONSIDERED THIS JOB... FUN.
YOU TELL ANYONE I USED THAT WORD, AND I'LL TURN YOU INTO FISH STICKS.
MY LIPS ARE SEALED.
BUT SINCE THE EVERAFTERING, THE WORKLOAD HAS GONE FROM UNBELIEVABLE TO UNTENABLE.
I'VE GOT THE BUSINESS ON ALCATRAZ THAT JUST WRAPPED.
URBAN LEGENDS ELBOWING THEIR WAY IN.
THE S VOLUME IS PRACTICALLY TEARING ITSELF APART, WITH "SPIRIT OF ST. LOUIS" AND "SPECKLAND, ROBERT" JOSTLING FOR SPACE.
THERE'S SUDDENLY A PLACEHOLDER FOR SOMETHING CALLED "NIBIRU," BUT IT'S JUST TWITCHING. NO INFORMATION THERE YET.
AND SUDDENLY Q--ALWAYS THE SLIMMEST, MOST WELL-BEHAVED BOOK ON THE SHELF--HAS MADE ROOM FOR AN EVENT AT "QUITTER'S INK."
CROSS-REFERENCED TO "YARESH, MICHAELA" AND "WITCHHUNTER GENERAL."
THE STORY IS GETTING AWAY FROM ME, SAFRIN.
THE WORLD MOVES FASTER THAN THE WORD.
DON'T WORRY.
I'LL BREW ANOTHER POT.

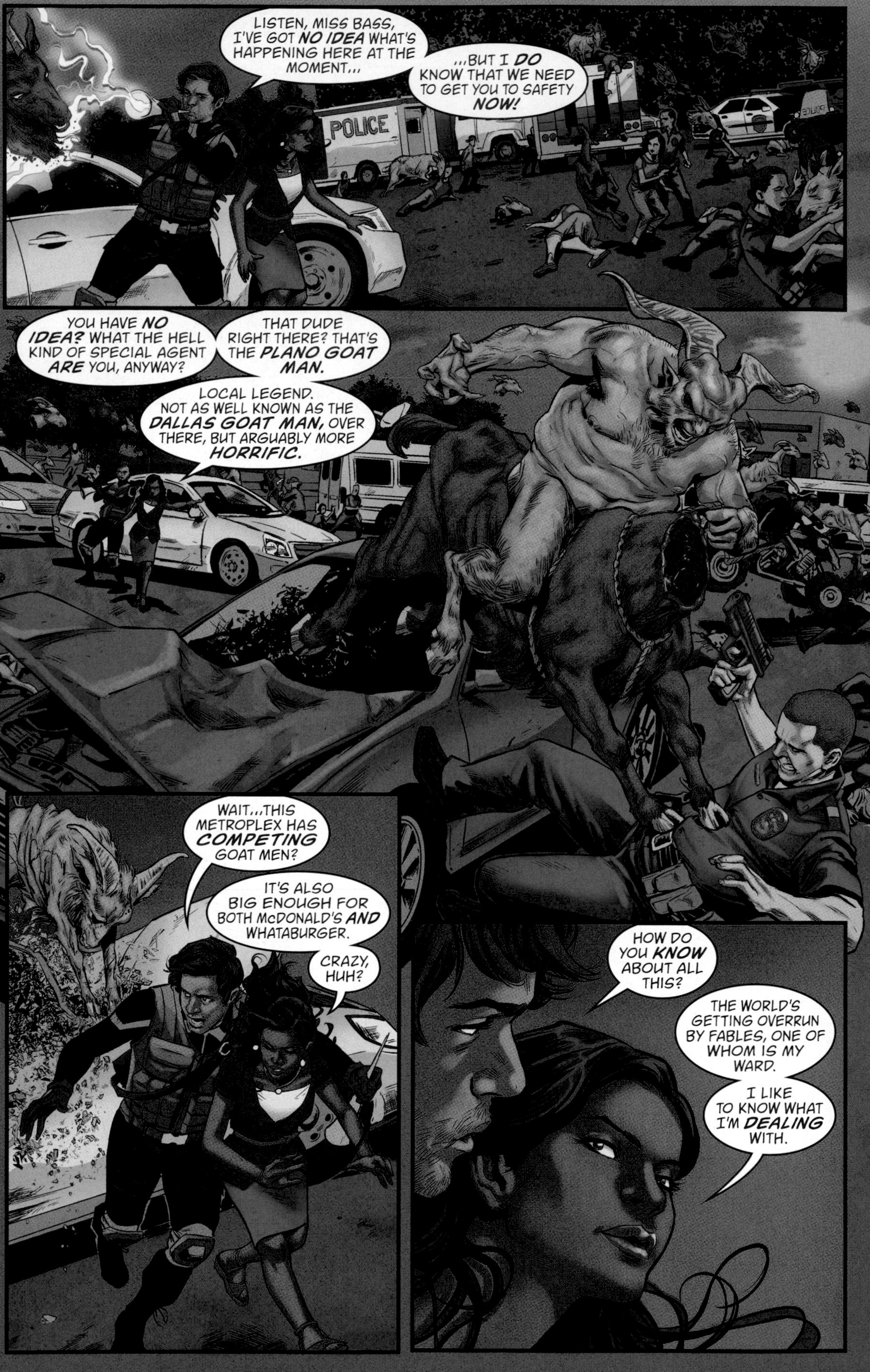

LISTEN, MISS BASS, I'VE GOT NO IDEA WHAT'S HAPPENING HERE AT THE MOMENT...
...BUT I DO KNOW THAT WE NEED TO GET YOU TO SAFETY NOW!
POLICE
YOU HAVE NO IDEA? WHAT THE HELL KIND OF SPECIAL AGENT ARE YOU, ANYWAY?
THAT DUDE RIGHT THERE? THAT'S THE PLANO GOAT MAN.
LOCAL LEGEND. NOT AS WELL KNOWN AS THE DALLAS GOAT MAN, OVER THERE, BUT ARGUABLY MORE HORRIFIC.
WAIT...THIS METROPLEX HAS COMPETING GOAT MEN?
IT'S ALSO BIG ENOUGH FOR BOTH McDONALD'S AND WHATABURGER.
CRAZY, HUH?
HOW DO YOU KNOW ABOUT ALL THIS?
THE WORLD'S GETTING OVERRUN BY FABLES, ONE OF WHOM IS MY WARD.
I LIKE TO KNOW WHAT I'M DEALING WITH.

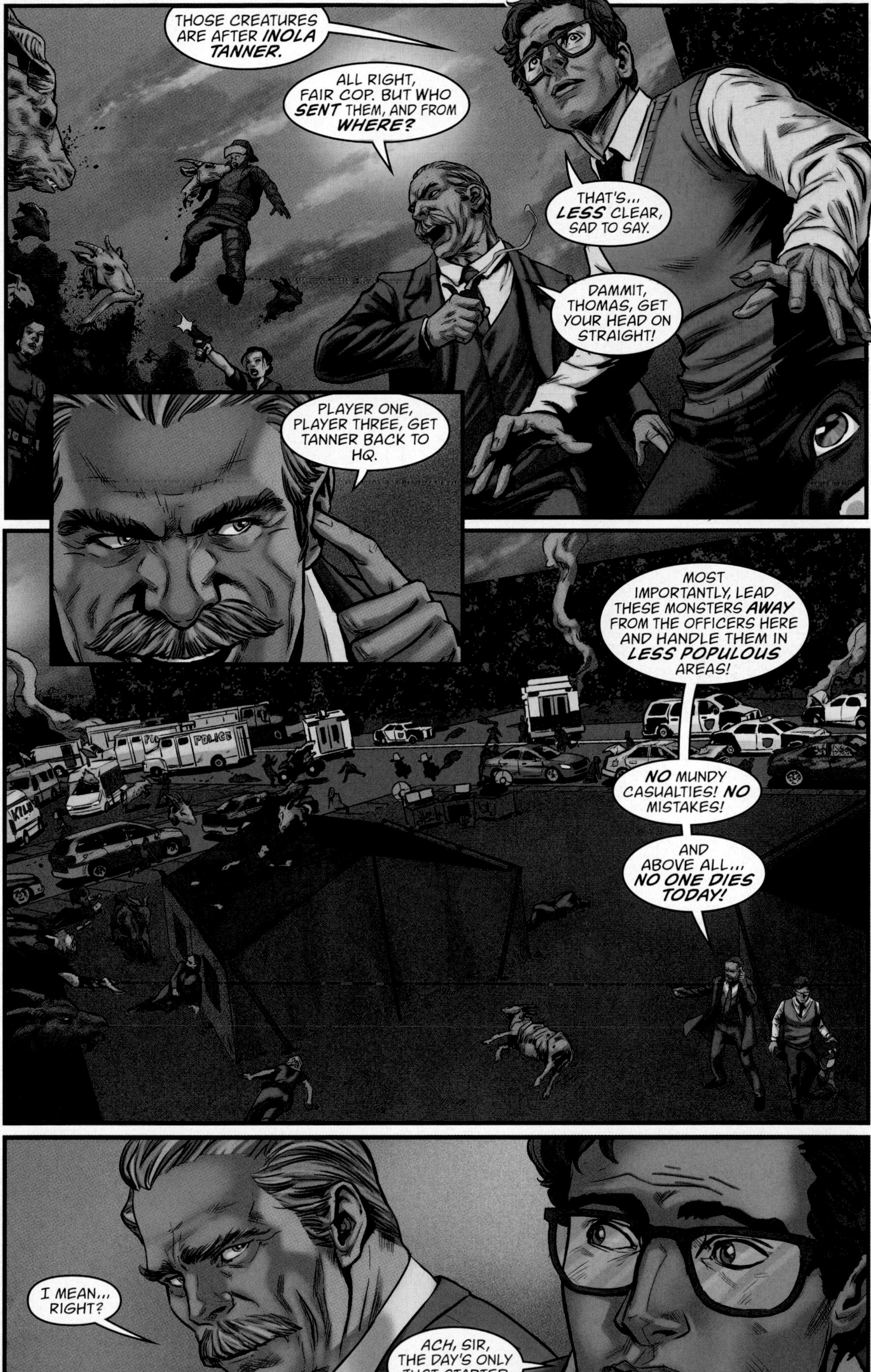
THOSE CREATURES ARE AFTER INOLA TANNER.
ALL RIGHT, FAIR COP. BUT WHO SENT THEM, AND FROM WHERE?
THAT'S... LESS CLEAR, SAD TO SAY.
DAMMIT, THOMAS, GET YOUR HEAD ON STRAIGHT!
PLAYER ONE, PLAYER THREE, GET TANNER BACK TO HQ.
MOST IMPORTANTLY, LEAD THESE MONSTERS AWAY FROM THE OFFICERS HERE AND HANDLE THEM IN LESS POPULOUS AREAS!
NO MUNDY CASUALTIES! NO MISTAKES!
AND ABOVE ALL... NO ONE DIES TODAY!
POLICE
I MEAN... RIGHT?
ACH, SIR, THE DAY'S ONLY JUST STARTED.

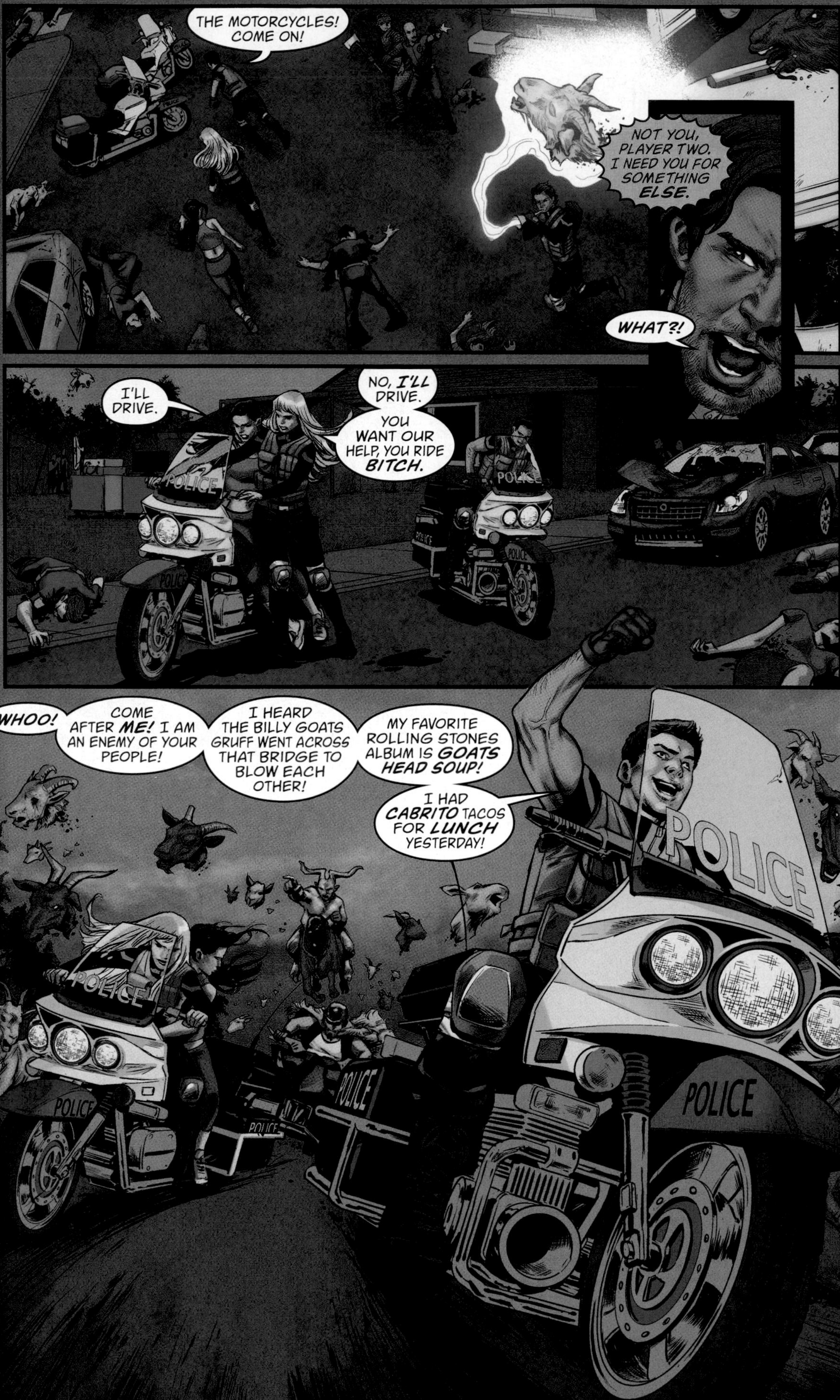
THE MOTORCYCLES! COME ON!
NOT YOU, PLAYER TWO. I NEED YOU FOR SOMETHING ELSE.
WHAT?!
I'LL DRIVE.
NO, I'LL DRIVE.
YOU WANT OUR HELP, YOU RIDE BITCH.
POLICE
WHOO!
COME AFTER ME! I AM AN ENEMY OF YOUR PEOPLE!
I HEARD THE BILLY GOATS GRUFF WENT ACROSS THAT BRIDGE TO BLOW EACH OTHER!
MY FAVORITE ROLLING STONES ALBUM IS GOATS HEAD SOUP!
I HAD CABRITO TACOS FOR LUNCH YESTERDAY!
POLICE

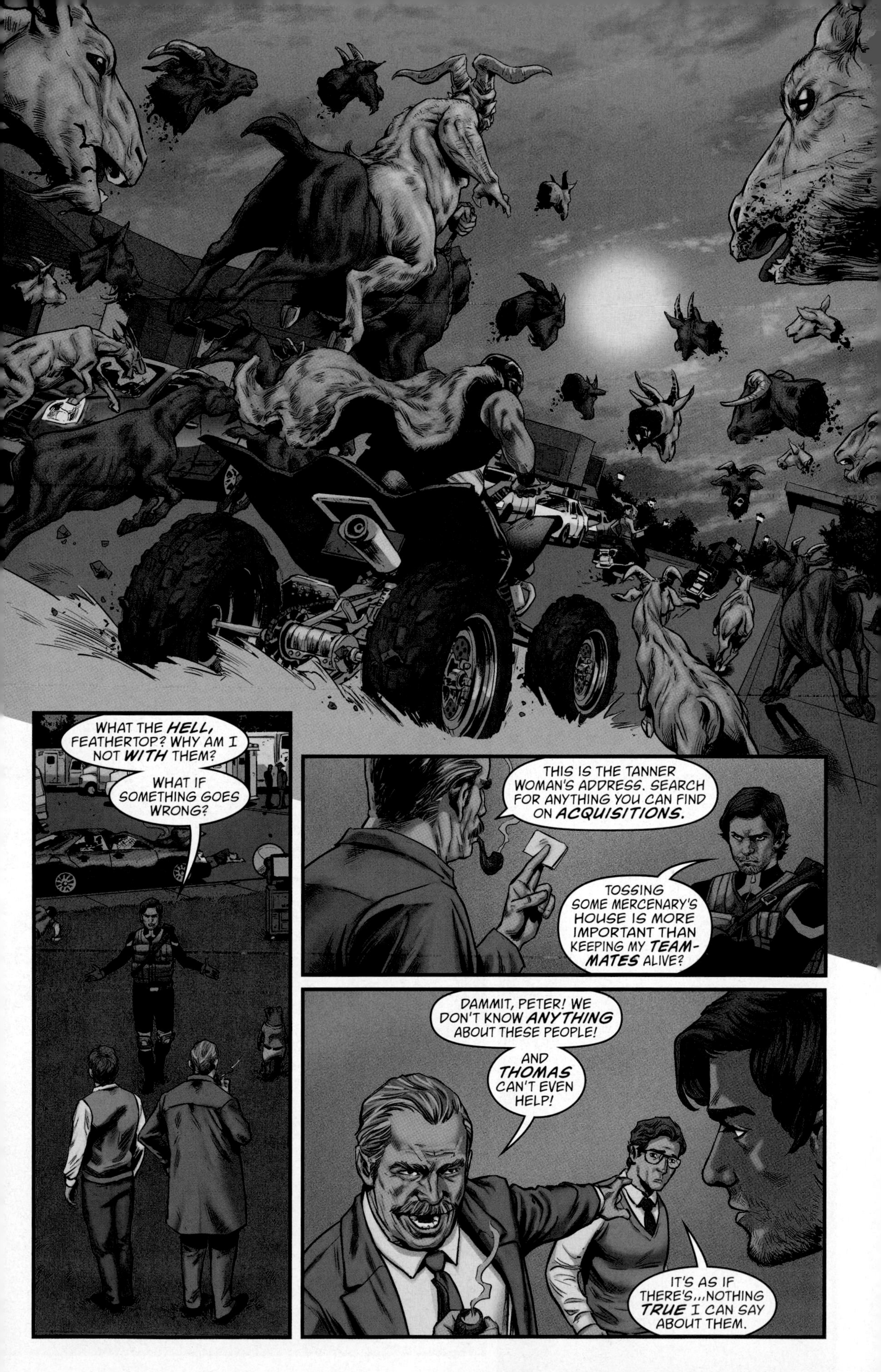
WHAT THE HELL, FEATHERTOP? WHY AM I NOT WITH THEM?
WHAT IF SOMETHING GOES WRONG?
THIS IS THE TANNER WOMAN'S ADDRESS. SEARCH FOR ANYTHING YOU CAN FIND ON ACQUISITIONS.
TOSSING SOME MERCENARY'S HOUSE IS MORE IMPORTANT THAN KEEPING MY TEAM-MATES ALIVE?
DAMMIT, PETER! WE DON'T KNOW ANYTHING ABOUT THESE PEOPLE!
AND THOMAS CAN'T EVEN HELP!
IT'S AS IF THERE'S...NOTHING TRUE I CAN SAY ABOUT THEM.

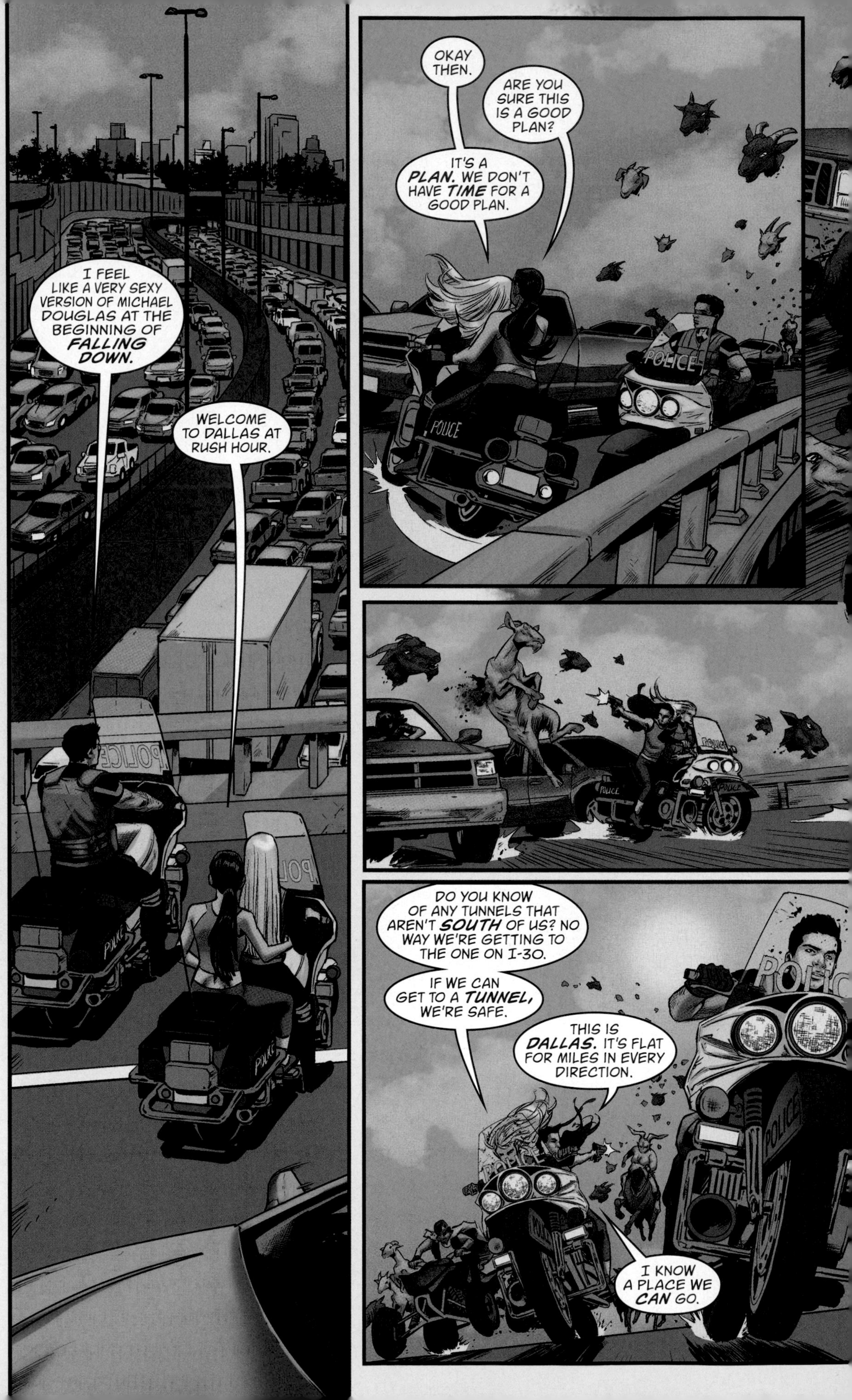

I FEEL LIKE A VERY SEXY VERSION OF MICHAEL DOUGLAS AT THE BEGINNING OF FALLING DOWN.
WELCOME TO DALLAS AT RUSH HOUR.
OKAY THEN.
ARE YOU SURE THIS IS A GOOD PLAN?
IT'S A PLAN. WE DON'T HAVE TIME FOR A GOOD PLAN.
POLICE
DO YOU KNOW OF ANY TUNNELS THAT AREN'T SOUTH OF US? NO WAY WE'RE GETTING TO THE ONE ON I-30.
IF WE CAN GET TO A TUNNEL, WE'RE SAFE.
THIS IS DALLAS. IT'S FLAT FOR MILES IN EVERY DIRECTION.
I KNOW A PLACE WE CAN GO.

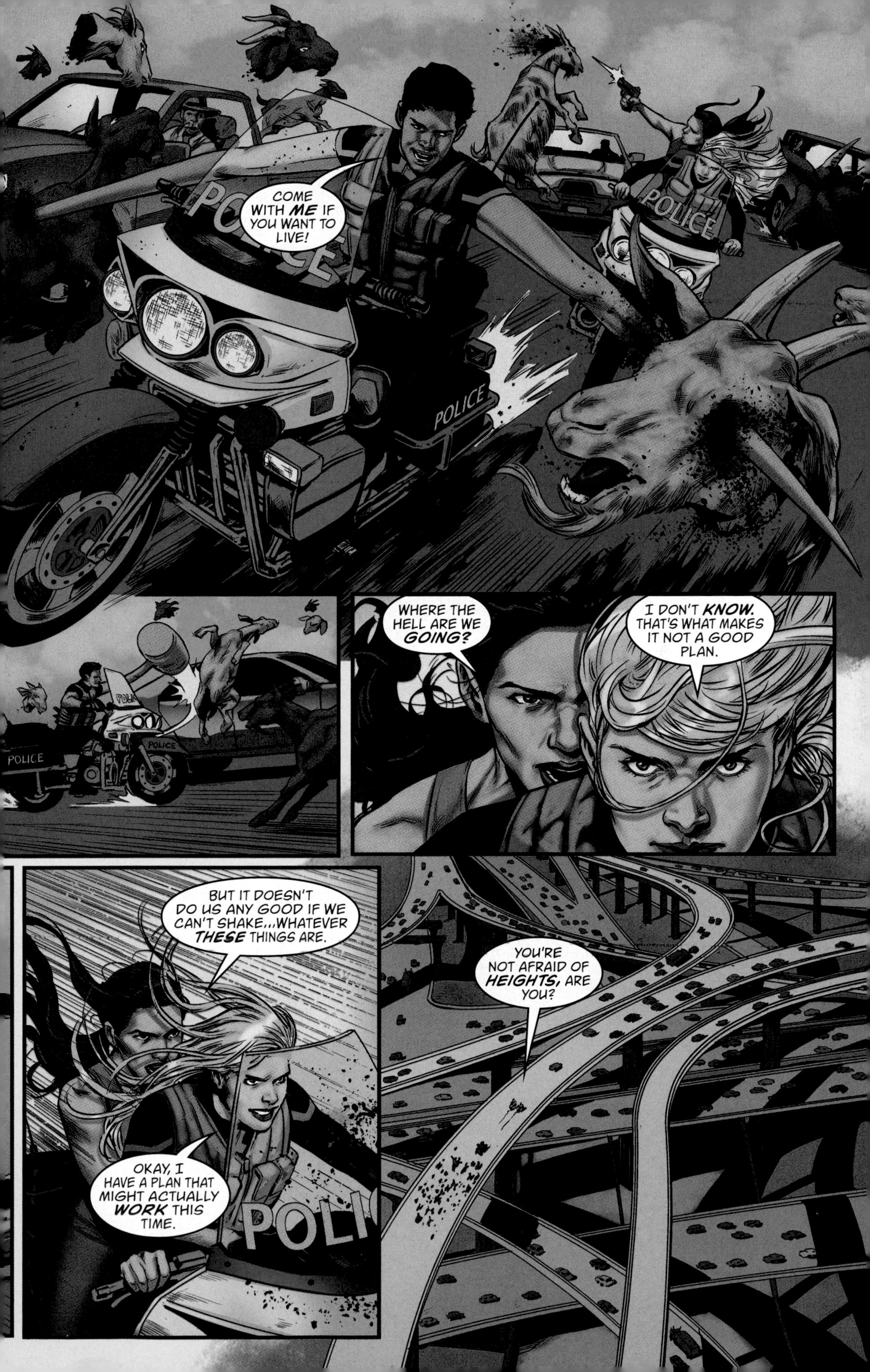
POLICE
COME WITH ME IF YOU WANT TO LIVE!
POLICE
POLICE
POLICE
POLICE
WHERE THE HELL ARE WE GOING?
I DON'T KNOW. THAT'S WHAT MAKES IT NOT A GOOD PLAN.
BUT IT DOESN'T DO US ANY GOOD IF WE CAN'T SHAKE...WHATEVER THESE THINGS ARE.
OKAY, I HAVE A PLAN THAT MIGHT ACTUALLY WORK THIS TIME.
POLI
YOU'RE NOT AFRAID OF HEIGHTS, ARE YOU?

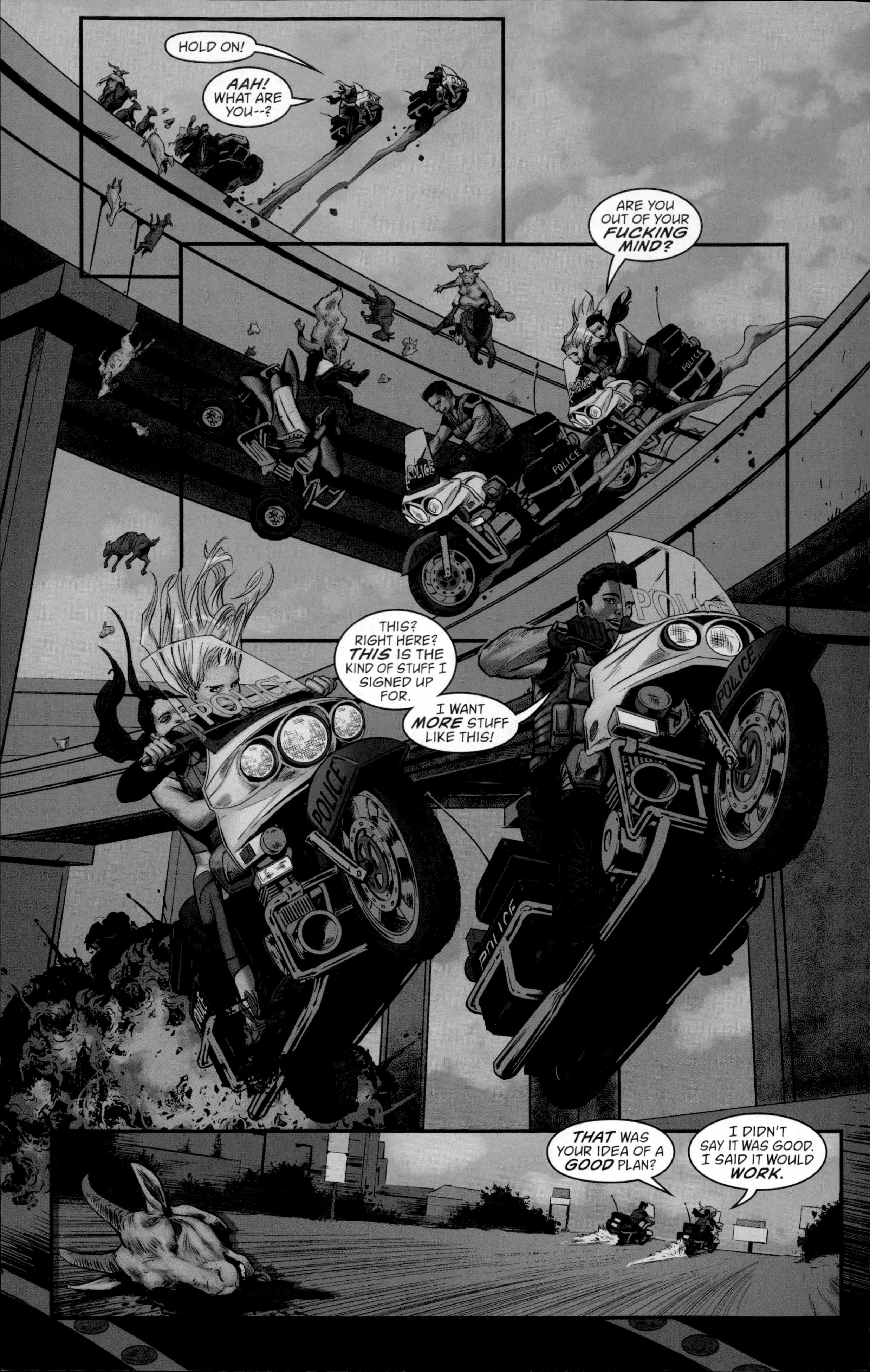
HOLD ON!
AAH! WHAT ARE YOU--?
ARE YOU OUT OF YOUR FUCKING MIND?
POLICE
THIS? RIGHT HERE? THIS IS THE KIND OF STUFF I SIGNED UP FOR.
I WANT MORE STUFF LIKE THIS!
THAT WAS YOUR IDEA OF A GOOD PLAN?
I DIDN'T SAY IT WAS GOOD. I SAID IT WOULD WORK.

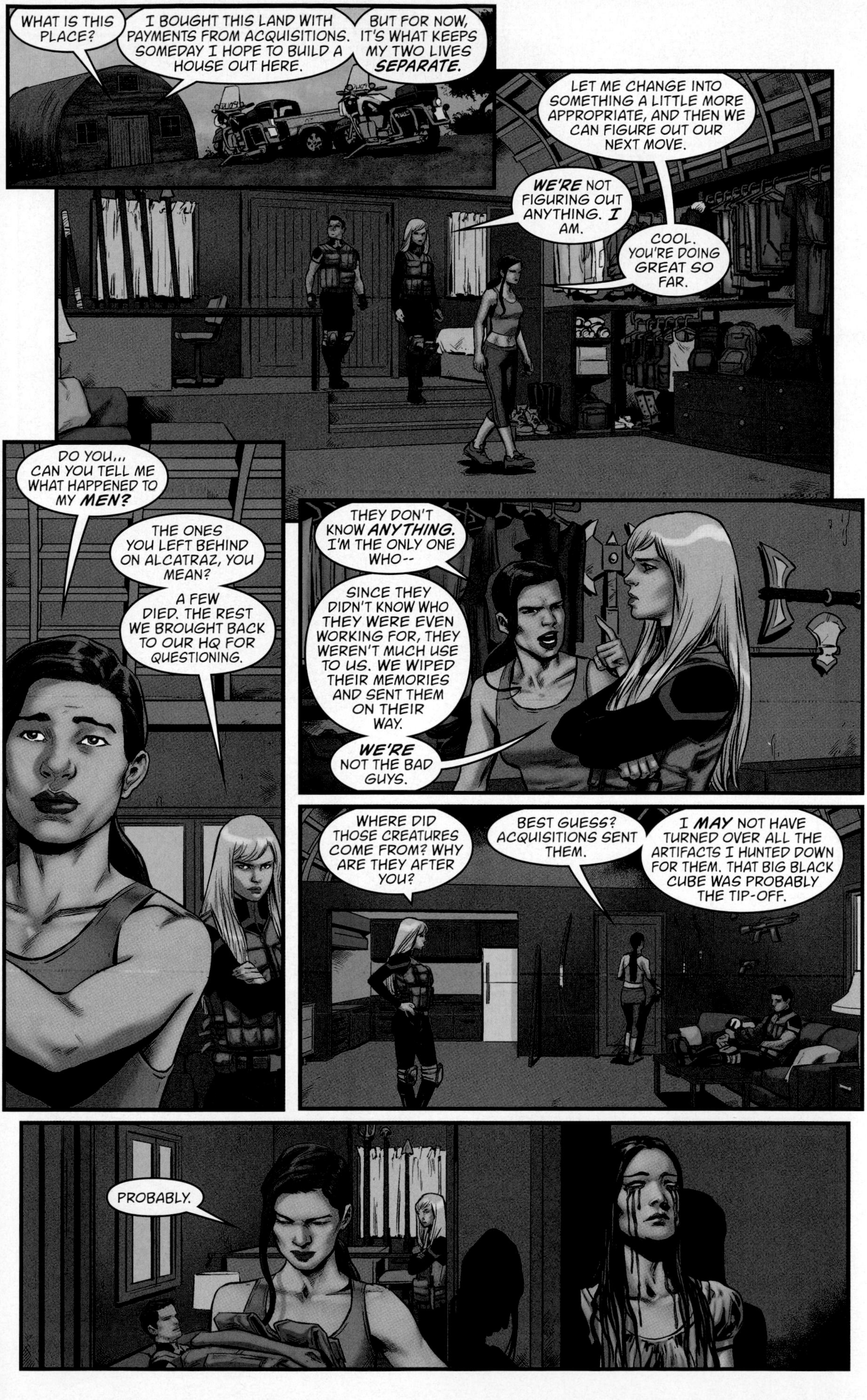
WHAT IS THIS PLACE?
I BOUGHT THIS LAND WITH PAYMENTS FROM ACQUISITIONS. SOMEDAY I HOPE TO BUILD A HOUSE OUT HERE.
BUT FOR NOW, IT'S WHAT KEEPS MY TWO LIVES SEPARATE.
LET ME CHANGE INTO SOMETHING A LITTLE MORE APPROPRIATE, AND THEN WE CAN FIGURE OUT OUR NEXT MOVE.
WE'RE NOT FIGURING OUT ANYTHING. I AM.
COOL. YOU'RE DOING GREAT SO FAR.
DO YOU... CAN YOU TELL ME WHAT HAPPENED TO MY MEN?
THE ONES YOU LEFT BEHIND ON ALCATRAZ, YOU MEAN?
A FEW DIED. THE REST WE BROUGHT BACK TO OUR HQ FOR QUESTIONING.
THEY DON'T KNOW ANYTHING. I'M THE ONLY ONE WHO--
SINCE THEY DIDN'T KNOW WHO THEY WERE EVEN WORKING FOR, THEY WEREN'T MUCH USE TO US. WE WIPED THEIR MEMORIES AND SENT THEM ON THEIR WAY.
WE'RE NOT THE BAD GUYS.
WHERE DID THOSE CREATURES COME FROM? WHY ARE THEY AFTER YOU?
BEST GUESS? ACQUISITIONS SENT THEM.
I MAY NOT HAVE TURNED OVER ALL THE ARTIFACTS I HUNTED DOWN FOR THEM. THAT BIG BLACK CUBE WAS PROBABLY THE TIP-OFF.
PROBABLY.

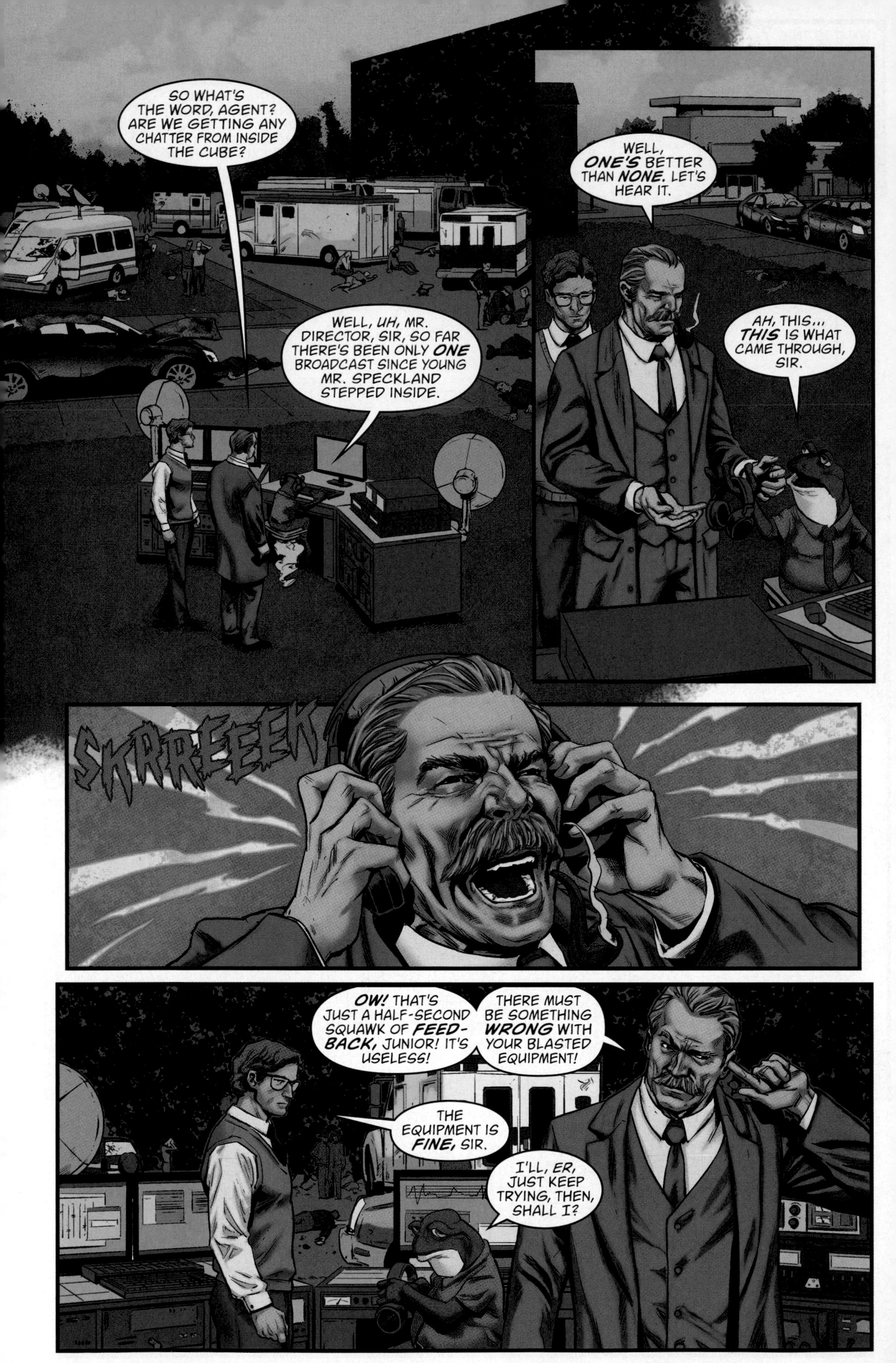

SO WHAT'S THE WORD, AGENT? ARE WE GETTING ANY CHATTER FROM INSIDE THE CUBE?
WELL, UH, MR. DIRECTOR, SIR, SO FAR THERE'S BEEN ONLY ONE BROADCAST SINCE YOUNG MR. SPECKLAND STEPPED INSIDE.
WELL, ONE'S BETTER THAN NONE. LET'S HEAR IT.
AH, THIS... THIS IS WHAT CAME THROUGH, SIR.
SKRREEEK
OW! THAT'S JUST A HALF-SECOND SQUAWK OF FEED-BACK, JUNIOR! IT'S USELESS!
THERE MUST BE SOMETHING WRONG WITH YOUR BLASTED EQUIPMENT!
THE EQUIPMENT IS FINE, SIR.
I'LL, ER, JUST KEEP TRYING, THEN, SHALL I?

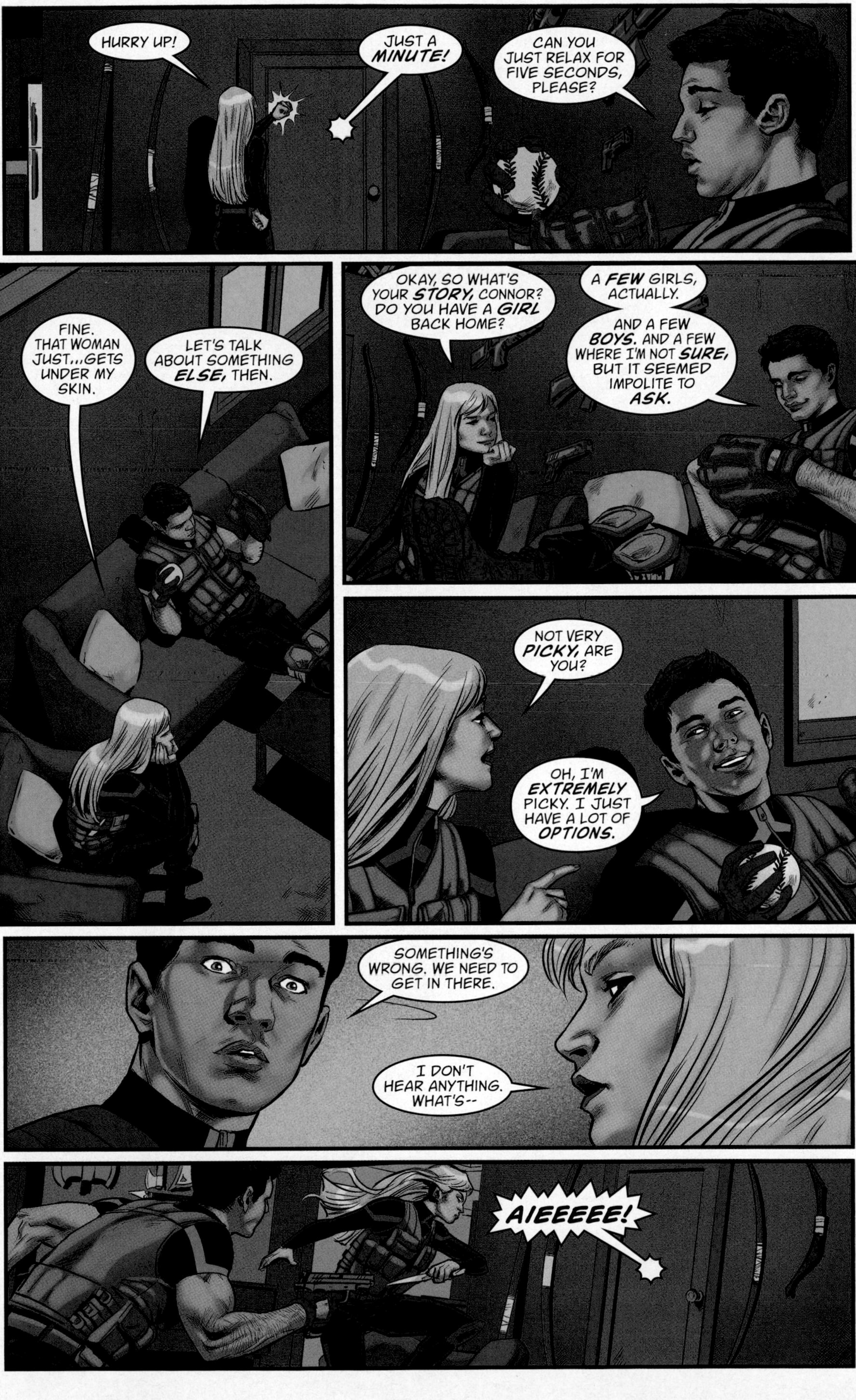
HURRY UP!
JUST A MINUTE!
CAN YOU JUST RELAX FOR FIVE SECONDS, PLEASE?
FINE. THAT WOMAN JUST...GETS UNDER MY SKIN.
LET'S TALK ABOUT SOMETHING ELSE, THEN.
OKAY, SO WHAT'S YOUR STORY, CONNOR? DO YOU HAVE A GIRL BACK HOME?
A FEW GIRLS, ACTUALLY.
AND A FEW BOYS. AND A FEW WHERE I'M NOT SURE, BUT IT SEEMED IMPOLITE TO ASK.
NOT VERY PICKY, ARE YOU?
OH, I'M EXTREMELY PICKY. I JUST HAVE A LOT OF OPTIONS.
SOMETHING'S WRONG. WE NEED TO GET IN THERE.
I DON'T HEAR ANYTHING. WHAT'S--
AIEEEEE!

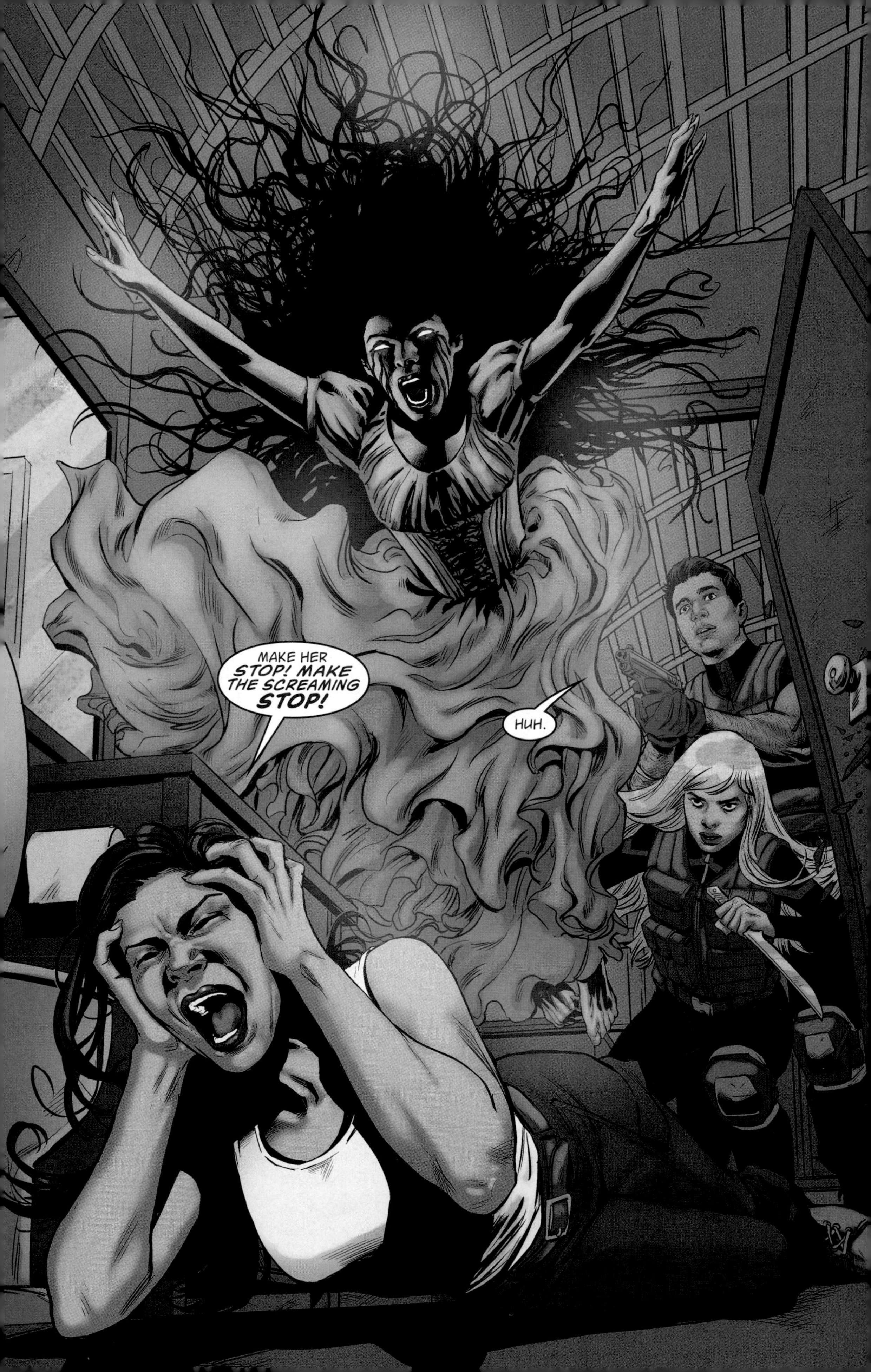
MAKE HER STOP! MAKE THE SCREAMING STOP!
HUH.

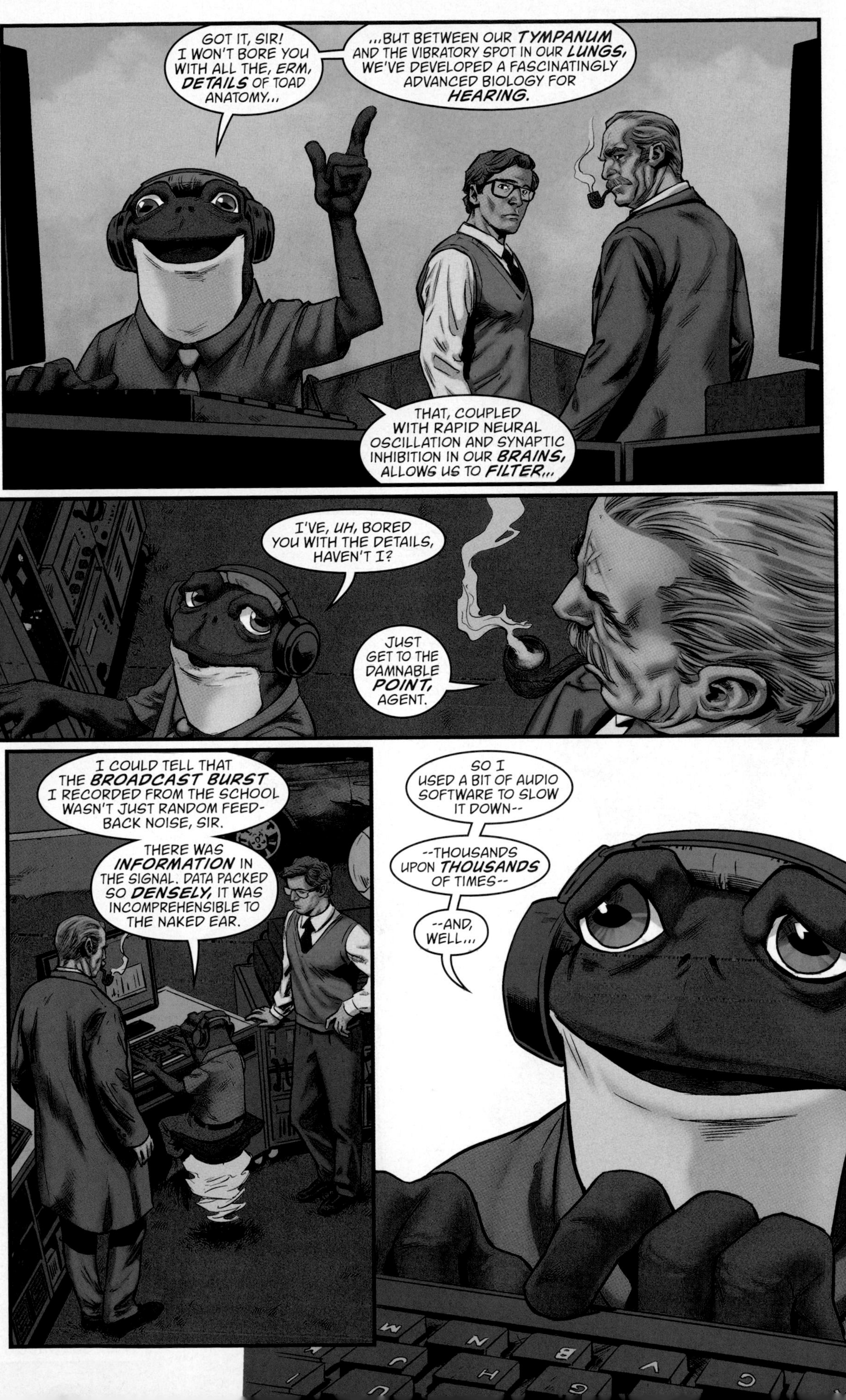
GOT IT, SIR! I WON'T BORE YOU WITH ALL THE, ERM, DETAILS OF TOAD ANATOMY...
...BUT BETWEEN OUR TYMPANUM AND THE VIBRATORY SPOT IN OUR LUNGS, WE'VE DEVELOPED A FASCINATINGLY ADVANCED BIOLOGY FOR HEARING.
THAT, COUPLED WITH RAPID NEURAL OSCILLATION AND SYNAPTIC INHIBITION IN OUR BRAINS, ALLOWS US TO FILTER...
I'VE, UH, BORED YOU WITH THE DETAILS, HAVEN'T I?
JUST GET TO THE DAMNABLE POINT, AGENT.
I COULD TELL THAT THE BROADCAST BURST I RECORDED FROM THE SCHOOL WASN'T JUST RANDOM FEED-BACK NOISE, SIR.
THERE WAS INFORMATION IN THE SIGNAL. DATA PACKED SO DENSELY, IT WAS INCOMPREHENSIBLE TO THE NAKED EAR.
SO I USED A BIT OF AUDIO SOFTWARE TO SLOW IT DOWN--
--THOUSANDS UPON THOUSANDS OF TIMES--
--AND, WELL...

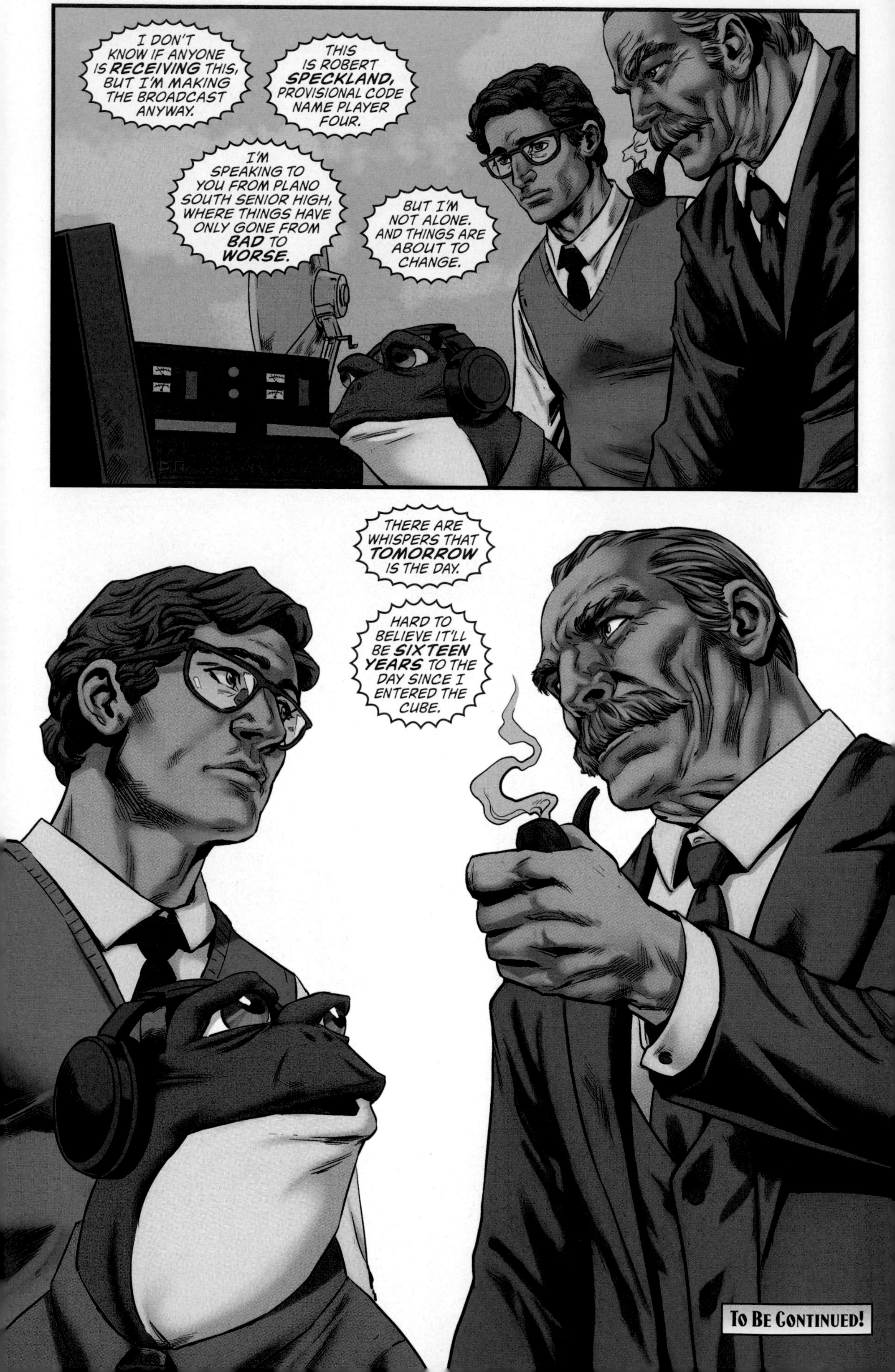
I DON'T KNOW IF ANYONE IS RECEIVING THIS, BUT I'M MAKING THE BROADCAST ANYWAY.
THIS IS ROBERT SPECKLAND, PROVISIONAL CODE NAME PLAYER FOUR.
I'M SPEAKING TO YOU FROM PLANO SOUTH SENIOR HIGH, WHERE THINGS HAVE ONLY GONE FROM BAD TO WORSE.
BUT I'M NOT ALONE. AND THINGS ARE ABOUT TO CHANGE.
THERE ARE WHISPERS THAT TOMORROW IS THE DAY.
HARD TO BELIEVE IT'LL BE SIXTEEN YEARS TO THE DAY SINCE I ENTERED THE CUBE.
TO BE CONTINUED!

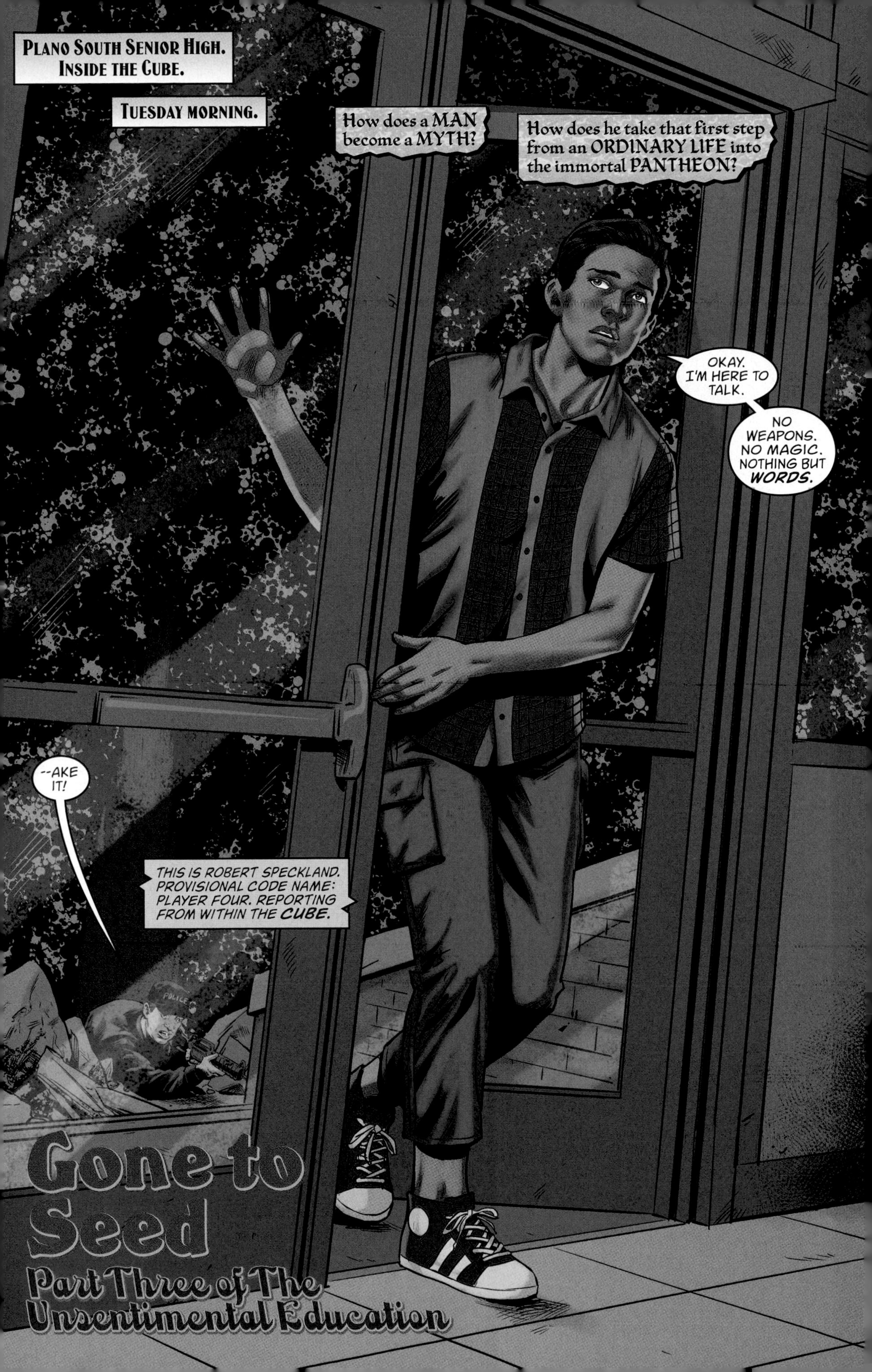

Plano South Senior High. Inside the Cube.
Tuesday morning.
How does a MAN become a MYTH?
How does he take that first step from an ORDINARY LIFE into the immortal PANTHEON?
OKAY. I'M HERE TO TALK.
NO WEAPONS. NO MAGIC. NOTHING BUT WORDS.
--AKE IT!
THIS IS ROBERT SPECKLAND. PROVISIONAL CODE NAME: PLAYER FOUR. REPORTING FROM WITHIN THE CUBE.
POLICE
Gone to Seed
Part Three of The Unsentimental Education

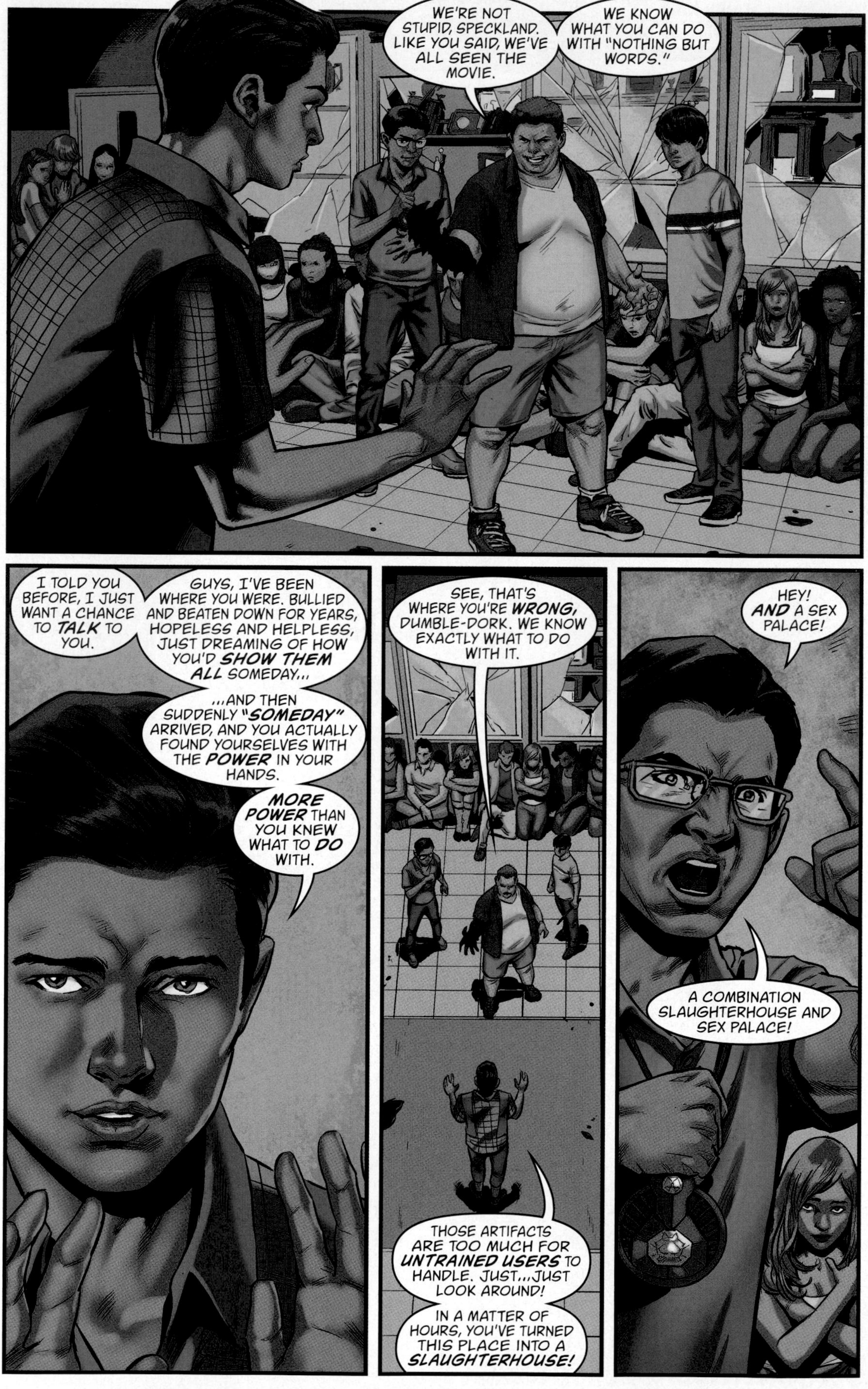
WE'RE NOT STUPID, SPECKLAND. LIKE YOU SAID, WE'VE ALL SEEN THE MOVIE.
WE KNOW WHAT YOU CAN DO WITH "NOTHING BUT WORDS."
I TOLD YOU BEFORE, I JUST WANT A CHANCE TO TALK TO YOU.
GUYS, I'VE BEEN WHERE YOU WERE. BULLIED AND BEATEN DOWN FOR YEARS, HOPELESS AND HELPLESS, JUST DREAMING OF HOW YOU'D SHOW THEM ALL SOMEDAY...
...AND THEN SUDDENLY "SOMEDAY" ARRIVED, AND YOU ACTUALLY FOUND YOURSELVES WITH THE POWER IN YOUR HANDS.
MORE POWER THAN YOU KNEW WHAT TO DO WITH.
SEE, THAT'S WHERE YOU'RE WRONG, DUMBLE-DORK. WE KNOW EXACTLY WHAT TO DO WITH IT.
THOSE ARTIFACTS ARE TOO MUCH FOR UNTRAINED USERS TO HANDLE. JUST...JUST LOOK AROUND!
IN A MATTER OF HOURS, YOU'VE TURNED THIS PLACE INTO A SLAUGHTERHOUSE!
A COMBINATION SLAUGHTERHOUSE AND SEX PALACE!
HEY! AND A SEX PALACE!

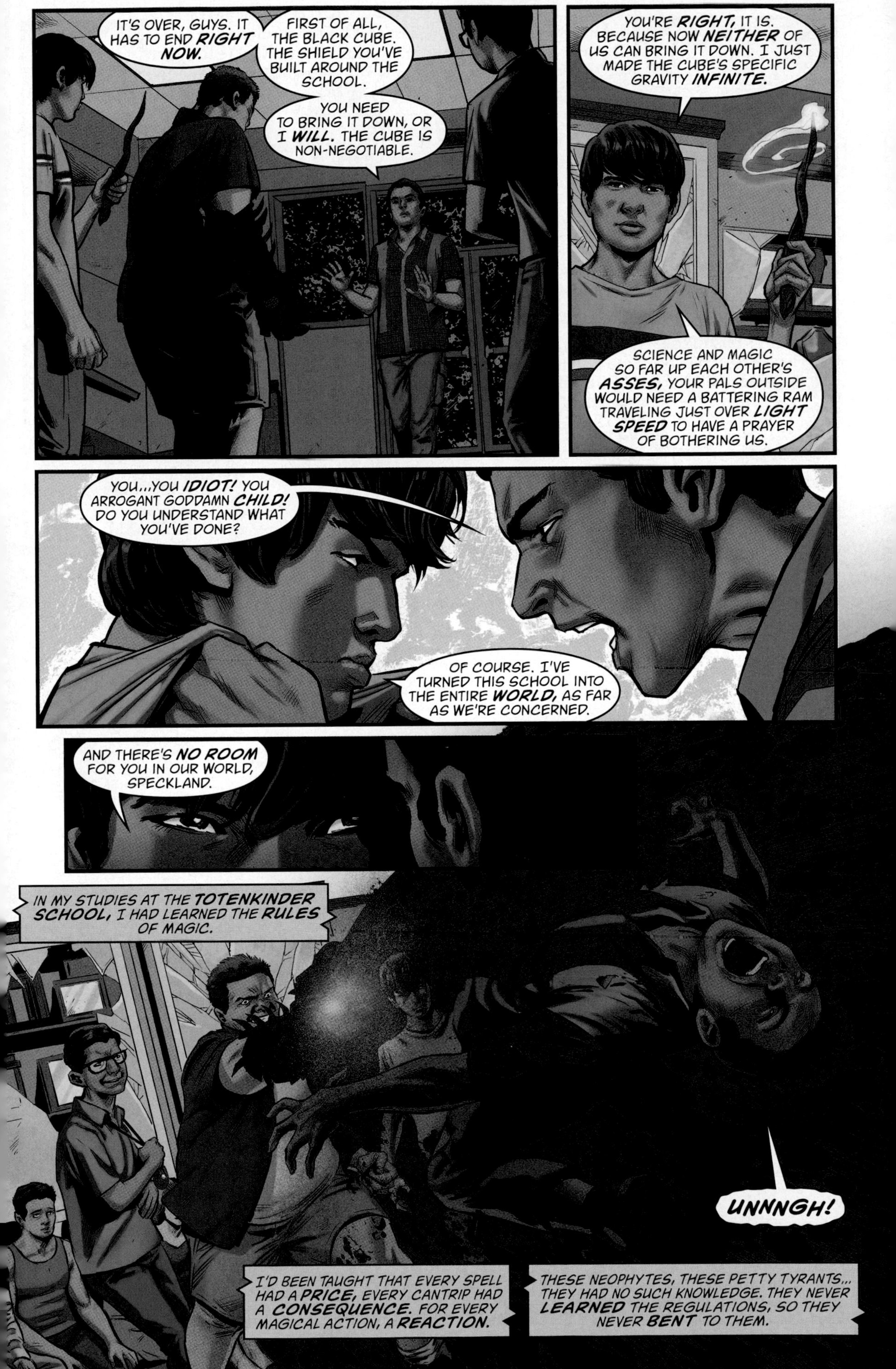
IT'S OVER, GUYS. IT HAS TO END RIGHT NOW.
FIRST OF ALL, THE BLACK CUBE. THE SHIELD YOU'VE BUILT AROUND THE SCHOOL.
YOU NEED TO BRING IT DOWN, OR I WILL. THE CUBE IS NON-NEGOTIABLE.
YOU'RE RIGHT, IT IS. BECAUSE NOW NEITHER OF US CAN BRING IT DOWN. I JUST MADE THE CUBE'S SPECIFIC GRAVITY INFINITE.
SCIENCE AND MAGIC SO FAR UP EACH OTHER'S ASSES, YOUR PALS OUTSIDE WOULD NEED A BATTERING RAM TRAVELING JUST OVER LIGHT SPEED TO HAVE A PRAYER OF BOTHERING US.
YOU...YOU IDIOT! YOU ARROGANT GODDAMN CHILD! DO YOU UNDERSTAND WHAT YOU'VE DONE?
OF COURSE. I'VE TURNED THIS SCHOOL INTO THE ENTIRE WORLD, AS FAR AS WE'RE CONCERNED.
AND THERE'S NO ROOM FOR YOU IN OUR WORLD, SPECKLAND.
IN MY STUDIES AT THE TOTENKINDER SCHOOL, I HAD LEARNED THE RULES OF MAGIC.
UNNNGH!
I'D BEEN TAUGHT THAT EVERY SPELL HAD A PRICE, EVERY CANTRIP HAD A CONSEQUENCE. FOR EVERY MAGICAL ACTION, A REACTION.
THESE NEOPHYTES, THESE PETTY TYRANTS... THEY HAD NO SUCH KNOWLEDGE. THEY NEVER LEARNED THE REGULATIONS, SO THEY NEVER BENT TO THEM.

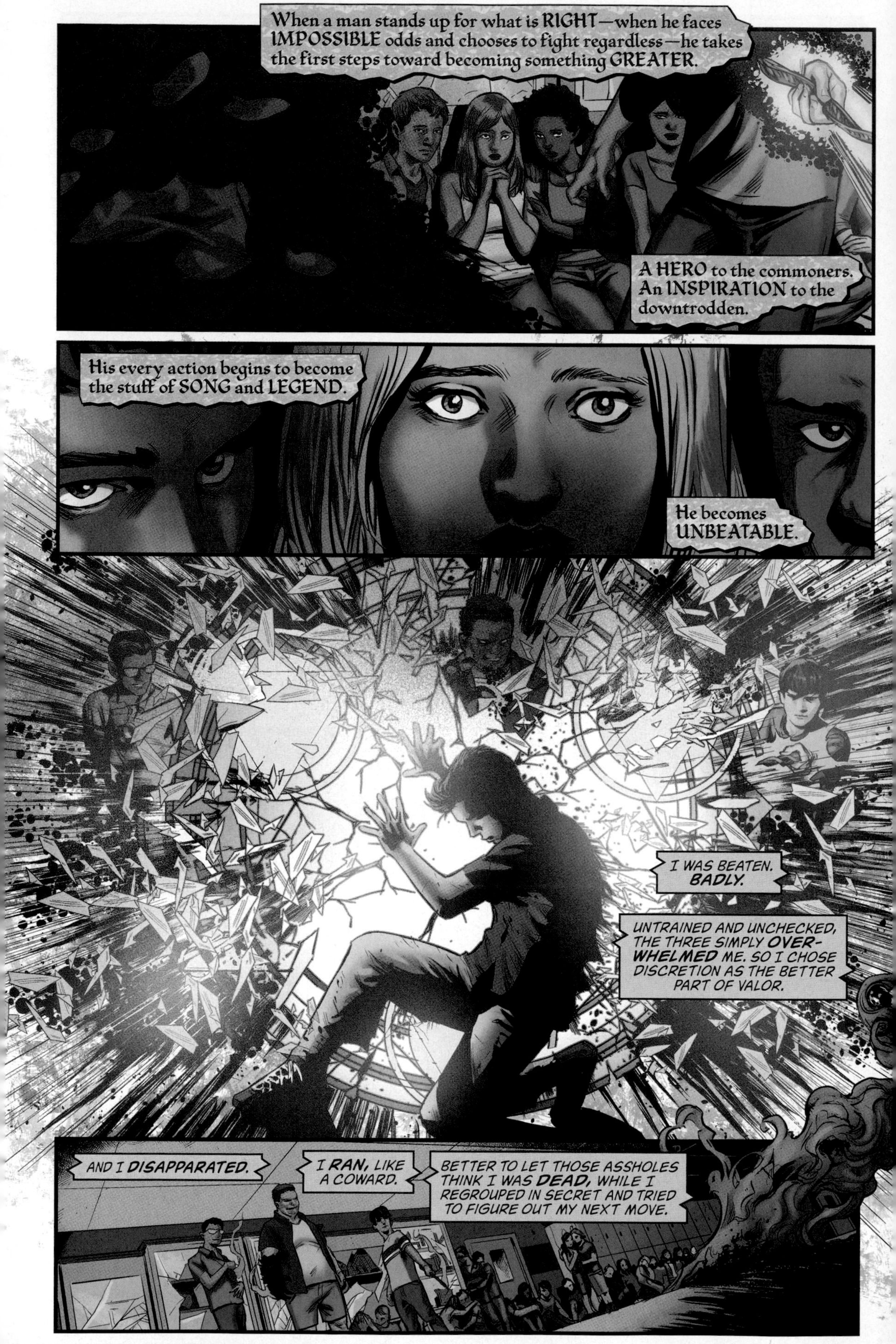
When a man stands up for what is RIGHT—when he faces IMPOSSIBLE odds and chooses to fight regardless—he takes the first steps toward becoming something GREATER.
A HERO to the commoners. An INSPIRATION to the downtrodden.
His every action begins to become the stuff of SONG and LEGEND.
He becomes UNBEATABLE.
I WAS BEATEN. BADLY.
UNTRAINED AND UNCHECKED, THE THREE SIMPLY OVER-WHELMED ME. SO I CHOSE DISCRETION AS THE BETTER PART OF VALOR.
AND I DISAPPARATED.
I RAN, LIKE A COWARD.
BETTER TO LET THOSE ASSHOLES THINK I WAS DEAD, WHILE I REGROUPED IN SECRET AND TRIED TO FIGURE OUT MY NEXT MOVE.

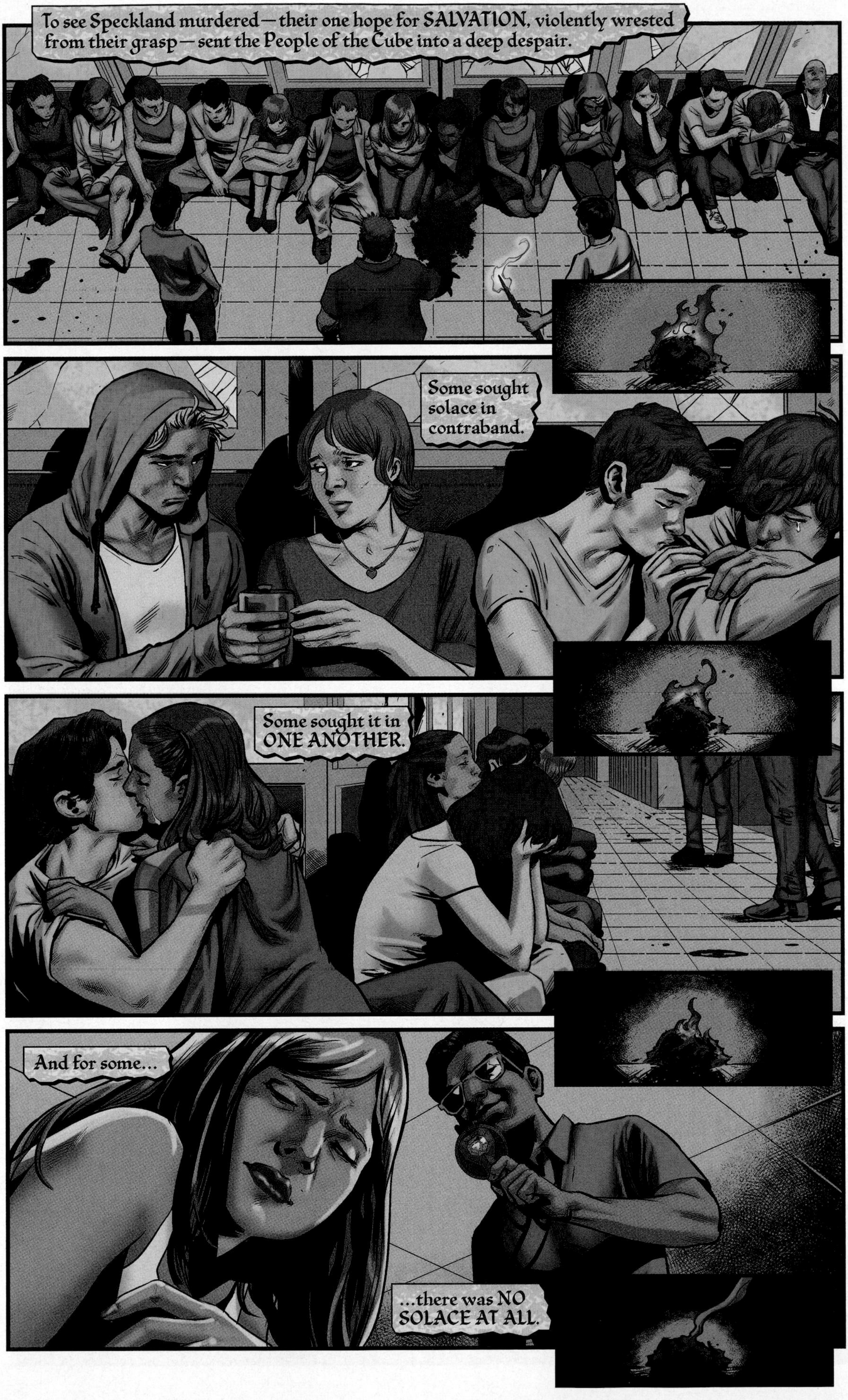
To see Speckland murdered—their one hope for SALVATION, violently wrested from their grasp—sent the People of the Cube into a deep despair.
Some sought solace in contraband.
Some sought it in ONE ANOTHER.
And for some...
...there was NO SOLACE AT ALL.

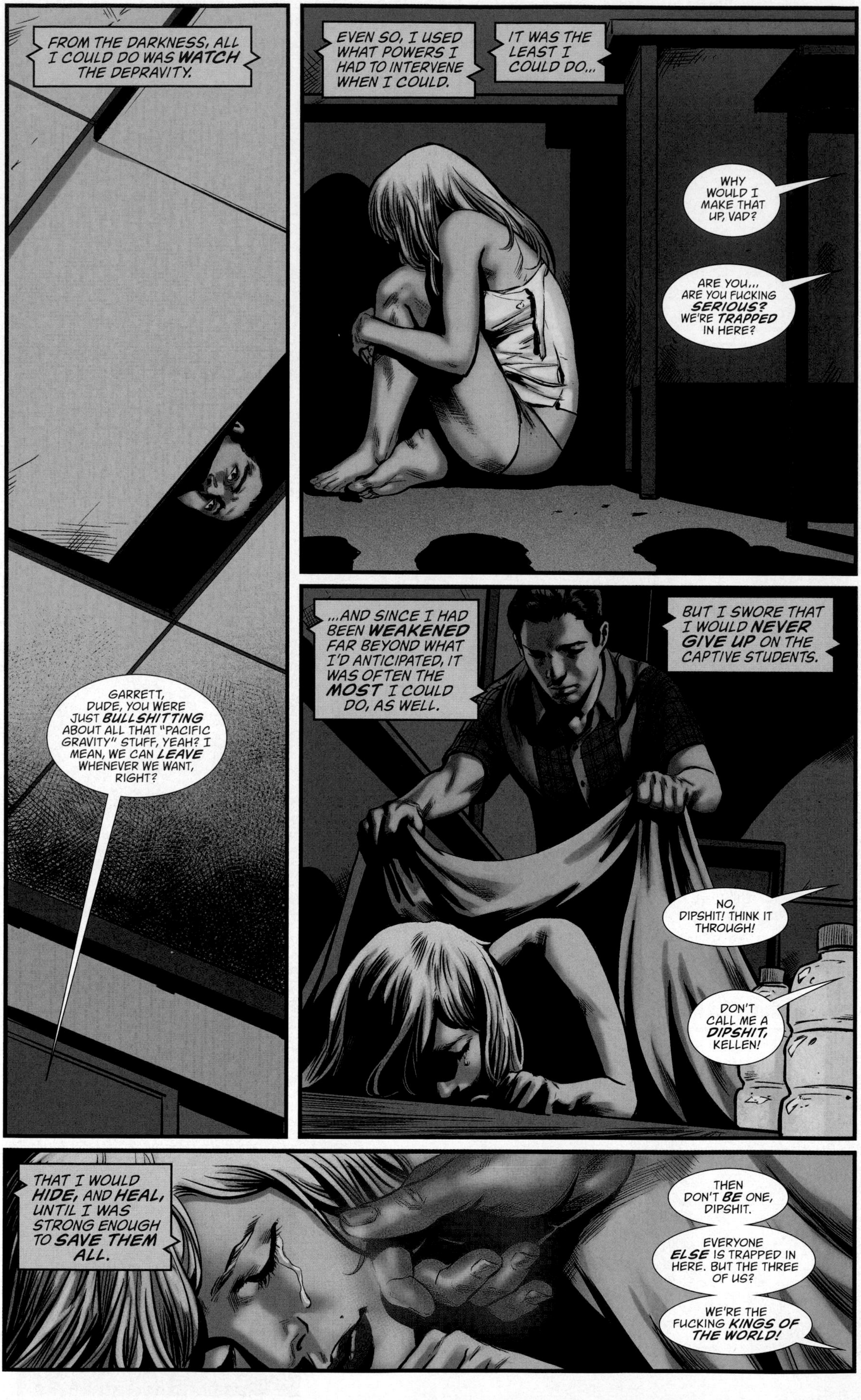
FROM THE DARKNESS, ALL I COULD DO WAS WATCH THE DEPRAVITY.
EVEN SO, I USED WHAT POWERS I HAD TO INTERVENE WHEN I COULD.
IT WAS THE LEAST I COULD DO...
WHY WOULD I MAKE THAT UP, VAD?
ARE YOU... ARE YOU FUCKING SERIOUS? WE'RE TRAPPED IN HERE?
GARRETT, DUDE, YOU WERE JUST BULLSHITTING ABOUT ALL THAT "PACIFIC GRAVITY" STUFF, YEAH? I MEAN, WE CAN LEAVE WHENEVER WE WANT, RIGHT?
...AND SINCE I HAD BEEN WEAKENED FAR BEYOND WHAT I'D ANTICIPATED, IT WAS OFTEN THE MOST I COULD DO, AS WELL.
BUT I SWORE THAT I WOULD NEVER GIVE UP ON THE CAPTIVE STUDENTS.
NO, DIPSHIT! THINK IT THROUGH!
DON'T CALL ME A DIPSHIT, KELLEN!
THAT I WOULD HIDE, AND HEAL, UNTIL I WAS STRONG ENOUGH TO SAVE THEM ALL.
THEN DON'T BE ONE, DIPSHIT.
EVERYONE ELSE IS TRAPPED IN HERE. BUT THE THREE OF US?
WE'RE THE FUCKING KINGS OF THE WORLD!

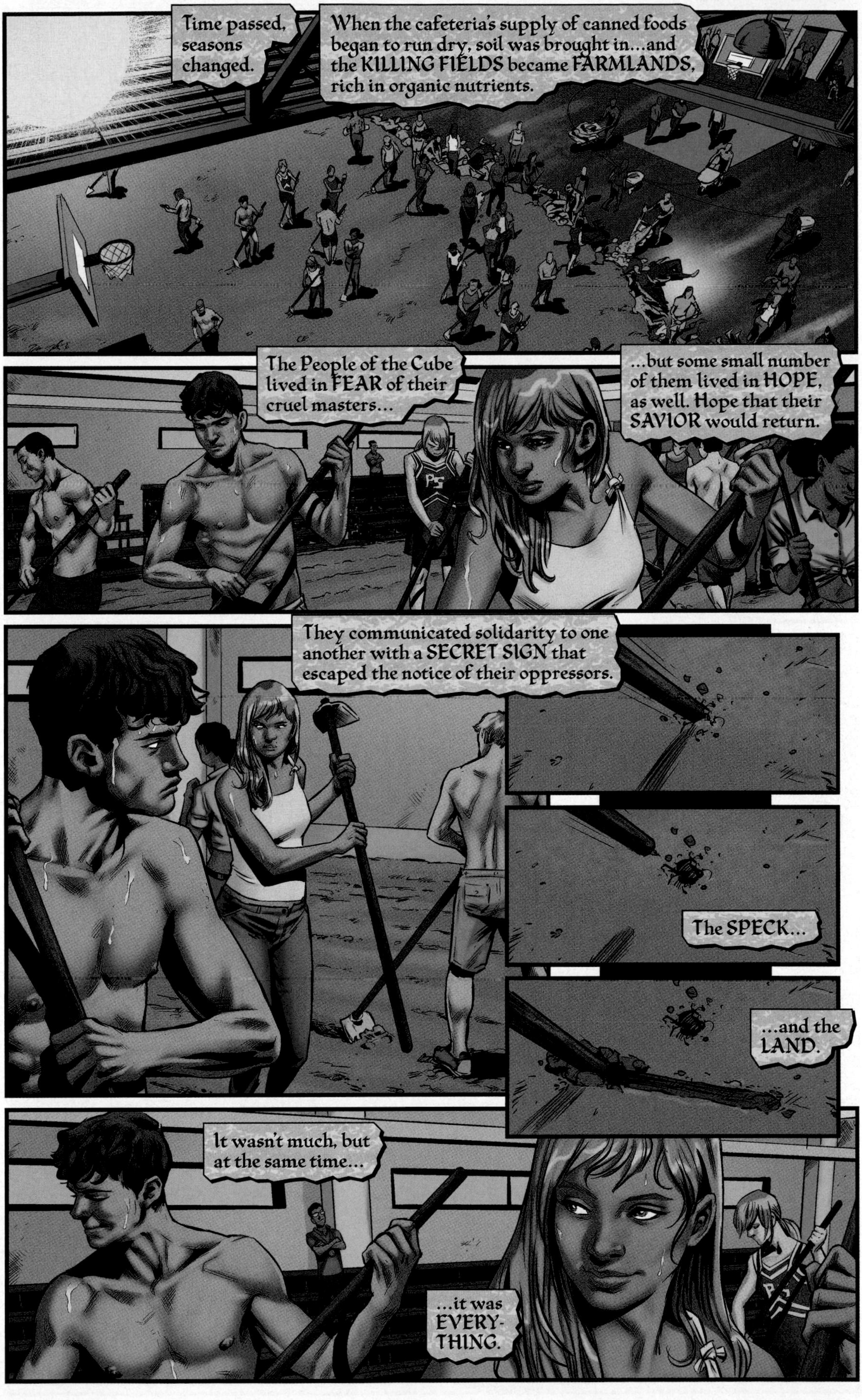
Time passed, seasons changed.
When the cafeteria's supply of canned foods began to run dry, soil was brought in...and the KILLING FIELDS became FARMLANDS, rich in organic nutrients.
The People of the Cube lived in FEAR of their cruel masters...
...but some small number of them lived in HOPE, as well. Hope that their SAVIOR would return.
They communicated solidarity to one another with a SECRET SIGN that escaped the notice of their oppressors.
The SPECK...
...and the LAND.
It wasn't much, but at the same time...
...it was EVERY-THING.

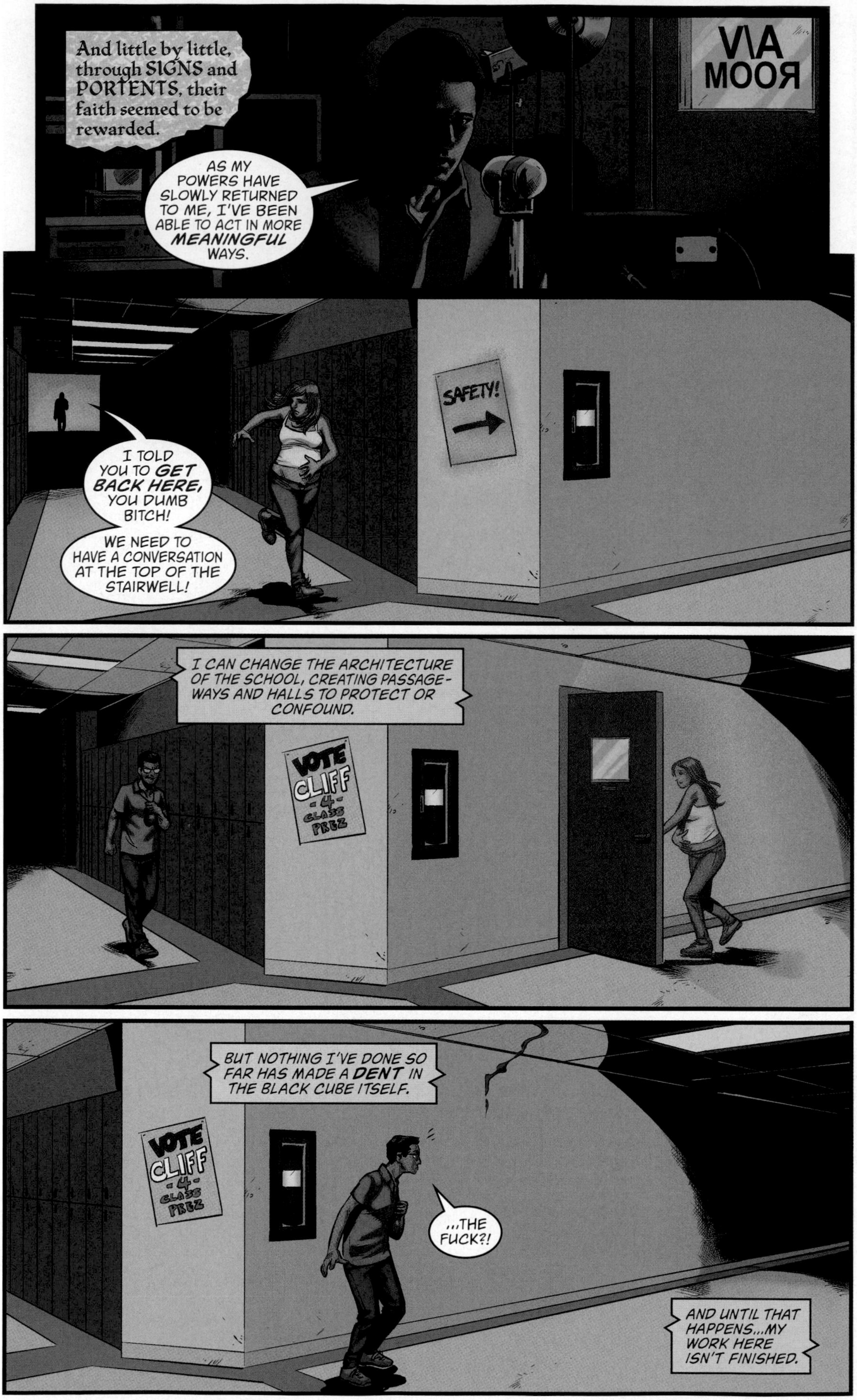
V\A
ROOM
And little by little, through SIGNS and PORTENTS, their faith seemed to be rewarded.
AS MY POWERS HAVE SLOWLY RETURNED TO ME, I'VE BEEN ABLE TO ACT IN MORE MEANINGFUL WAYS.
SAFETY!
I TOLD YOU TO GET BACK HERE, YOU DUMB BITCH!
WE NEED TO HAVE A CONVERSATION AT THE TOP OF THE STAIRWELL!
I CAN CHANGE THE ARCHITECTURE OF THE SCHOOL, CREATING PASSAGE-WAYS AND HALLS TO PROTECT OR CONFOUND.
VOTE CLIFF -4- CLASS PREZ
BUT NOTHING I'VE DONE SO FAR HAS MADE A DENT IN THE BLACK CUBE ITSELF.
VOTE CLIFF -4- CLASS PREZ
...THE FUCK?!
AND UNTIL THAT HAPPENS...MY WORK HERE ISN'T FINISHED.

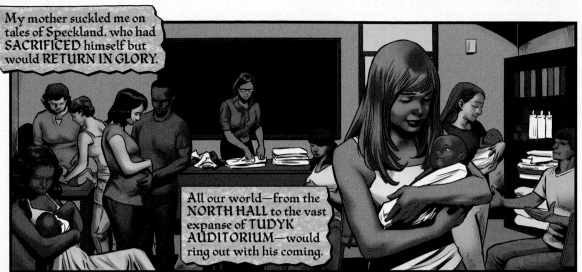

My mother suckled me on tales of Speckland, who had SACRIFICED himself but would RETURN IN GLORY.

All our world—from the NORTH HALL to the vast expanse of TUDYK AUDITORIUM—would ring out with his coming.

We attended CHURCH in secret, invoking his name, hoping that our PRAYERS somehow reached his ears.

Every week we grew a little LOUDER, a little BOLDER. Every week our numbers increased.

Every week the TITHE was just a little more, as people who had NOTHING gave all that they had.

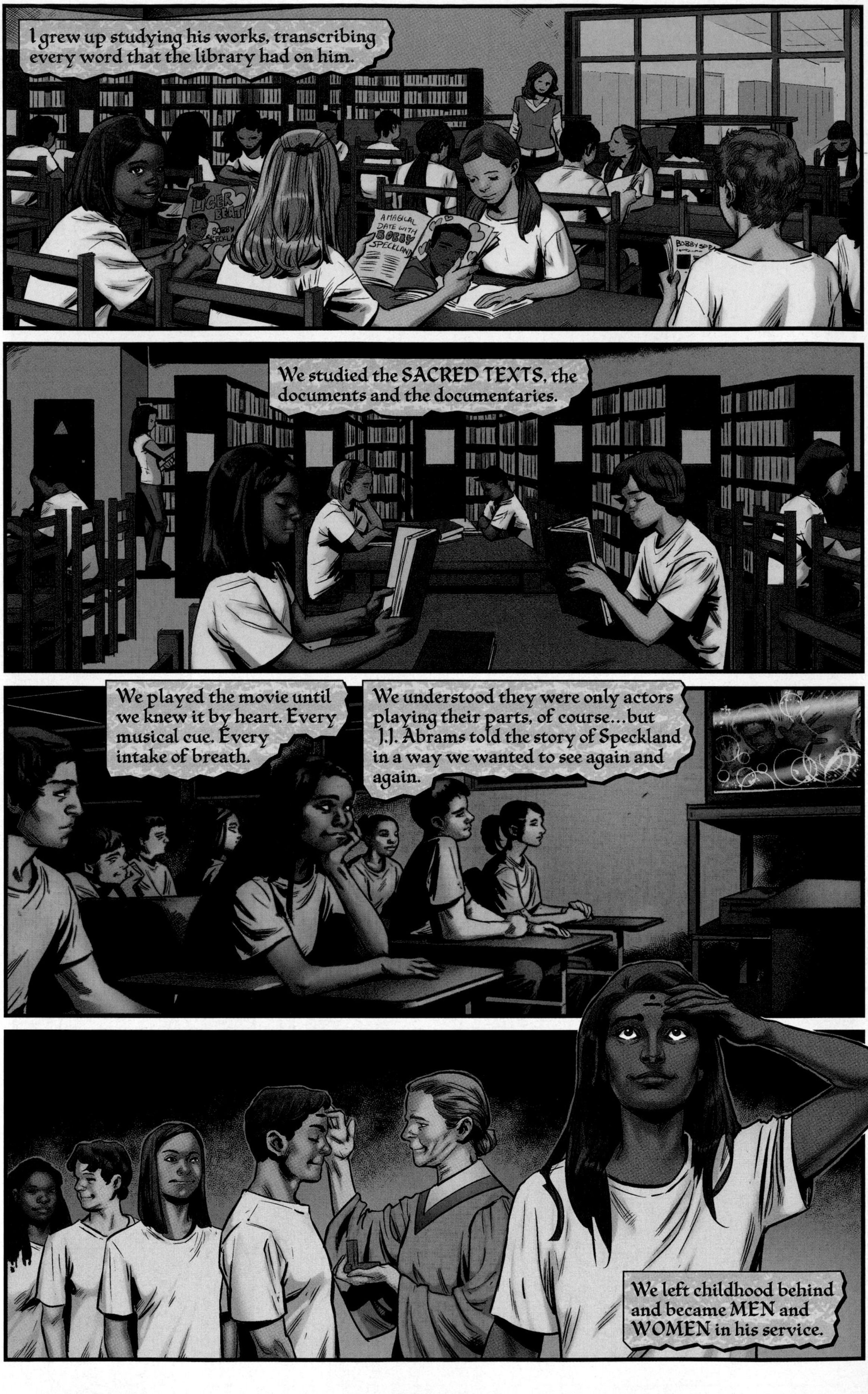
I grew up studying his works, transcribing every word that the library had on him.
LIGER BEAT
A MAGICAL DATE WITH BOBBY SPECKLAND
We studied the SACRED TEXTS, the documents and the documentaries.
We played the movie until we knew it by heart. Every musical cue. Every intake of breath.
We understood they were only actors playing their parts, of course...but J.J. Abrams told the story of Speckland in a way we wanted to see again and again.
We left childhood behind and became MEN and WOMEN in his service.

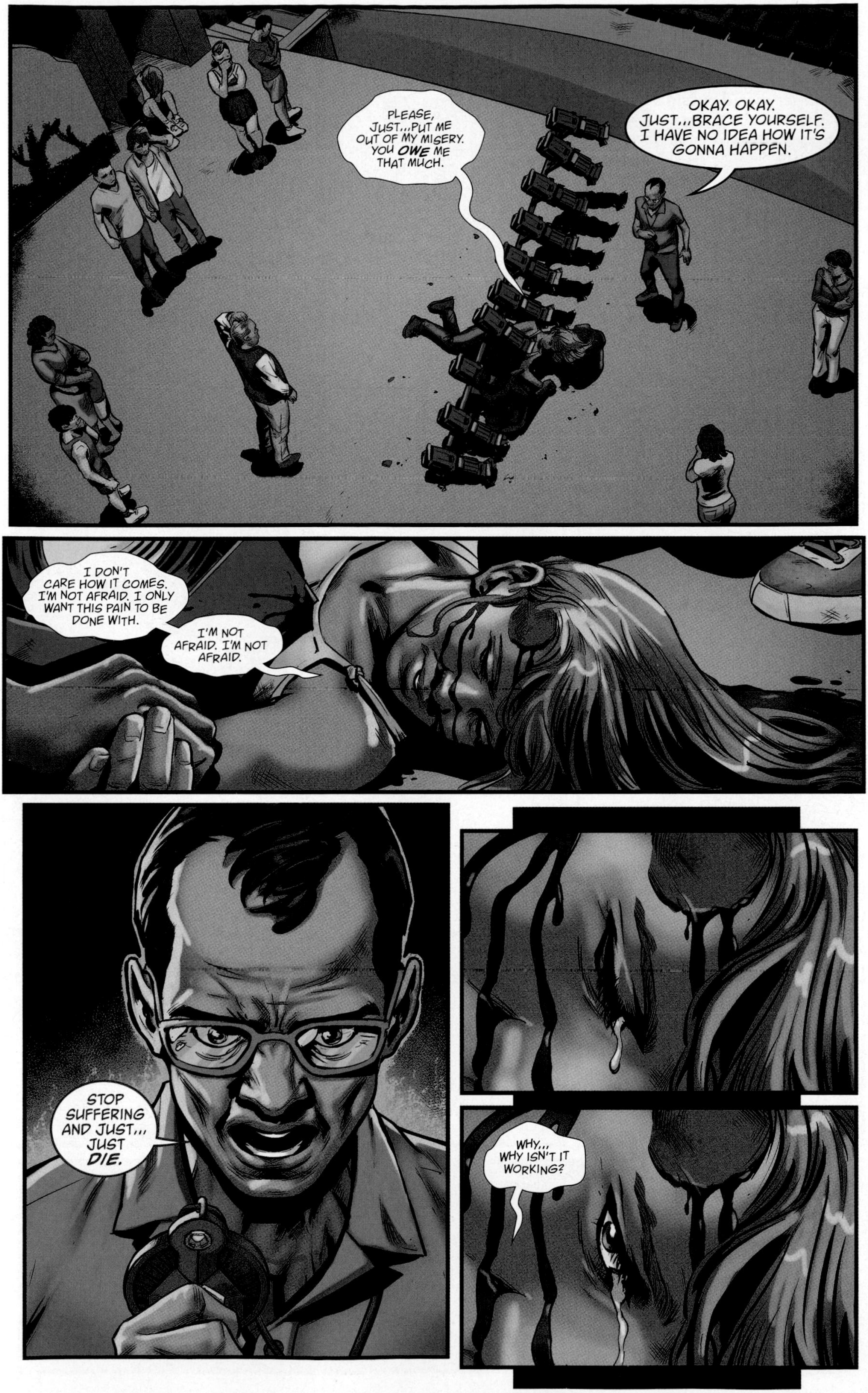
PLEASE, JUST...PUT ME OUT OF MY MISERY. YOU OWE ME THAT MUCH.
OKAY. OKAY. JUST...BRACE YOURSELF. I HAVE NO IDEA HOW IT'S GONNA HAPPEN.
I DON'T CARE HOW IT COMES. I'M NOT AFRAID. I ONLY WANT THIS PAIN TO BE DONE WITH.
I'M NOT AFRAID. I'M NOT AFRAID.
STOP SUFFERING AND JUST... JUST DIE.
WHY... WHY ISN'T IT WORKING?

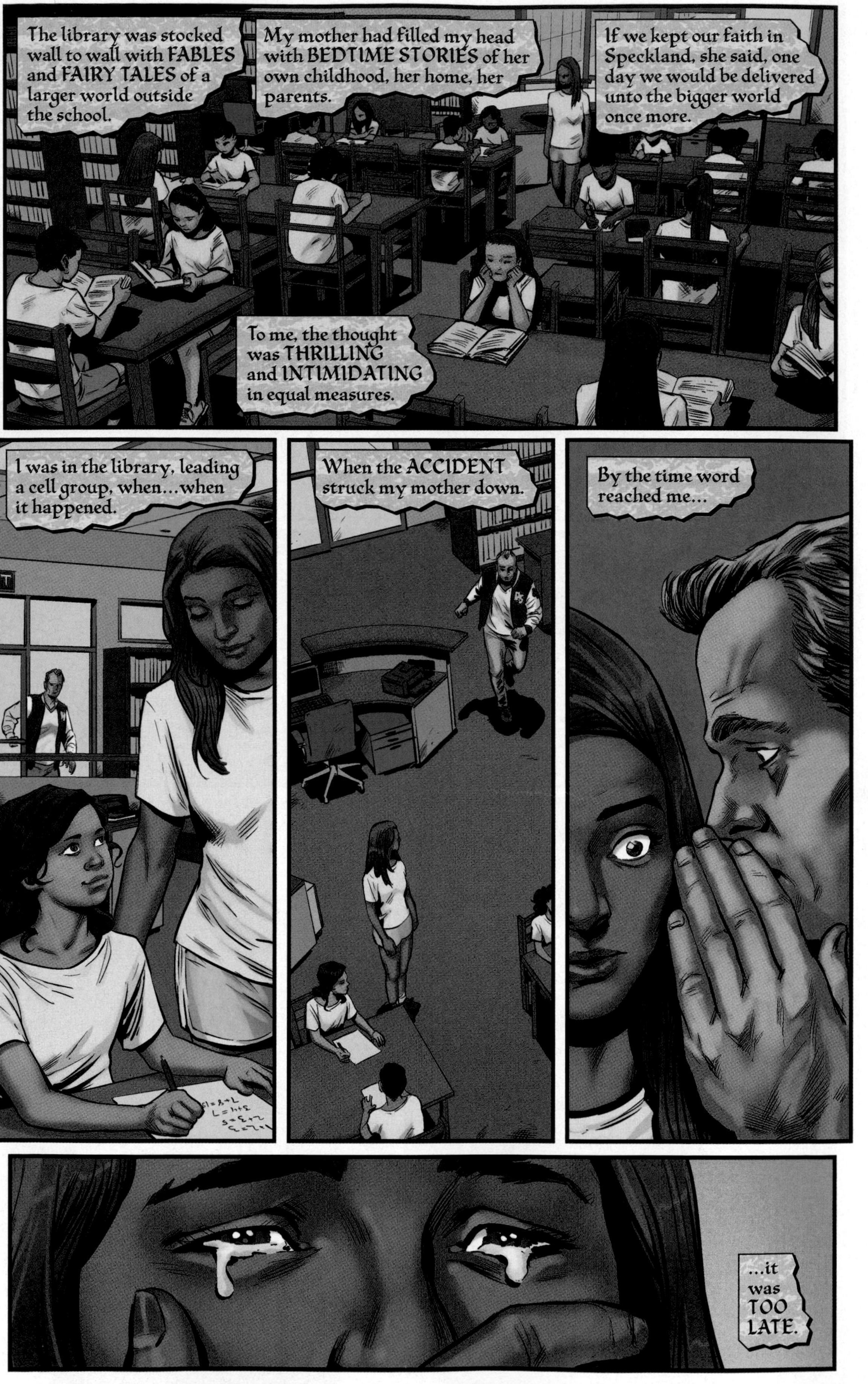

The library was stocked wall to wall with FABLES and FAIRY TALES of a larger world outside the school.
My mother had filled my head with BEDTIME STORIES of her own childhood, her home, her parents.
If we kept our faith in Speckland, she said, one day we would be delivered unto the bigger world once more.
To me, the thought was THRILLING and INTIMIDATING in equal measures.
I was in the library, leading a cell group, when...when it happened.
When the ACCIDENT struck my mother down.
By the time word reached me...
...it was TOO LATE.

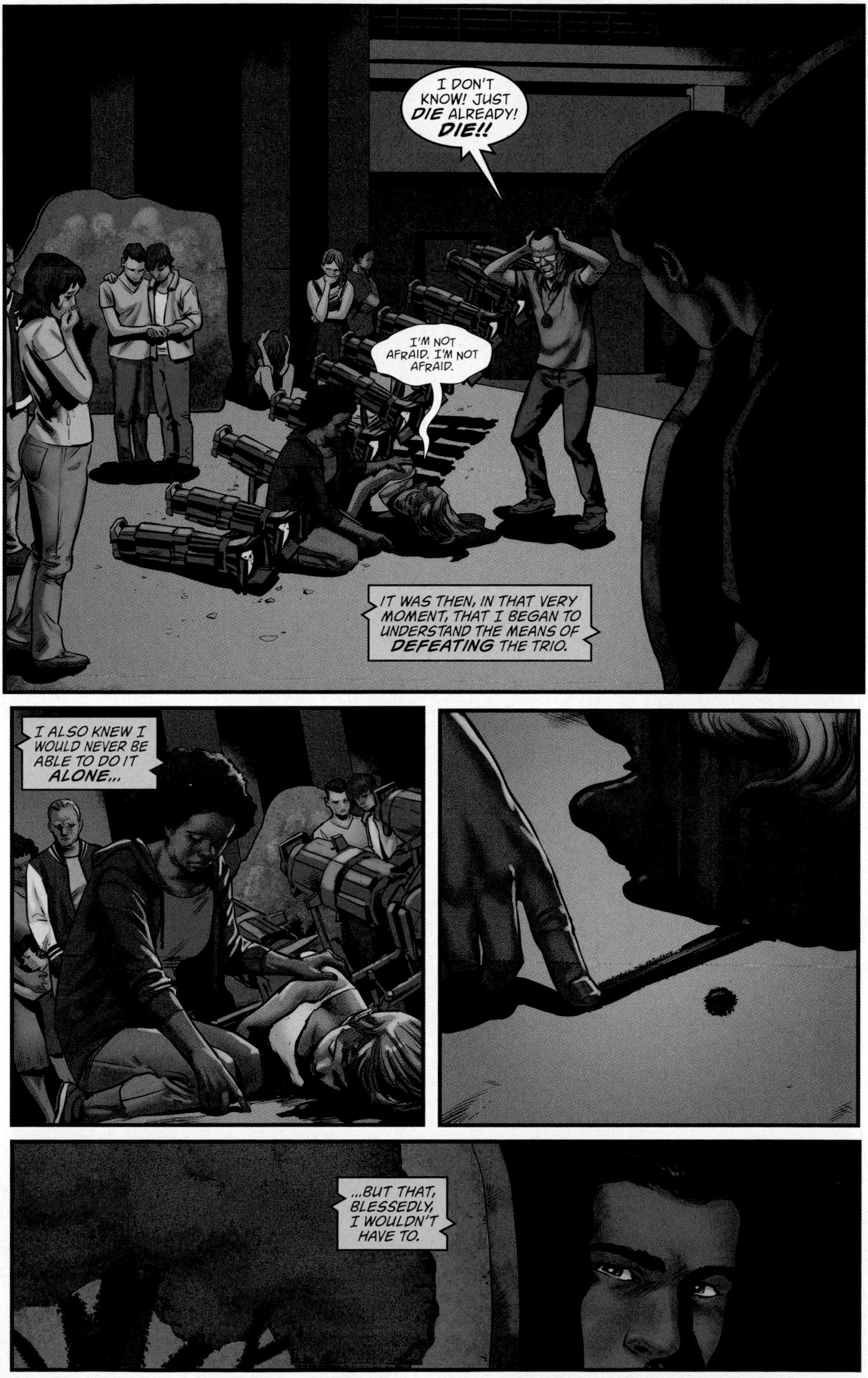
I DON'T KNOW! JUST DIE ALREADY! DIE!!
I'M NOT AFRAID. I'M NOT AFRAID.
IT WAS THEN, IN THAT VERY MOMENT, THAT I BEGAN TO UNDERSTAND THE MEANS OF DEFEATING THE TRIO.
I ALSO KNEW I WOULD NEVER BE ABLE TO DO IT ALONE...
...BUT THAT, BLESSEDLY, I WOULDN'T HAVE TO.

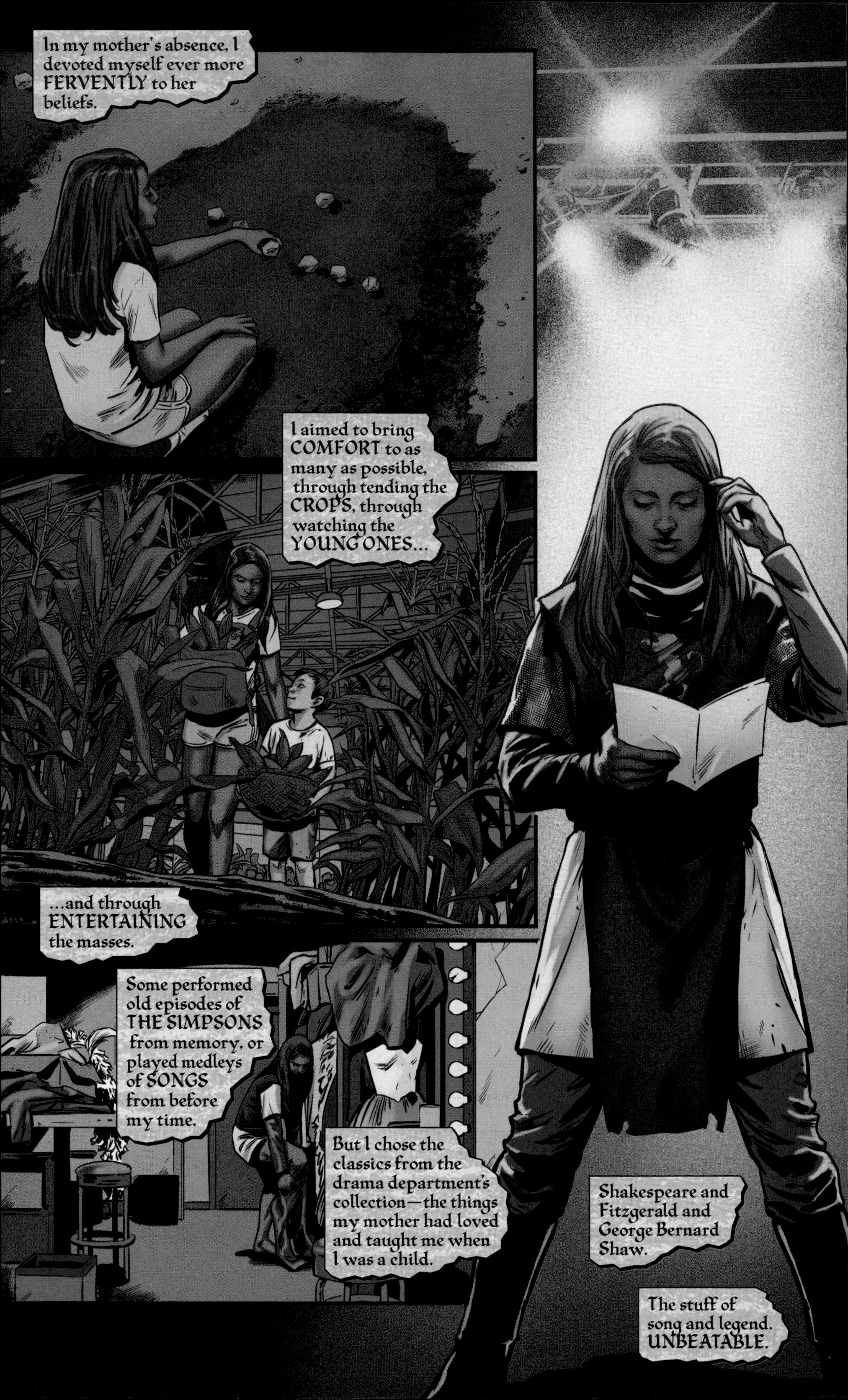
In my mother's absence, I devoted myself ever more FERVENTLY to her beliefs.
I aimed to bring COMFORT to as many as possible, through tending the CROPS, through watching the YOUNG ONES...
...and through ENTERTAINING the masses.
Some performed old episodes of THE SIMPSONS from memory, or played medleys of SONGS from before my time.
But I chose the classics from the drama department's collection—the things my mother had loved and taught me when I was a child.
Shakespeare and Fitzgerald and George Bernard Shaw.
The stuff of song and legend. UNBEATABLE.

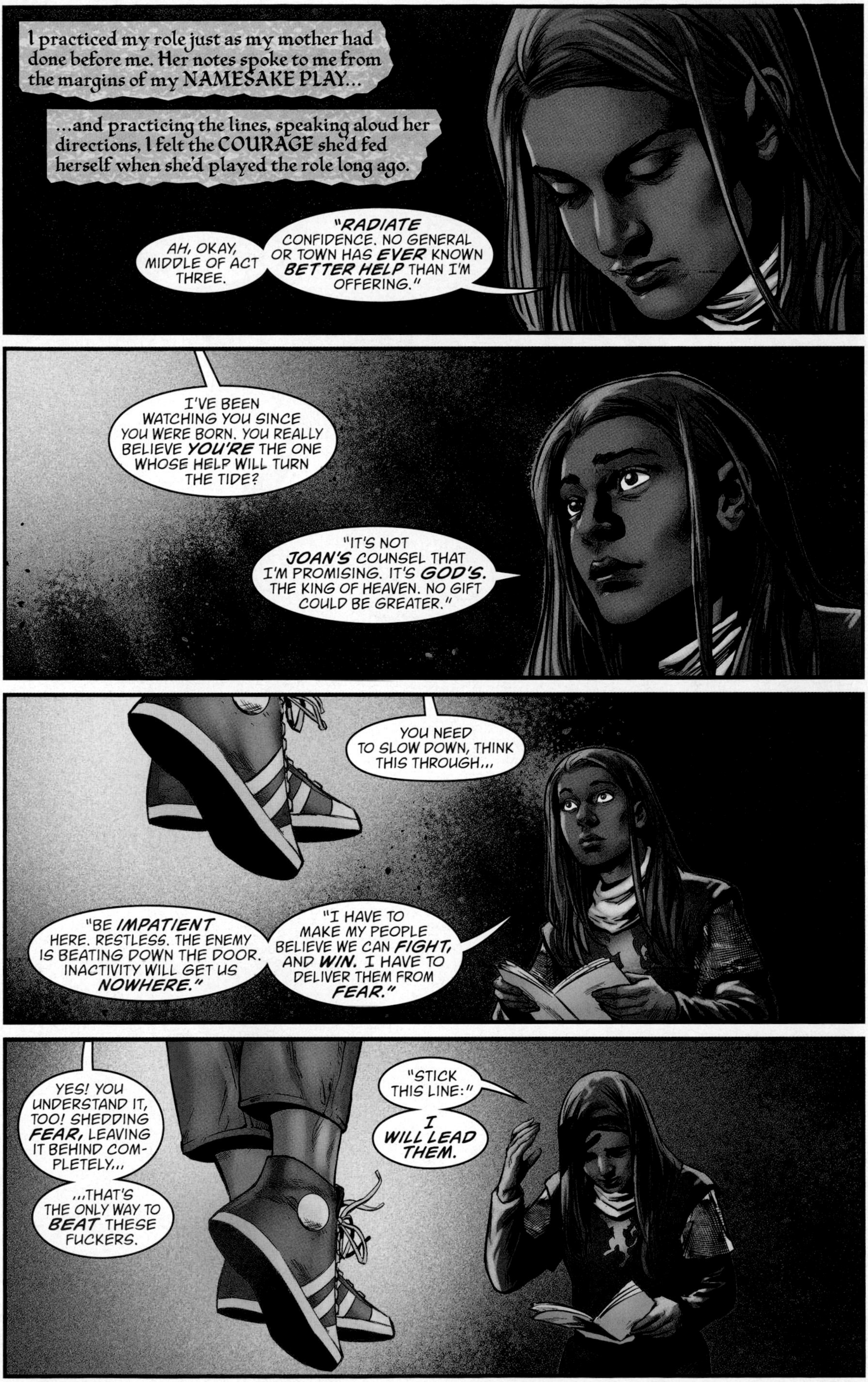
I practiced my role just as my mother had done before me. Her notes spoke to me from the margins of my NAMESAKE PLAY...
...and practicing the lines, speaking aloud her directions, I felt the COURAGE she'd fed herself when she'd played the role long ago.
AH, OKAY, MIDDLE OF ACT THREE.
"RADIATE CONFIDENCE. NO GENERAL OR TOWN HAS EVER KNOWN BETTER HELP THAN I'M OFFERING."
I'VE BEEN WATCHING YOU SINCE YOU WERE BORN. YOU REALLY BELIEVE YOU'RE THE ONE WHOSE HELP WILL TURN THE TIDE?
"IT'S NOT JOAN'S COUNSEL THAT I'M PROMISING. IT'S GOD'S. THE KING OF HEAVEN. NO GIFT COULD BE GREATER."
YOU NEED TO SLOW DOWN, THINK THIS THROUGH...
"BE IMPATIENT HERE. RESTLESS. THE ENEMY IS BEATING DOWN THE DOOR. INACTIVITY WILL GET US NOWHERE."
"I HAVE TO MAKE MY PEOPLE BELIEVE WE CAN FIGHT, AND WIN. I HAVE TO DELIVER THEM FROM FEAR."
YES! YOU UNDERSTAND IT, TOO! SHEDDING FEAR, LEAVING IT BEHIND COMPLETELY...
...THAT'S THE ONLY WAY TO BEAT THESE FUCKERS.
"STICK THIS LINE:"
I WILL LEAD THEM.

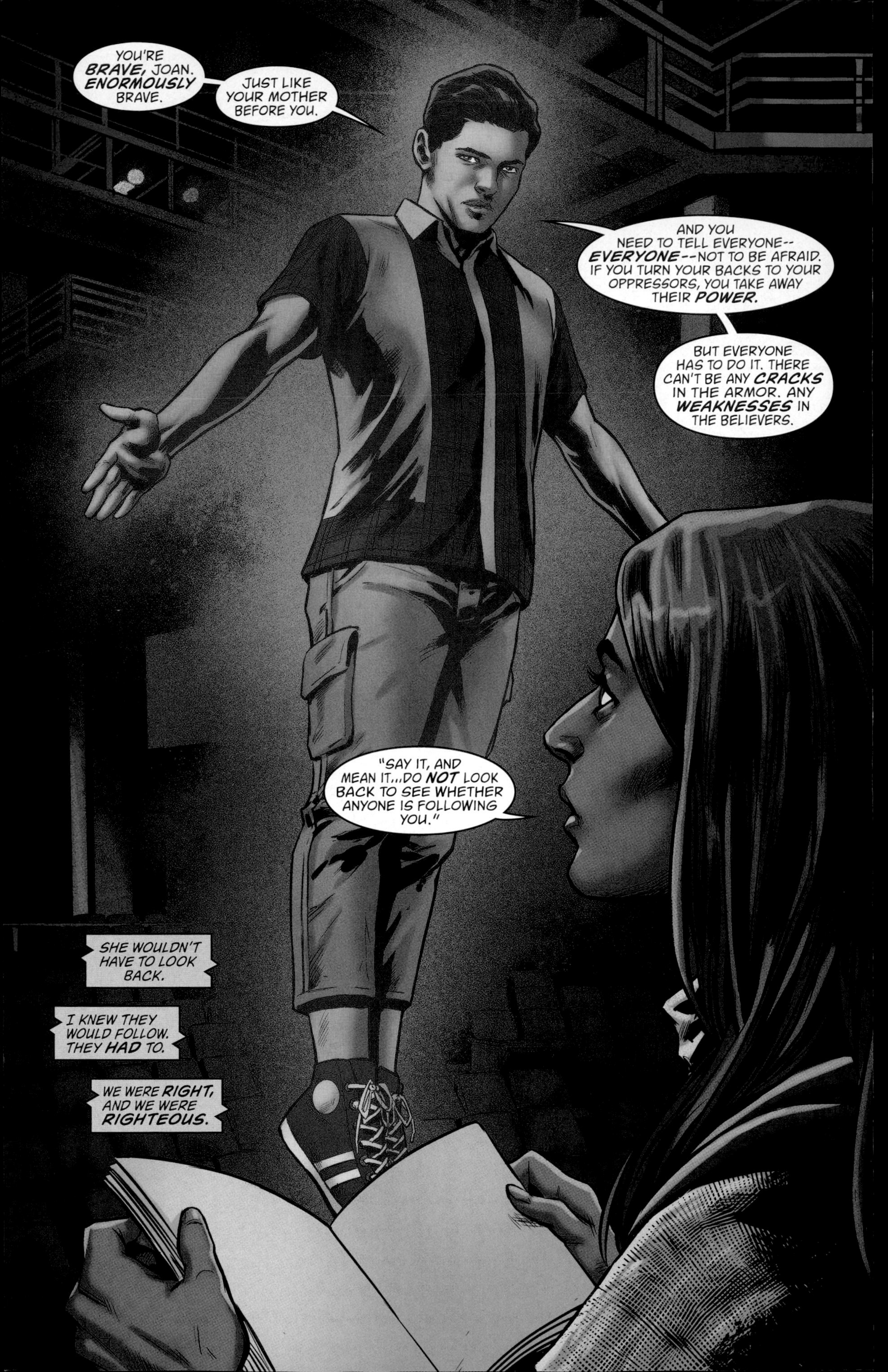
YOU'RE BRAVE, JOAN. ENORMOUSLY BRAVE.
JUST LIKE YOUR MOTHER BEFORE YOU.
AND YOU NEED TO TELL EVERYONE-- EVERYONE--NOT TO BE AFRAID. IF YOU TURN YOUR BACKS TO YOUR OPPRESSORS, YOU TAKE AWAY THEIR POWER.
BUT EVERYONE HAS TO DO IT. THERE CAN'T BE ANY CRACKS IN THE ARMOR. ANY WEAKNESSES IN THE BELIEVERS.
"SAY IT, AND MEAN IT...DO NOT LOOK BACK TO SEE WHETHER ANYONE IS FOLLOWING YOU."
SHE WOULDN'T HAVE TO LOOK BACK.
I KNEW THEY WOULD FOLLOW. THEY HAD TO.
WE WERE RIGHT, AND WE WERE RIGHTEOUS.

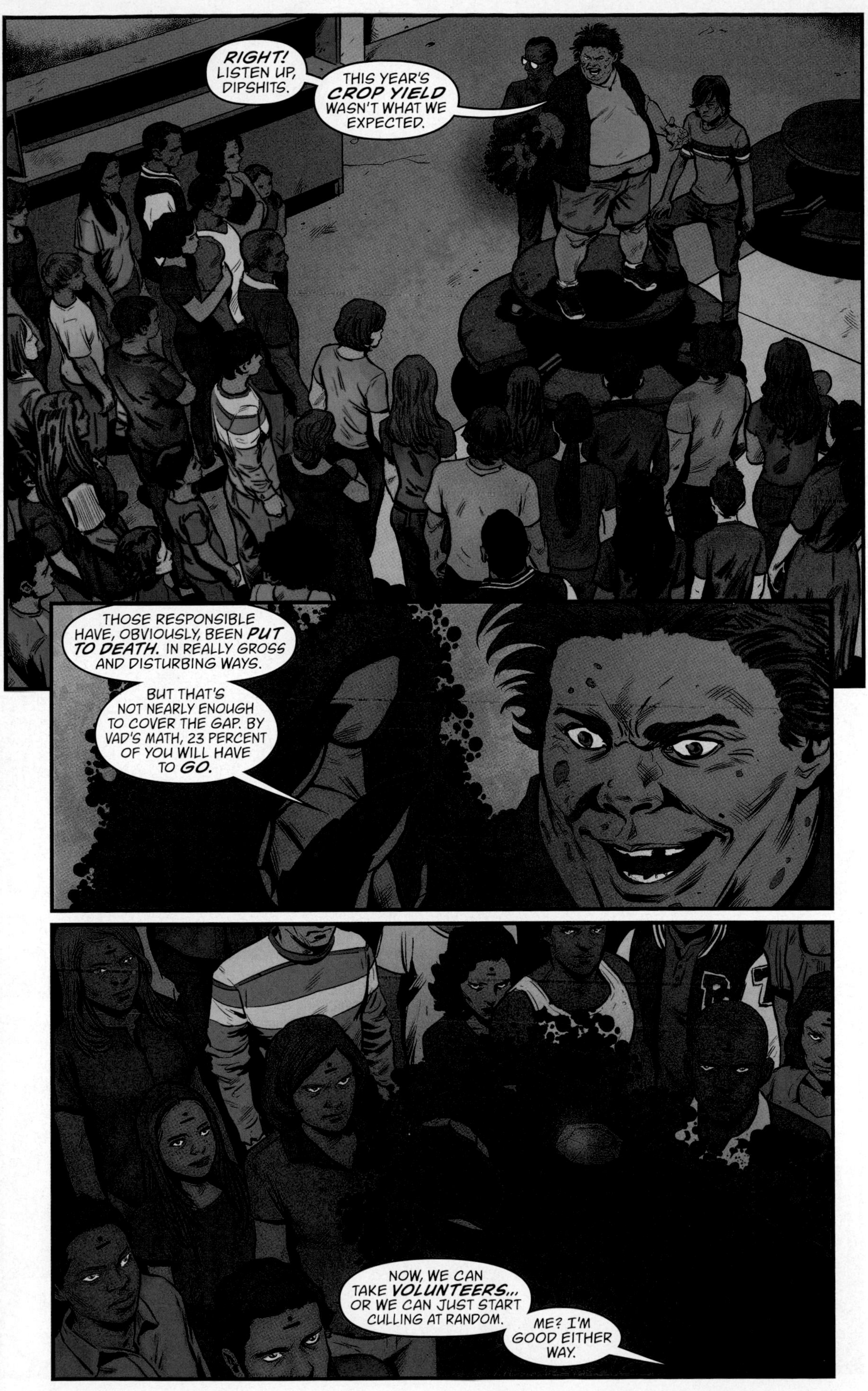
RIGHT! LISTEN UP, DIPSHITS.
THIS YEAR'S CROP YIELD WASN'T WHAT WE EXPECTED.
THOSE RESPONSIBLE HAVE, OBVIOUSLY, BEEN PUT TO DEATH. IN REALLY GROSS AND DISTURBING WAYS.
BUT THAT'S NOT NEARLY ENOUGH TO COVER THE GAP. BY VAD'S MATH, 23 PERCENT OF YOU WILL HAVE TO GO.
NOW, WE CAN TAKE VOLUNTEERS... OR WE CAN JUST START CULLING AT RANDOM.
ME? I'M GOOD EITHER WAY.

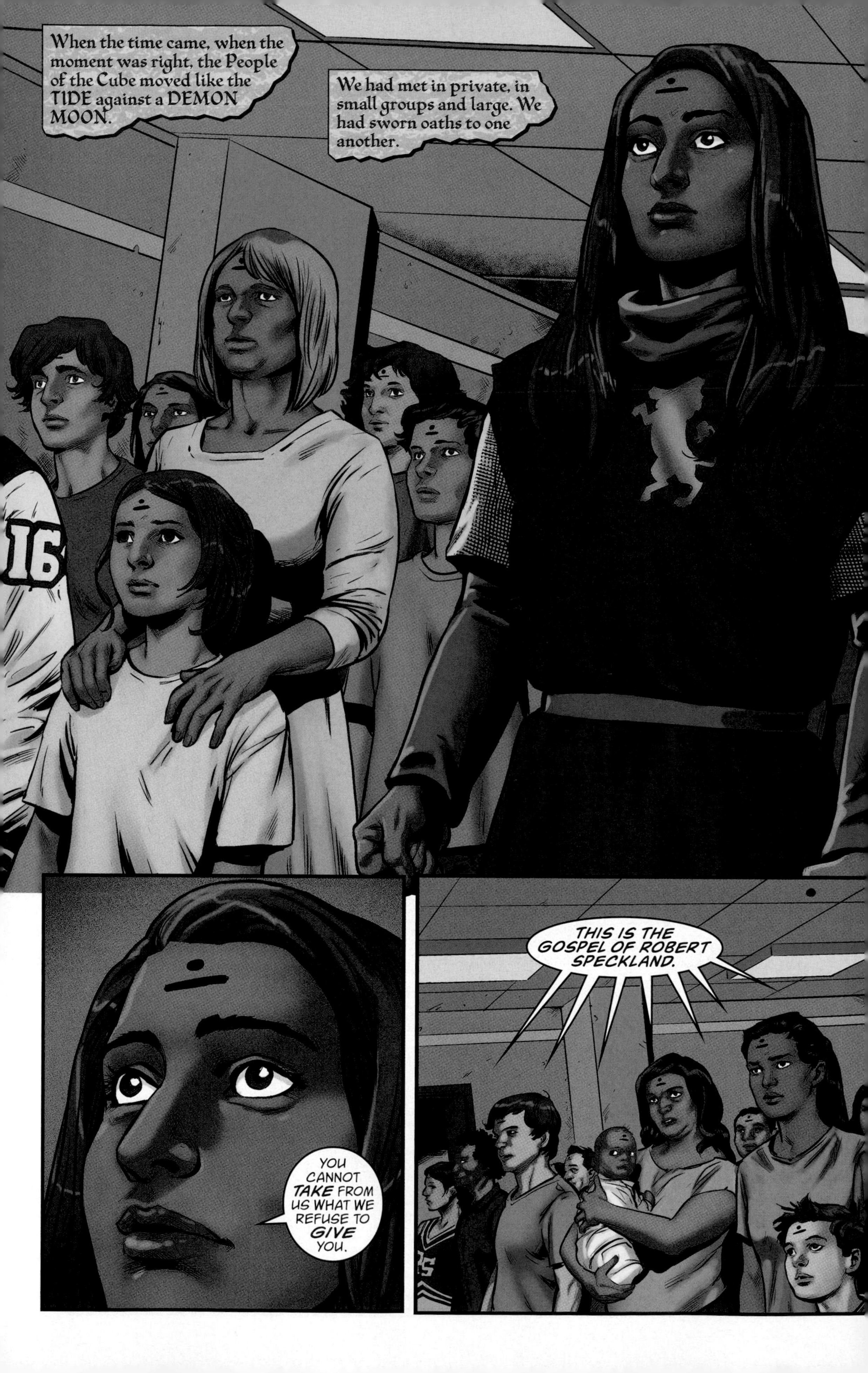

When the time came, when the moment was right, the People of the Cube moved like the TIDE against a DEMON MOON.
We had met in private, in small groups and large. We had sworn oaths to one another.
16
YOU CANNOT TAKE FROM US WHAT WE REFUSE TO GIVE YOU.
THIS IS THE GOSPEL OF ROBERT SPECKLAND.

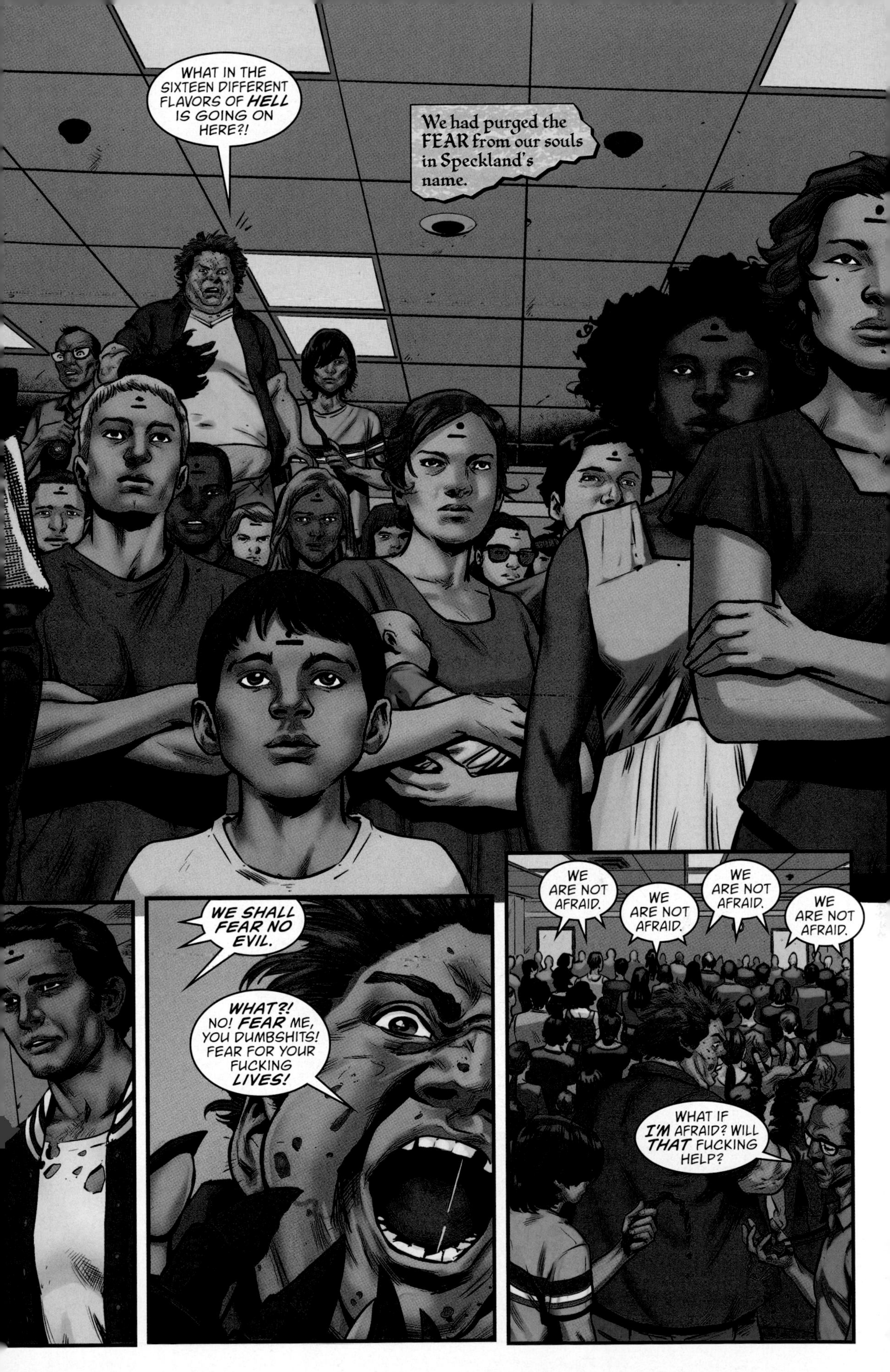
WHAT IN THE SIXTEEN DIFFERENT FLAVORS OF HELL IS GOING ON HERE?!
We had purged the FEAR from our souls in Speckland's name.
WE SHALL FEAR NO EVIL.
WHAT?! NO! FEAR ME, YOU DUMBSHITS! FEAR FOR YOUR FUCKING LIVES!
WE ARE NOT AFRAID.
WE ARE NOT AFRAID.
WE ARE NOT AFRAID.
WE ARE NOT AFRAID.
WHAT IF I'M AFRAID? WILL THAT FUCKING HELP?

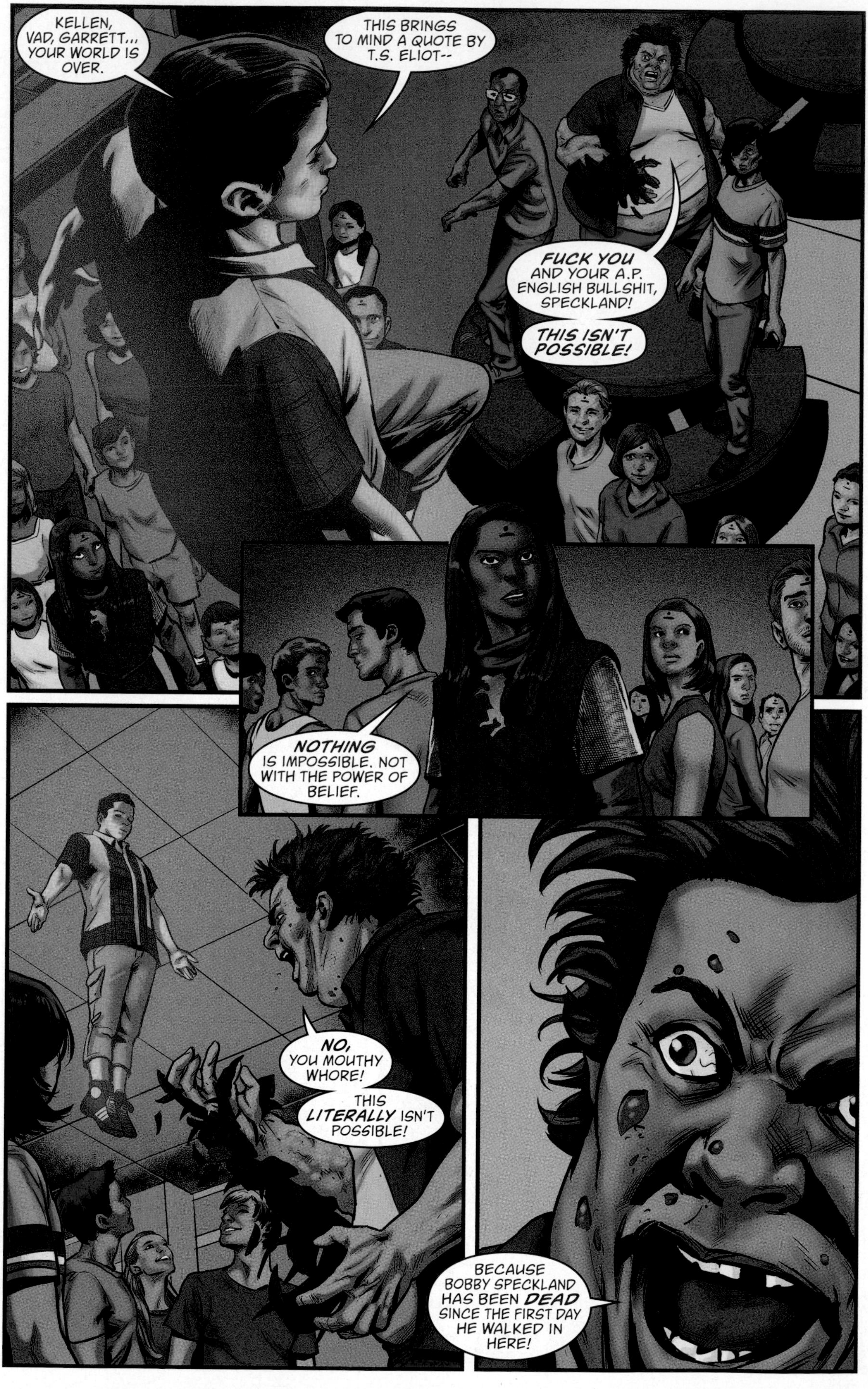
KELLEN, VAD, GARRETT... YOUR WORLD IS OVER.
THIS BRINGS TO MIND A QUOTE BY T.S. ELIOT--
FUCK YOU AND YOUR A.P. ENGLISH BULLSHIT, SPECKLAND!
THIS ISN'T POSSIBLE!
NOTHING IS IMPOSSIBLE. NOT WITH THE POWER OF BELIEF.
NO, YOU MOUTHY WHORE!
THIS LITERALLY ISN'T POSSIBLE!
BECAUSE BOBBY SPECKLAND HAS BEEN DEAD SINCE THE FIRST DAY HE WALKED IN HERE!

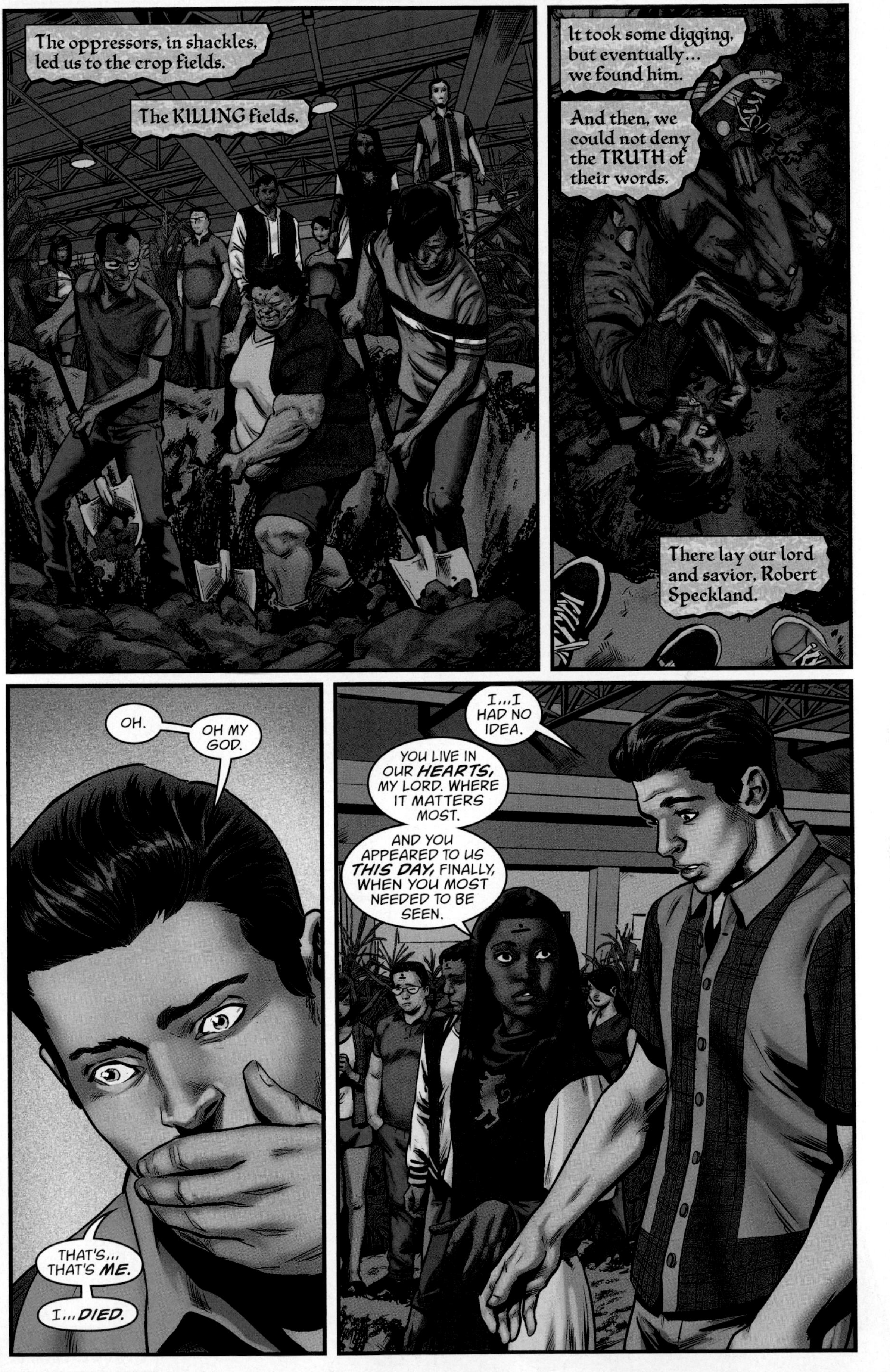

The oppressors, in shackles, led us to the crop fields.
The KILLING fields.
It took some digging, but eventually... we found him.
And then, we could not deny the TRUTH of their words.
There lay our lord and savior, Robert Speckland.
OH.
OH MY GOD.
THAT'S... THAT'S ME.
I... DIED.
I... I HAD NO IDEA.
YOU LIVE IN OUR HEARTS, MY LORD. WHERE IT MATTERS MOST.
AND YOU APPEARED TO US THIS DAY, FINALLY, WHEN YOU MOST NEEDED TO BE SEEN.

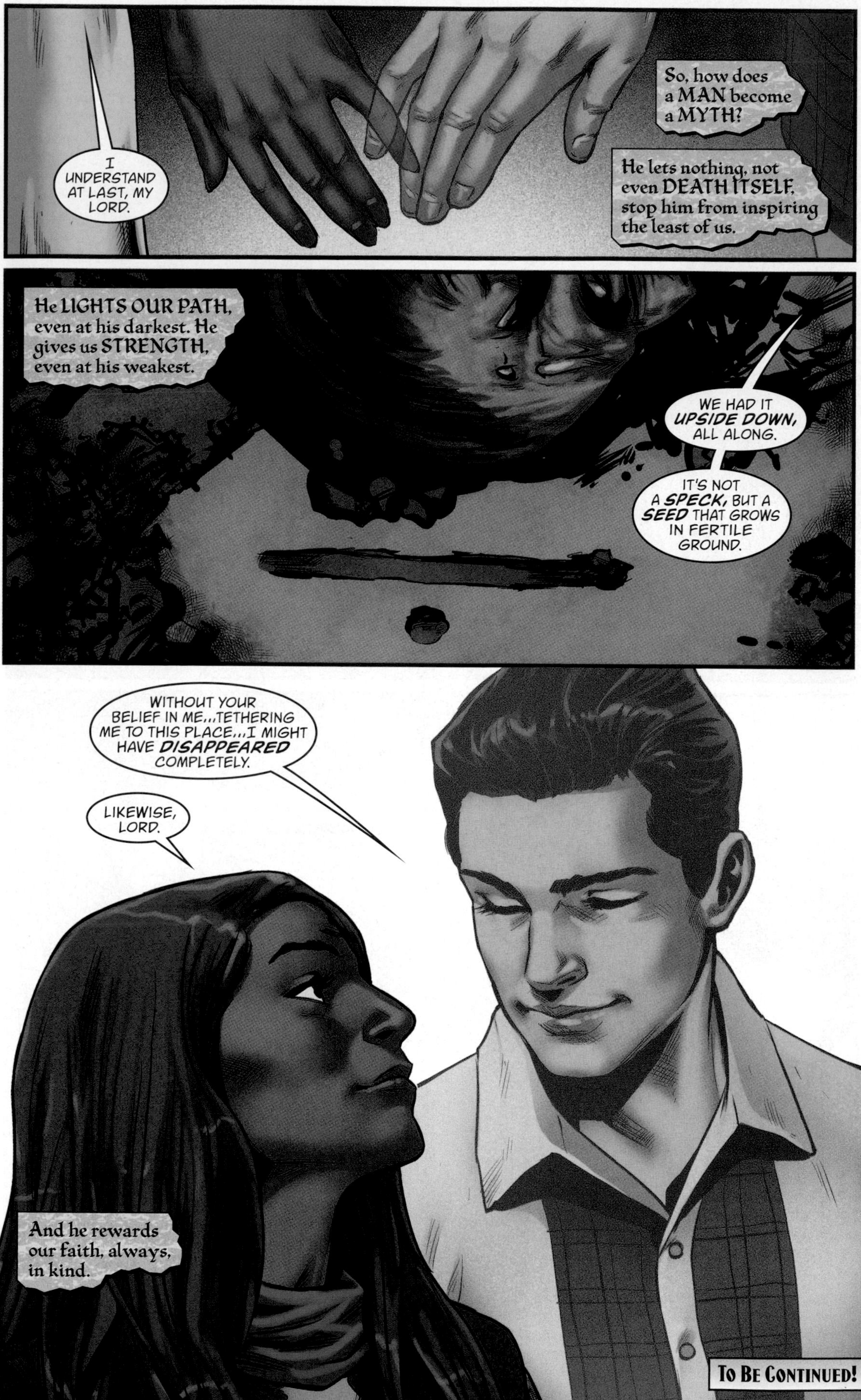
So, how does a MAN become a MYTH?
I UNDERSTAND AT LAST, MY LORD.
He lets nothing, not even DEATH ITSELF, stop him from inspiring the least of us.
He LIGHTS OUR PATH, even at his darkest. He gives us STRENGTH, even at his weakest.
WE HAD IT UPSIDE DOWN, ALL ALONG.
IT'S NOT A SPECK, BUT A SEED THAT GROWS IN FERTILE GROUND.
WITHOUT YOUR BELIEF IN ME...TETHERING ME TO THIS PLACE...I MIGHT HAVE DISAPPEARED COMPLETELY.
LIKEWISE, LORD.
And he rewards our faith, always, in kind.
TO BE CONTINUED!

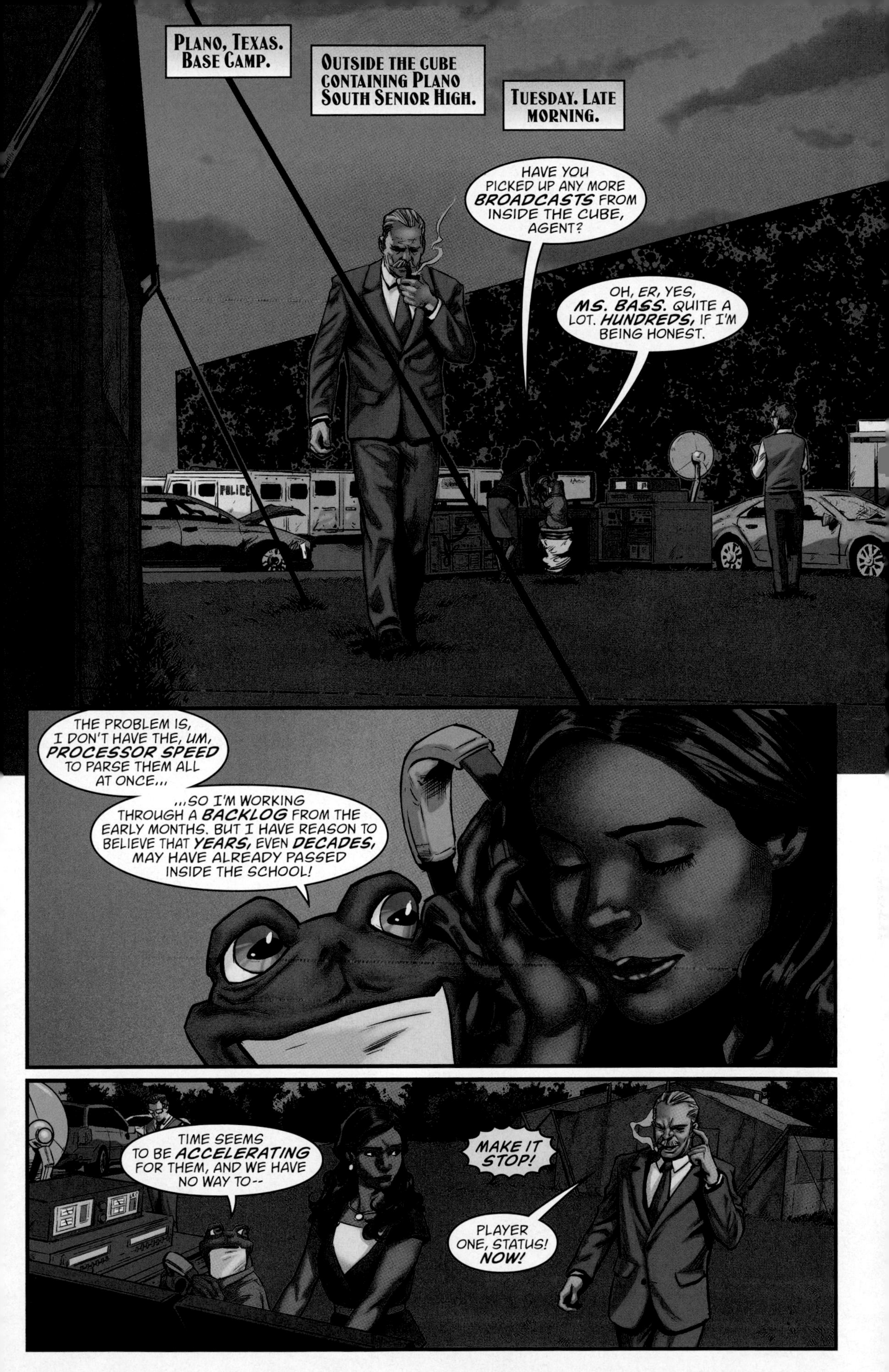
PLANO, TEXAS. BASE CAMP.
OUTSIDE THE CUBE CONTAINING PLANO SOUTH SENIOR HIGH.
TUESDAY. LATE MORNING.
HAVE YOU PICKED UP ANY MORE BROADCASTS FROM INSIDE THE CUBE, AGENT?
OH, ER, YES, MS. BASS. QUITE A LOT. HUNDREDS, IF I'M BEING HONEST.
THE PROBLEM IS, I DON'T HAVE THE, UM, PROCESSOR SPEED TO PARSE THEM ALL AT ONCE...
...SO I'M WORKING THROUGH A BACKLOG FROM THE EARLY MONTHS. BUT I HAVE REASON TO BELIEVE THAT YEARS, EVEN DECADES, MAY HAVE ALREADY PASSED INSIDE THE SCHOOL!
TIME SEEMS TO BE ACCELERATING FOR THEM, AND WE HAVE NO WAY TO--
MAKE IT STOP!
PLAYER ONE, STATUS! NOW!

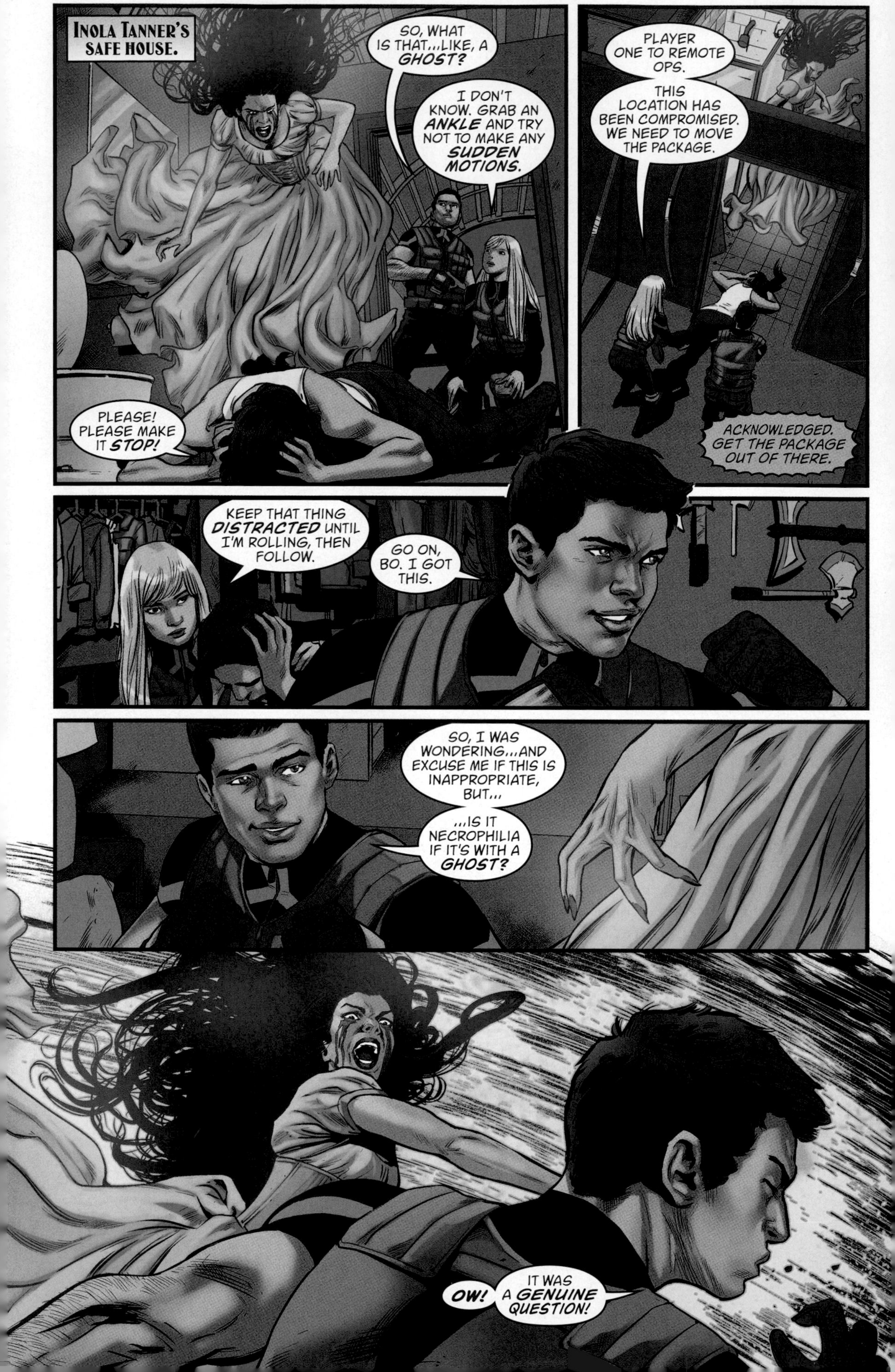
INOLA TANNER'S SAFE HOUSE.
SO, WHAT IS THAT...LIKE, A GHOST?
I DON'T KNOW. GRAB AN ANKLE AND TRY NOT TO MAKE ANY SUDDEN MOTIONS.
PLEASE! PLEASE MAKE IT STOP!
PLAYER ONE TO REMOTE OPS.
THIS LOCATION HAS BEEN COMPROMISED. WE NEED TO MOVE THE PACKAGE.
ACKNOWLEDGED. GET THE PACKAGE OUT OF THERE.
KEEP THAT THING DISTRACTED UNTIL I'M ROLLING, THEN FOLLOW.
GO ON, BO. I GOT THIS.
SO, I WAS WONDERING...AND EXCUSE ME IF THIS IS INAPPROPRIATE, BUT...
...IS IT NECROPHILIA IF IT'S WITH A GHOST?
OW!
IT WAS A GENUINE QUESTION!

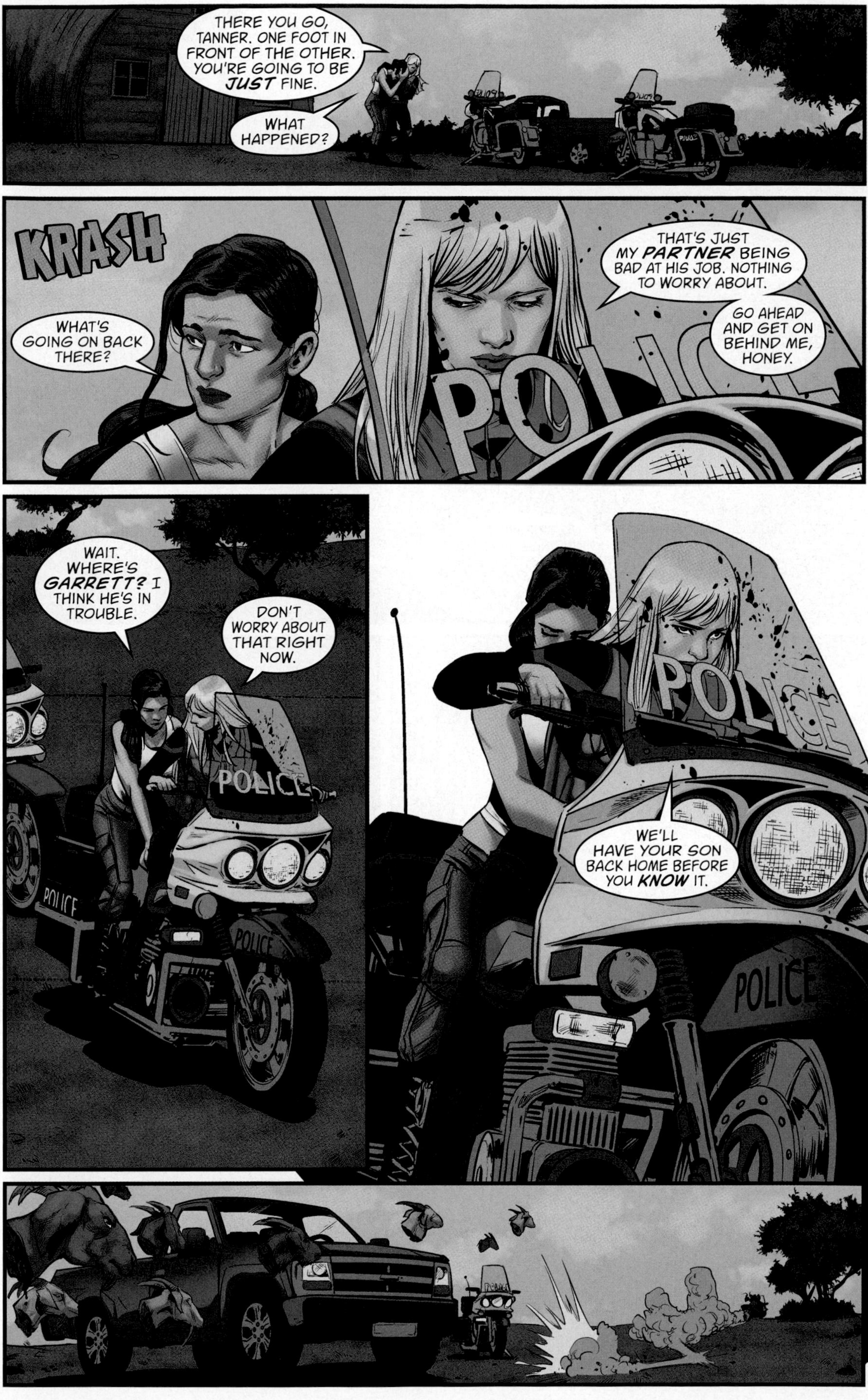
THERE YOU GO, TANNER. ONE FOOT IN FRONT OF THE OTHER. YOU'RE GOING TO BE JUST FINE.
WHAT HAPPENED?
KRASH
WHAT'S GOING ON BACK THERE?
THAT'S JUST MY PARTNER BEING BAD AT HIS JOB. NOTHING TO WORRY ABOUT.
GO AHEAD AND GET ON BEHIND ME, HONEY.
POLICE
WAIT. WHERE'S GARRETT? I THINK HE'S IN TROUBLE.
DON'T WORRY ABOUT THAT RIGHT NOW.
POLICE
WE'LL HAVE YOUR SON BACK HOME BEFORE YOU KNOW IT.
POLICE

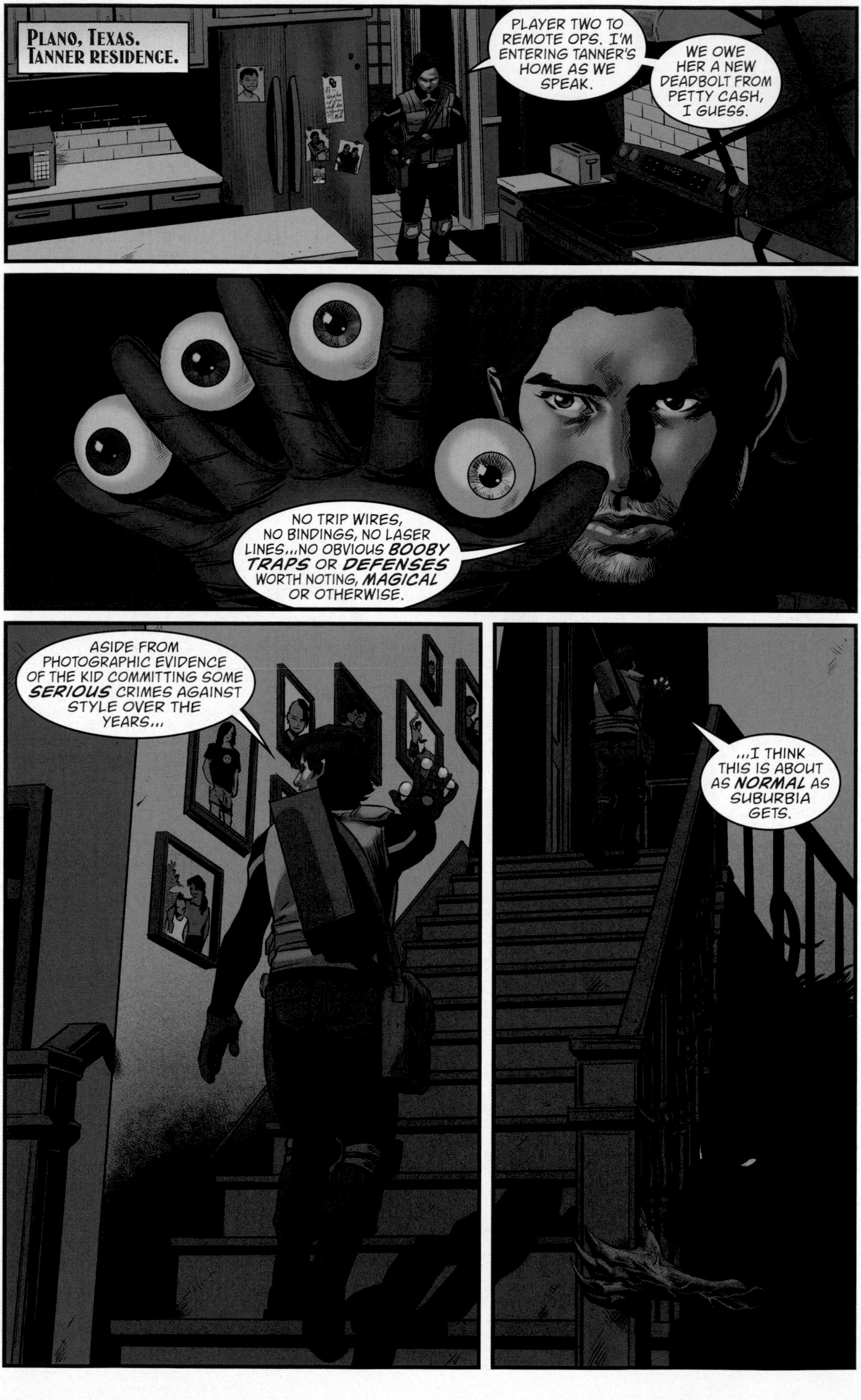
PLANO, TEXAS. TANNER RESIDENCE.
PLAYER TWO TO REMOTE OPS. I'M ENTERING TANNER'S HOME AS WE SPEAK.
WE OWE HER A NEW DEADBOLT FROM PETTY CASH, I GUESS.
NO TRIP WIRES, NO BINDINGS, NO LASER LINES...NO OBVIOUS BOOBY TRAPS OR DEFENSES WORTH NOTING, MAGICAL OR OTHERWISE.
ASIDE FROM PHOTOGRAPHIC EVIDENCE OF THE KID COMMITTING SOME SERIOUS CRIMES AGAINST STYLE OVER THE YEARS...
...I THINK THIS IS ABOUT AS NORMAL AS SUBURBIA GETS.

KEEP YOUR HEAD ON A **SWIVEL**, PLAYER TWO. IT WON'T TAKE THESE **ACQUISITIONS** PEOPLE LONG TO INVESTIGATE WHAT ELSE TANNER MIGHT HAVE STOLEN, IF THEY HAVEN'T ALREADY.

REMEMBER, WE DON'T HAVE THE FIRST CLUE WHAT THEY'RE CAPABLE OF.

MAYBE NOT...

...BUT THEN AGAIN, **THEY** DON'T KNOW WHAT **WE'RE** CAPABLE OF, EITHER.

PLAYER TWO OUT.

HELL, **I** DON'T EVEN KNOW WHAT WE'RE CAPABLE OF THESE DAYS.

WHAT CAN YOU TELL ME ABOUT THE CUBE, THOMAS?

VERY LITTLE, I'M AFRAID.

ANYTHING I TRY TO SAY ABOUT IT IS **TRUE,** OF COURSE...

...BUT THE OPPOSITE IS **ALSO** TRUE.

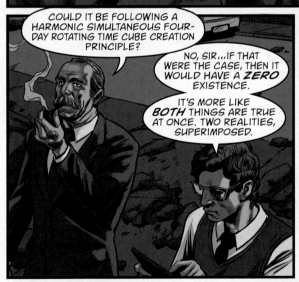

COULD IT BE FOLLOWING A HARMONIC SIMULTANEOUS FOUR-DAY ROTATING TIME CUBE CREATION PRINCIPLE?

NO, SIR...IF THAT WERE THE CASE, THEN IT WOULD HAVE A **ZERO** EXISTENCE.

IT'S MORE LIKE **BOTH** THINGS ARE TRUE AT ONCE. TWO REALITIES, SUPERIMPOSED.

HMMM...NOW, **THAT** RINGS A BELL...

PLAYER THREE TO REMOTE OPS. LITTLE HELP?

ANY OF YOU DASHING GENTLEMEN AT BASE CAMP WANNA GIVE ME SOME ADVICE ON HOW TO **HANDLE** THIS CHICK?

FIRST, DON'T CALL HER A **CHICK.**

THEN TELL ME WHAT SHE LOOKS LIKE. THE MORE DESCRIPTIVE, THE BETTER. WHAT'S THIS CHICK WEARING?

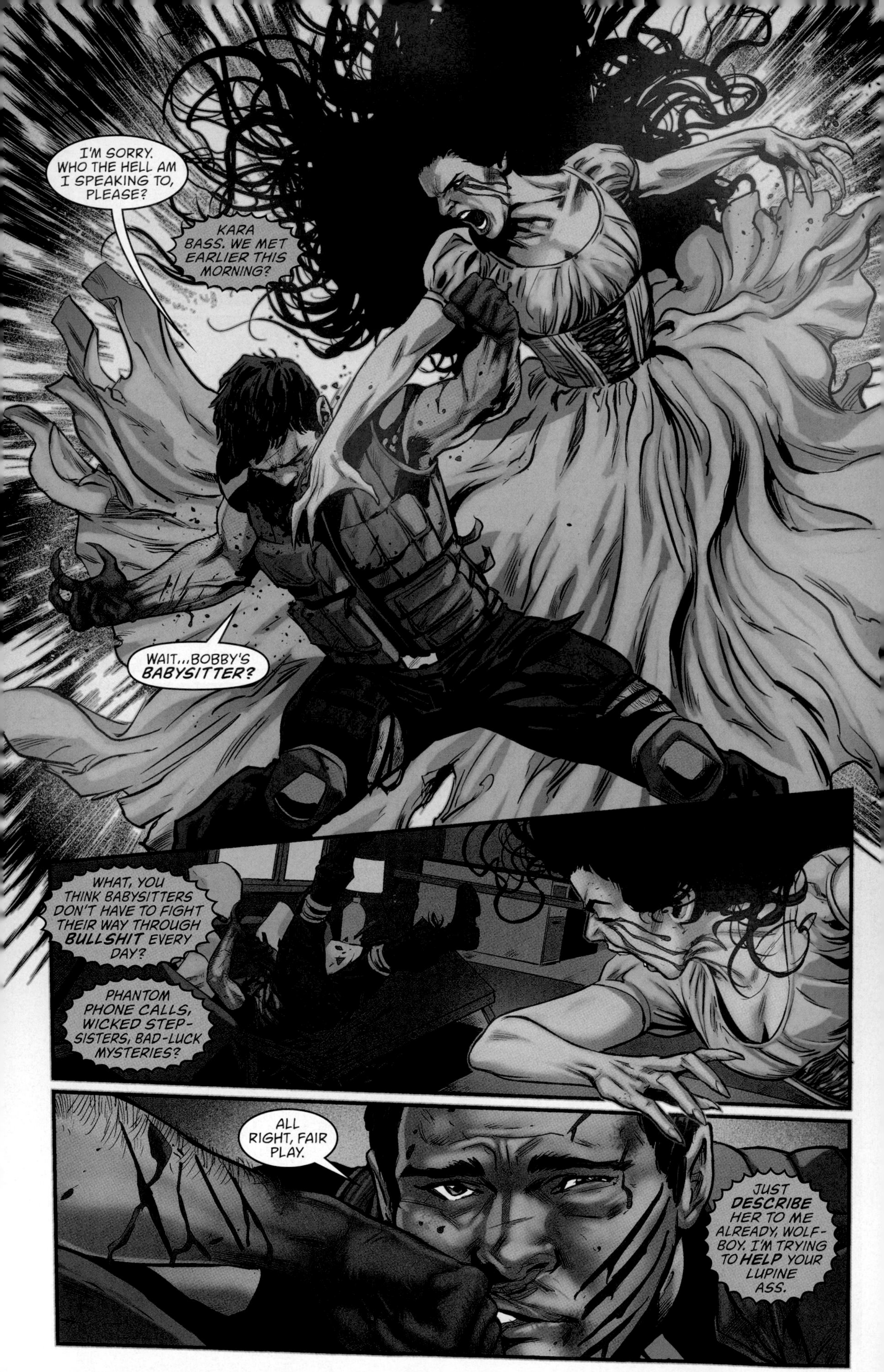
I'M SORRY. WHO THE HELL AM I SPEAKING TO, PLEASE?
KARA BASS. WE MET EARLIER THIS MORNING?
WAIT...BOBBY'S **BABYSITTER?**
WHAT, YOU THINK BABYSITTERS DON'T HAVE TO FIGHT THEIR WAY THROUGH **BULLSHIT** EVERY DAY?
PHANTOM PHONE CALLS, WICKED STEP-SISTERS, BAD-LUCK MYSTERIES?
ALL RIGHT, FAIR PLAY.
JUST **DESCRIBE** HER TO ME ALREADY, WOLF-BOY. I'M TRYING TO **HELP** YOUR LUPINE ASS.

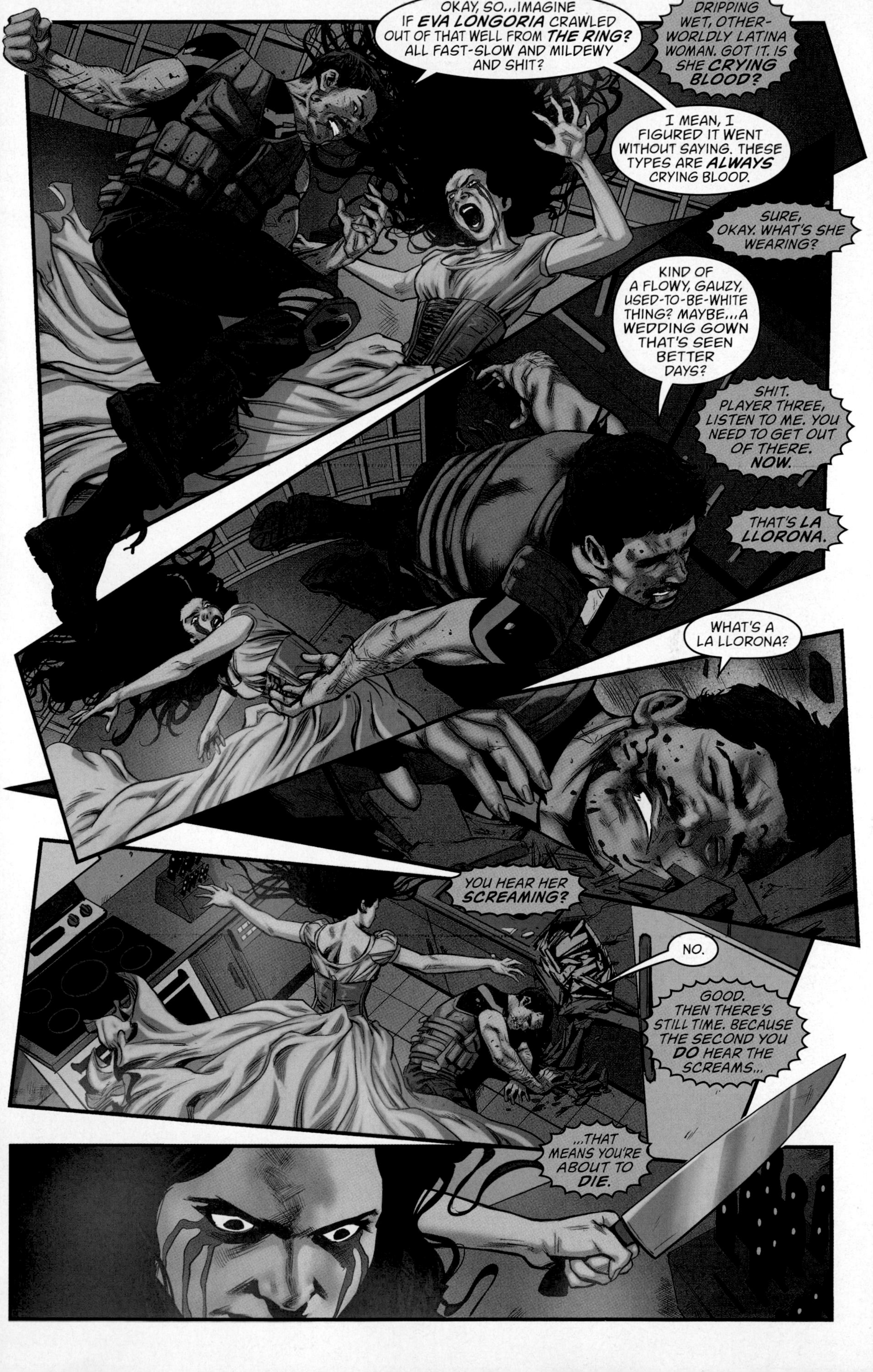

OKAY, SO...IMAGINE IF EVA LONGORIA CRAWLED OUT OF THAT WELL FROM THE RING? ALL FAST-SLOW AND MILDEWY AND SHIT?
DRIPPING WET, OTHER-WORLDLY LATINA WOMAN. GOT IT. IS SHE CRYING BLOOD?
I MEAN, I FIGURED IT WENT WITHOUT SAYING. THESE TYPES ARE ALWAYS CRYING BLOOD.
SURE, OKAY. WHAT'S SHE WEARING?
KIND OF A FLOWY, GAUZY, USED-TO-BE-WHITE THING? MAYBE...A WEDDING GOWN THAT'S SEEN BETTER DAYS?
SHIT. PLAYER THREE, LISTEN TO ME. YOU NEED TO GET OUT OF THERE. NOW.
THAT'S LA LLORONA.
WHAT'S A LA LLORONA?
YOU HEAR HER SCREAMING?
NO.
GOOD. THEN THERE'S STILL TIME. BECAUSE THE SECOND YOU DO HEAR THE SCREAMS...
...THAT MEANS YOU'RE ABOUT TO DIE.

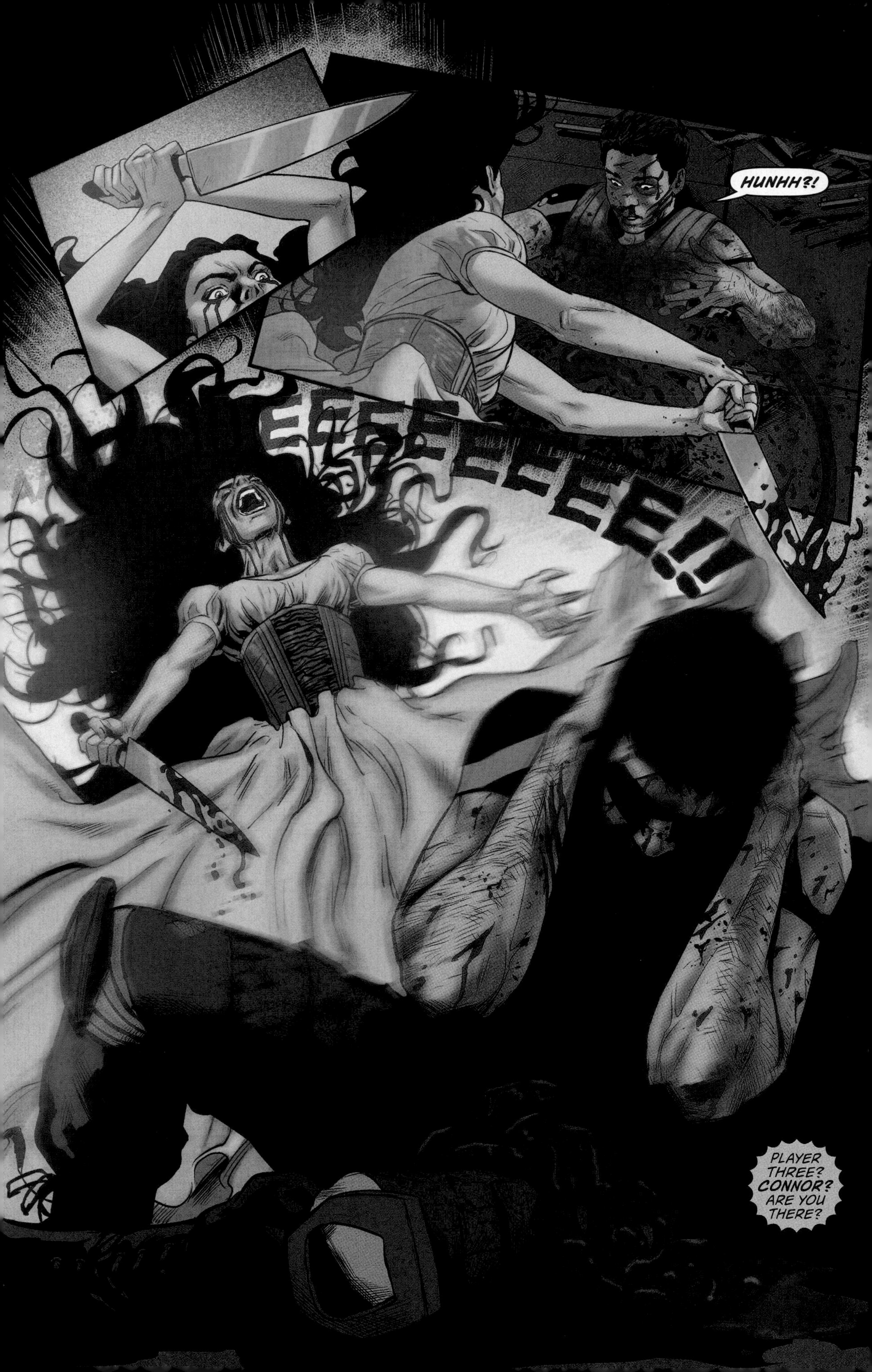
HUNHH?!
EEEEEEEEEEEEE!!!
PLAYER THREE? CONNOR? ARE YOU THERE?

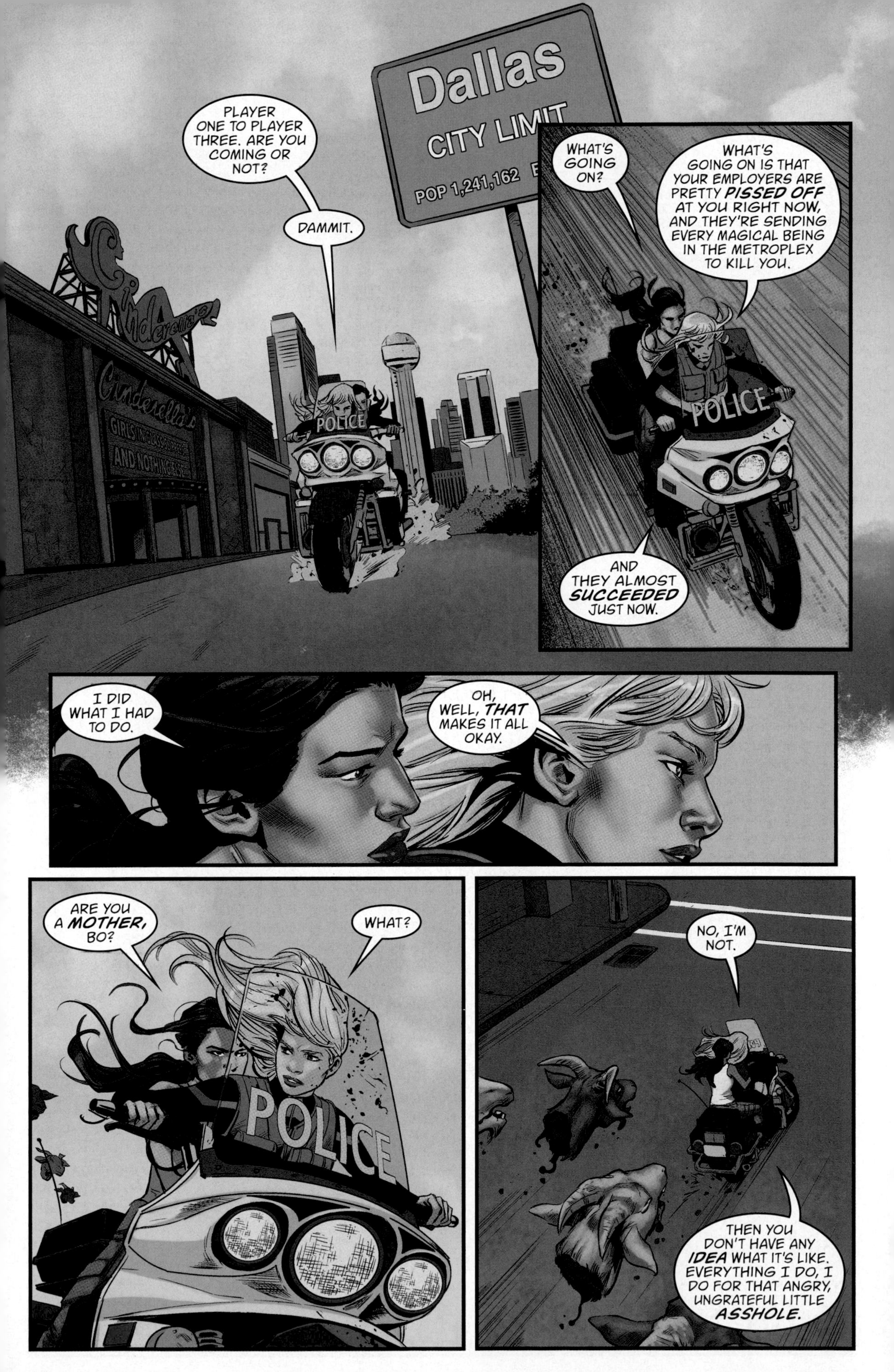

Dallas
CITY LIMIT
POP 1,241,162
Cinderella's
PLAYER ONE TO PLAYER THREE. ARE YOU COMING OR NOT?
DAMMIT.
POLICE
WHAT'S GOING ON?
WHAT'S GOING ON IS THAT YOUR EMPLOYERS ARE PRETTY ***PISSED OFF*** AT YOU RIGHT NOW, AND THEY'RE SENDING EVERY MAGICAL BEING IN THE METROPLEX TO KILL YOU.
AND THEY ALMOST ***SUCCEEDED*** JUST NOW.
I DID WHAT I HAD TO DO.
OH, WELL, ***THAT*** MAKES IT ALL OKAY.
ARE YOU A ***MOTHER,*** BO?
WHAT?
POLICE
NO, I'M NOT.
THEN YOU DON'T HAVE ANY ***IDEA*** WHAT IT'S LIKE. EVERYTHING I DO, I DO FOR THAT ANGRY, UNGRATEFUL LITTLE ***ASSHOLE.***

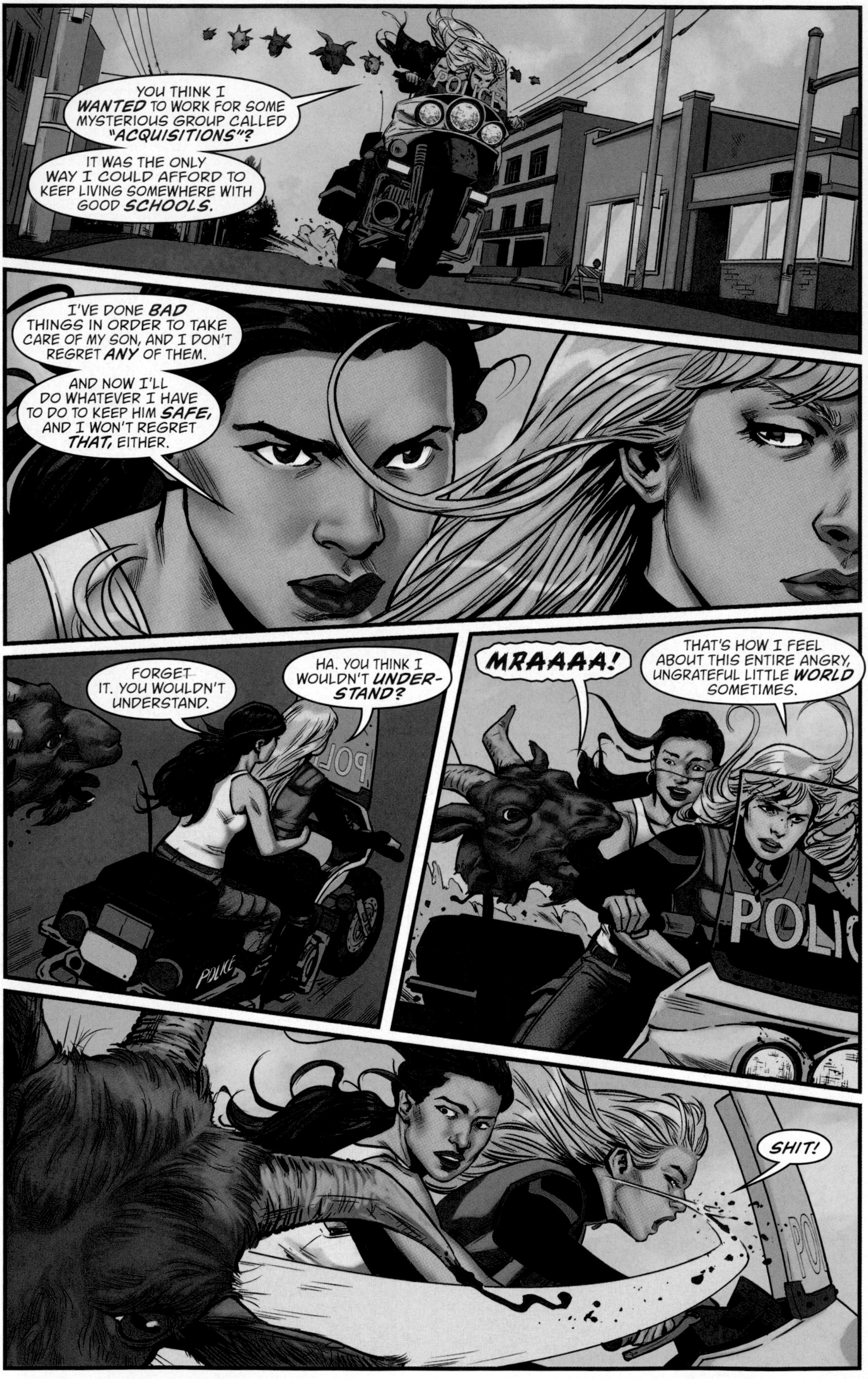
YOU THINK I WANTED TO WORK FOR SOME MYSTERIOUS GROUP CALLED "ACQUISITIONS"?
IT WAS THE ONLY WAY I COULD AFFORD TO KEEP LIVING SOMEWHERE WITH GOOD SCHOOLS.
POLICE
I'VE DONE BAD THINGS IN ORDER TO TAKE CARE OF MY SON, AND I DON'T REGRET ANY OF THEM.
AND NOW I'LL DO WHATEVER I HAVE TO DO TO KEEP HIM SAFE, AND I WON'T REGRET THAT, EITHER.
FORGET IT. YOU WOULDN'T UNDERSTAND.
HA. YOU THINK I WOULDN'T UNDERSTAND?
POLICE
MRAAAA!
THAT'S HOW I FEEL ABOUT THIS ENTIRE ANGRY, UNGRATEFUL LITTLE WORLD SOMETIMES.
POLIC
SHIT!

OW!

PLAYER ONE, THIS IS PLAYER TWO. IS EVERYTHING OKAY?

HUNKY-DORY. I NEED TO GET TO THE I-30 TUNNEL AND EVERYTHING WILL BE JUST FINE.

GOT A FEW OF THE MORE *TENACIOUS* FLYING GOAT HEADS STILL IN PURSUIT, BUT I CAN HANDLE THEM.

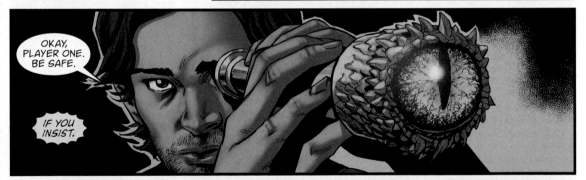

OKAY, PLAYER ONE. BE SAFE.

IF YOU INSIST.

HOLY HELL.

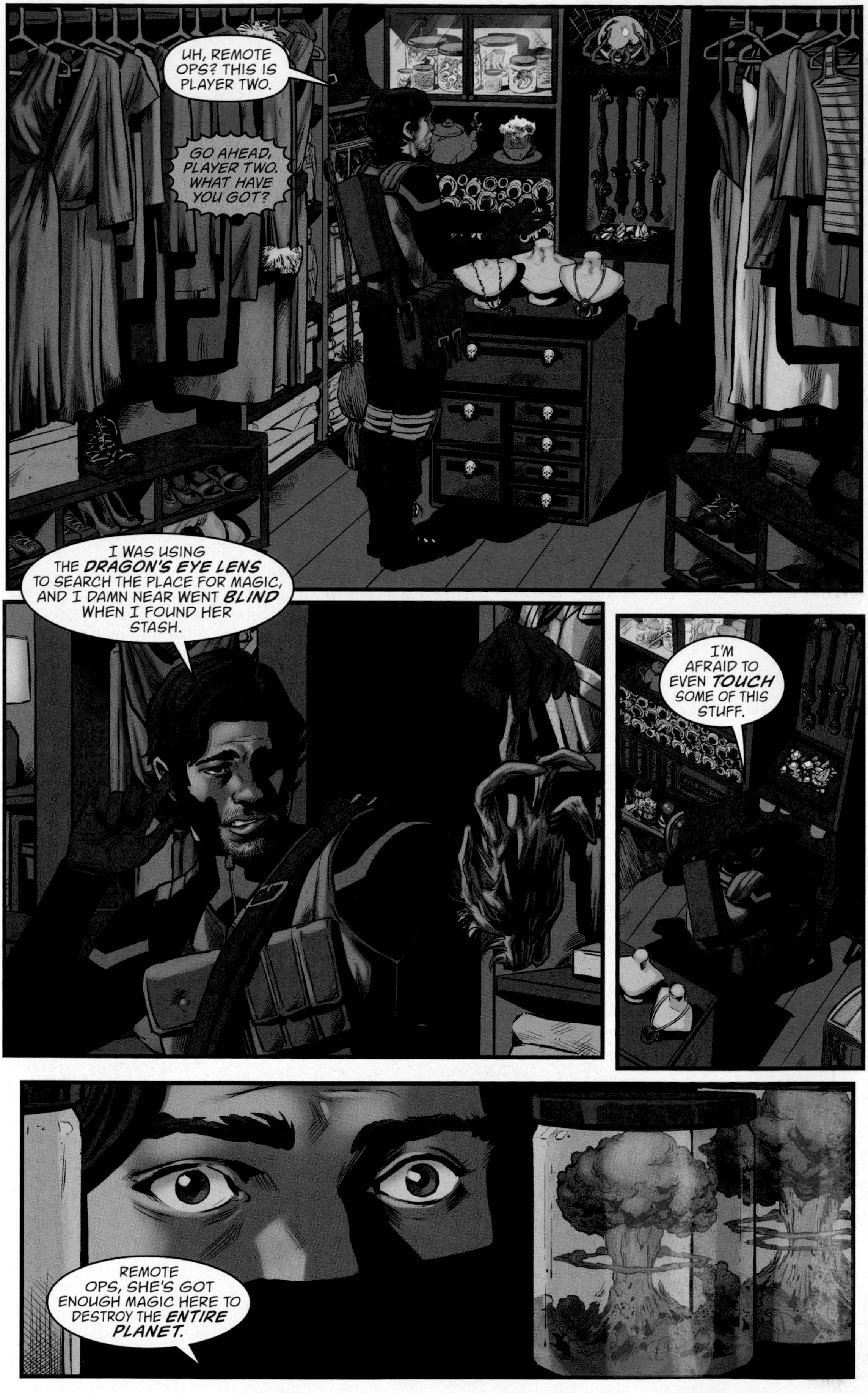
UH, REMOTE OPS? THIS IS PLAYER TWO.
GO AHEAD, PLAYER TWO. WHAT HAVE YOU GOT?
I WAS USING THE **DRAGON'S EYE LENS** TO SEARCH THE PLACE FOR MAGIC, AND I DAMN NEAR WENT **BLIND** WHEN I FOUND HER STASH.
I'M AFRAID TO EVEN **TOUCH** SOME OF THIS STUFF.
REMOTE OPS, SHE'S GOT ENOUGH MAGIC HERE TO DESTROY THE **ENTIRE PLANET**.

I TAKE IT THERE'S MORE THAN YOU CAN CARRY OUT ON YOUR OWN?

UH, YEAH. WE'LL NEED A *TEAM* TO RETRIEVE--

NO. PUT IT ALL DOWN THE WELL.

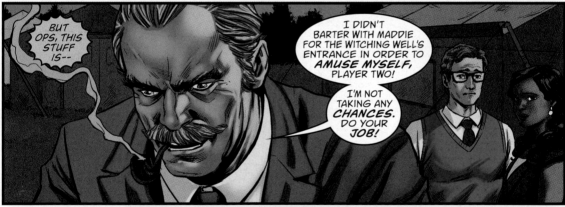

BUT OPS, THIS STUFF IS--

I DIDN'T BARTER WITH MADDIE FOR THE WITCHING WELL'S ENTRANCE IN ORDER TO *AMUSE MYSELF,* PLAYER TWO!

I'M NOT TAKING ANY *CHANCES.* DO YOUR *JOB!*

WHATEVER YOU--

REMOTE OPS *OUT.*

≋CLICK≋

PLAYER THREE. *REPORT.*

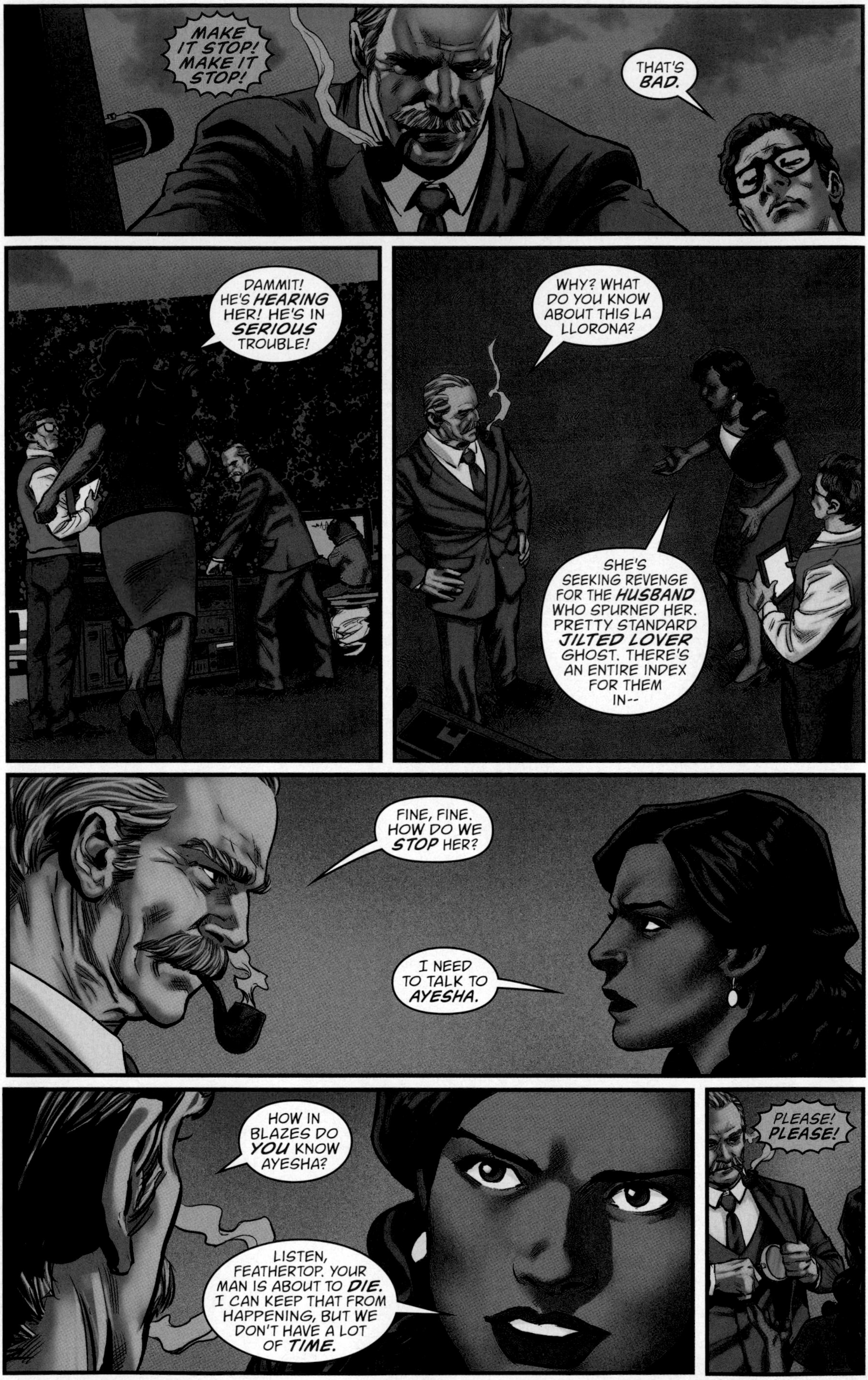
MAKE IT STOP! MAKE IT STOP!
THAT'S BAD.
DAMMIT! HE'S HEARING HER! HE'S IN SERIOUS TROUBLE!
WHY? WHAT DO YOU KNOW ABOUT THIS LA LLORONA?
SHE'S SEEKING REVENGE FOR THE HUSBAND WHO SPURNED HER. PRETTY STANDARD JILTED LOVER GHOST. THERE'S AN ENTIRE INDEX FOR THEM IN--
FINE, FINE. HOW DO WE STOP HER?
I NEED TO TALK TO AYESHA.
HOW IN BLAZES DO YOU KNOW AYESHA?
LISTEN, FEATHERTOP. YOUR MAN IS ABOUT TO DIE. I CAN KEEP THAT FROM HAPPENING, BUT WE DON'T HAVE A LOT OF TIME.
PLEASE! PLEASE!

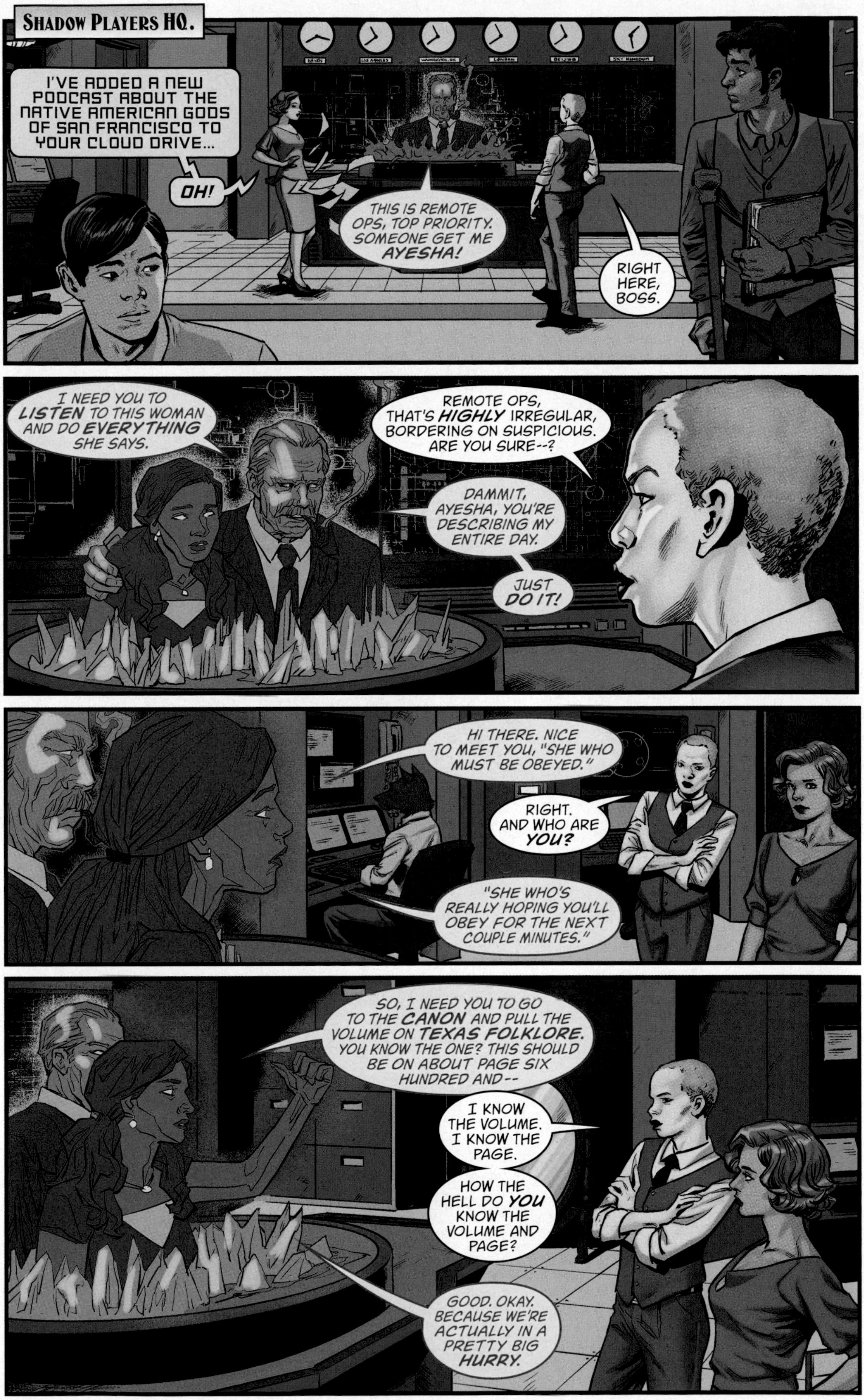
SHADOW PLAYERS HQ.
I'VE ADDED A NEW PODCAST ABOUT THE NATIVE AMERICAN GODS OF SAN FRANCISCO TO YOUR CLOUD DRIVE...
OH!
THIS IS REMOTE OPS, TOP PRIORITY. SOMEONE GET ME AYESHA!
RIGHT HERE, BOSS.
I NEED YOU TO LISTEN TO THIS WOMAN AND DO EVERYTHING SHE SAYS.
REMOTE OPS, THAT'S HIGHLY IRREGULAR, BORDERING ON SUSPICIOUS. ARE YOU SURE--?
DAMMIT, AYESHA, YOU'RE DESCRIBING MY ENTIRE DAY.
JUST DO IT!
HI THERE. NICE TO MEET YOU, "SHE WHO MUST BE OBEYED."
RIGHT. AND WHO ARE YOU?
"SHE WHO'S REALLY HOPING YOU'LL OBEY FOR THE NEXT COUPLE MINUTES."
SO, I NEED YOU TO GO TO THE CANON AND PULL THE VOLUME ON TEXAS FOLKLORE. YOU KNOW THE ONE? THIS SHOULD BE ON ABOUT PAGE SIX HUNDRED AND--
I KNOW THE VOLUME. I KNOW THE PAGE.
HOW THE HELL DO YOU KNOW THE VOLUME AND PAGE?
GOOD. OKAY. BECAUSE WE'RE ACTUALLY IN A PRETTY BIG HURRY.

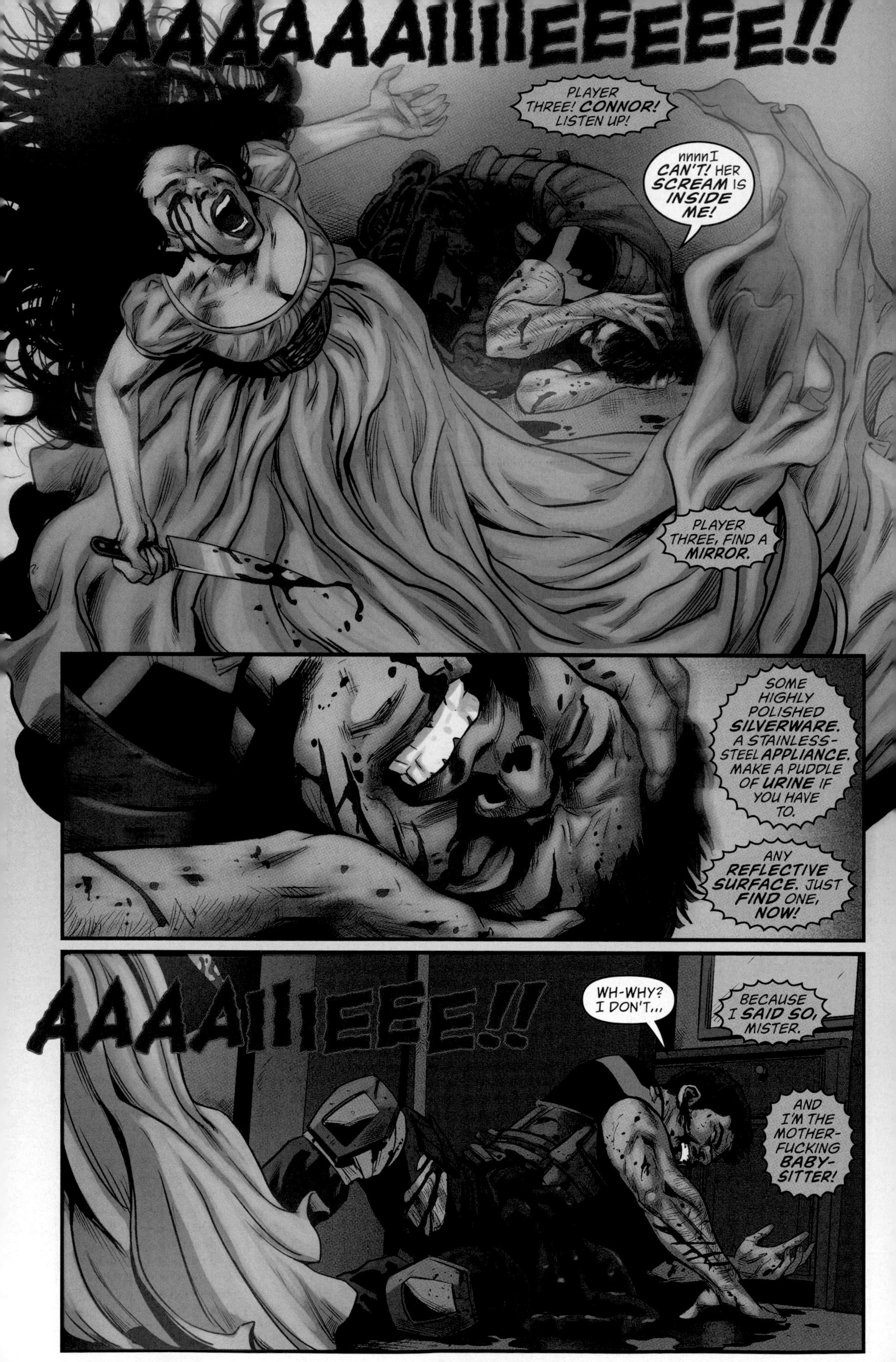
AAAAAAAIIIEEEEEE!!
PLAYER THREE! CONNOR! LISTEN UP!
nnnnI CAN'T! HER SCREAM IS INSIDE ME!
PLAYER THREE, FIND A MIRROR.
SOME HIGHLY POLISHED SILVERWARE. A STAINLESS-STEEL APPLIANCE. MAKE A PUDDLE OF URINE IF YOU HAVE TO.
ANY REFLECTIVE SURFACE. JUST FIND ONE, NOW!
AAAAIIIEEE!!
WH-WHY? I DON'T...
BECAUSE I SAID SO, MISTER.
AND I'M THE MOTHER-FUCKING BABY-SITTER!

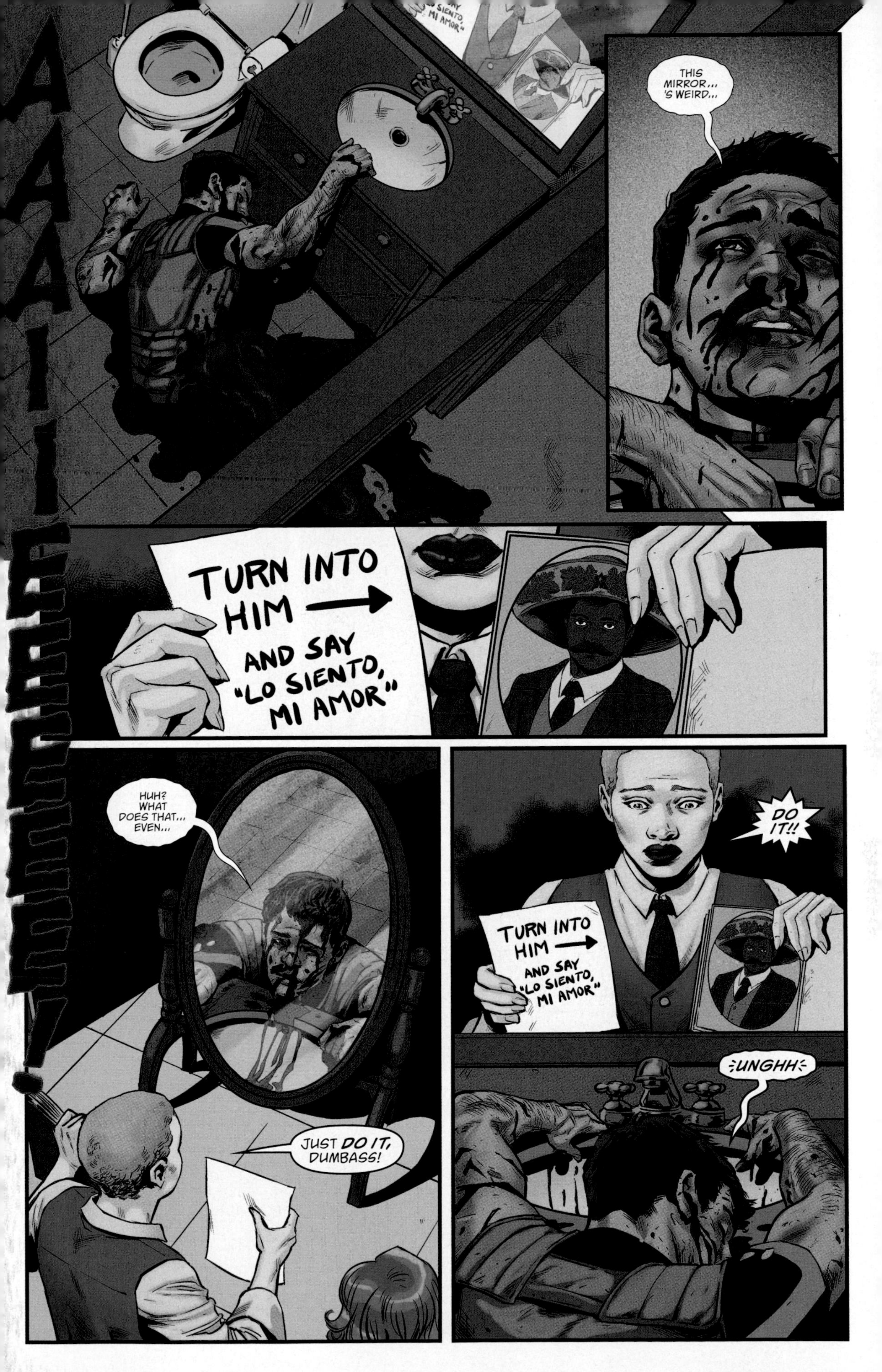
AAIIEEEE!
"LO SIENTO, MI AMOR"
THIS MIRROR... 'S WEIRD...
TURN INTO HIM → AND SAY "LO SIENTO, MI AMOR"
HUH? WHAT DOES THAT... EVEN...
JUST DO IT, DUMBASS!
DO IT!!
TURN INTO HIM → AND SAY "LO SIENTO, MI AMOR"
UNGHH

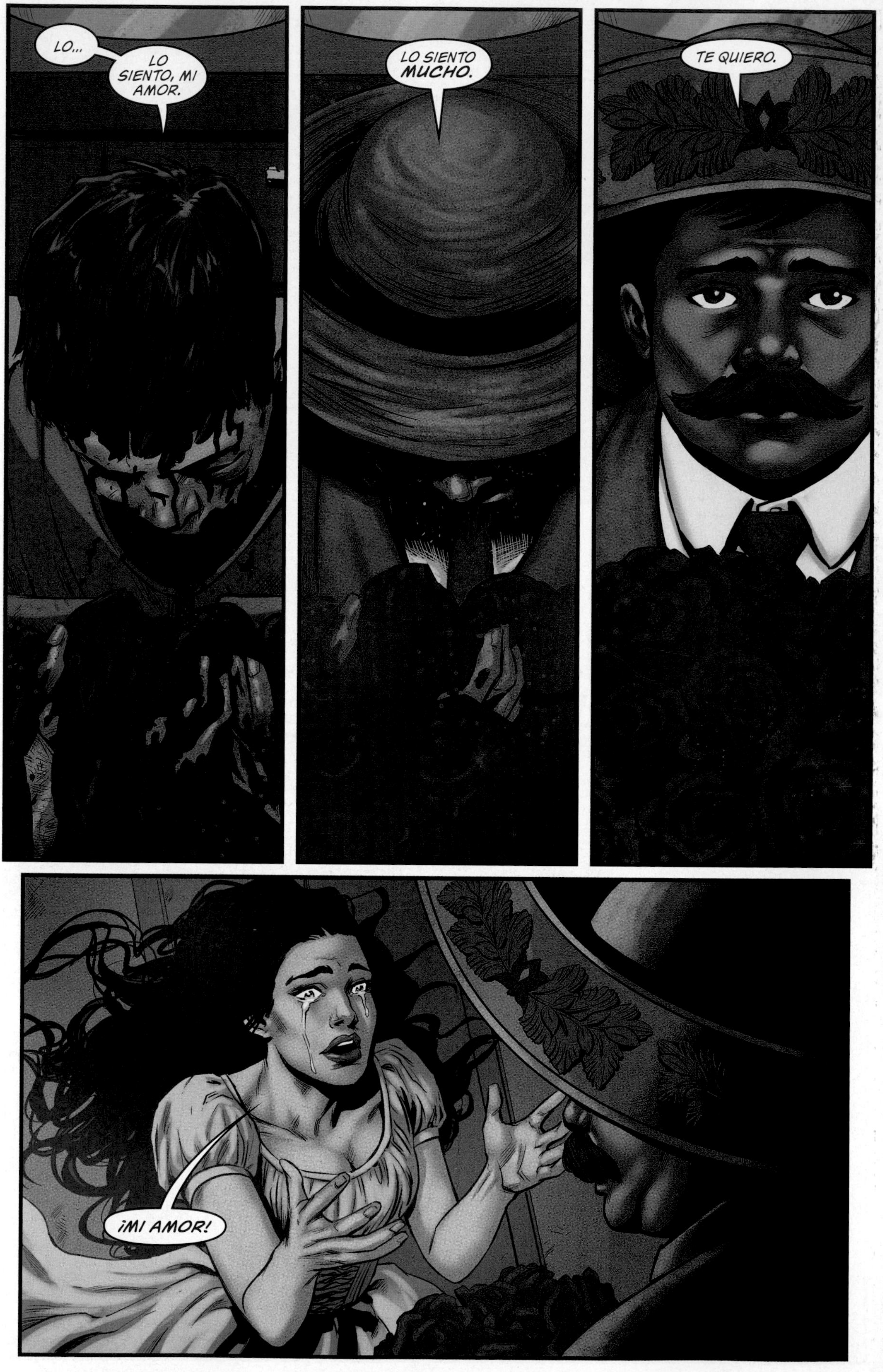
LO...
LO SIENTO, MI AMOR.
LO SIENTO MUCHO.
TE QUIERO.
¡MI AMOR!

SOLVED OUR WEE LA LLORONA PROBLEM, DID YOU, MISS BASS? DISARMED HER WITH AN OLD LOVER, EH?
OOH, THOMAS, I COULD LISTEN TO YOUR SCOTTISH TONGUE TRY TO PRONOUNCE "LA LLORONA" ALL DAY AND NEVER GET BORED.
ACH. CRACKS CASES AND CRACKS JOKES. DON'T YOU LOOK JUST LIKE THE CAT THAT ATE THE CANARY?
WHAT CAN I SAY? I KNOW A THING OR TWO ABOUT A THING OR TWO.
THAT YOU DO. TRUER WORDS WERE NEVER--
THE CAT! OF COURSE! I NEED THE CAT!
MADDIE. YES. YES! NO TIME FOR SMALL TALK, WOMAN.
I NEED TO SPEAK TO A FRIEND OF YOURS. RIGHT AWAY.
PLAYER ONE TO REMOTE OPS. I HAVE A PROBLEM!

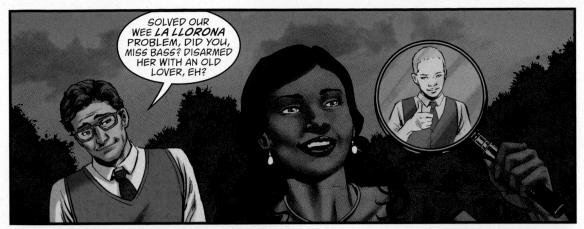

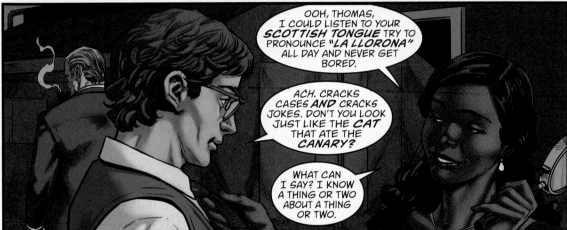

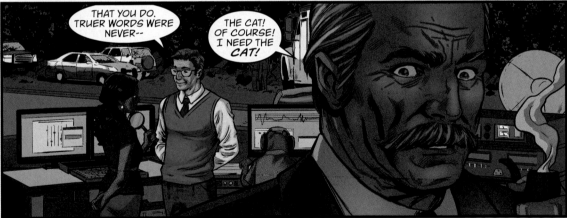

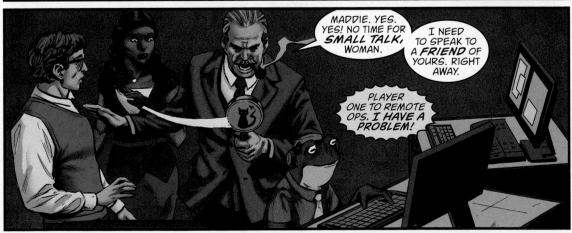

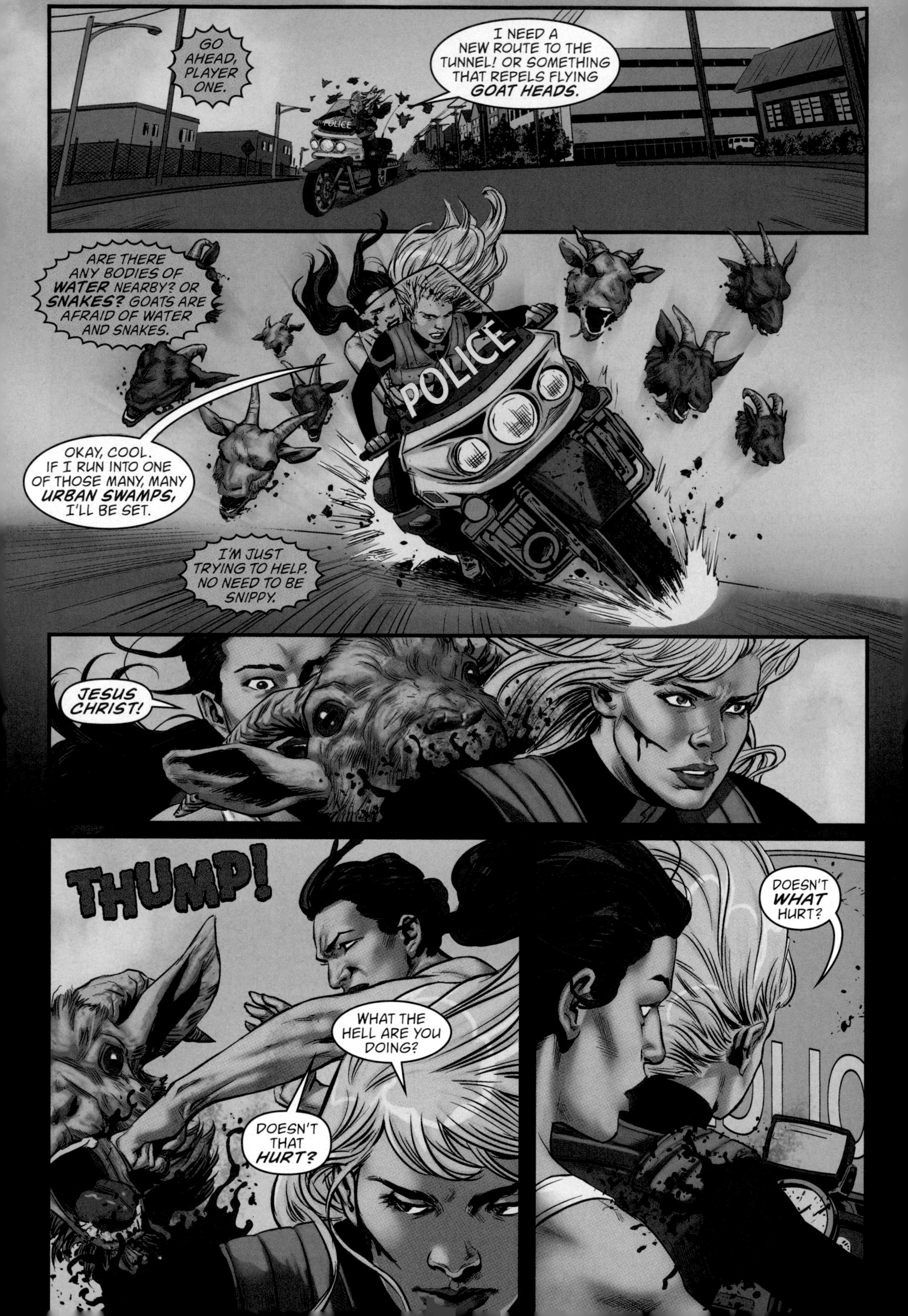

GO AHEAD, PLAYER ONE.
I NEED A NEW ROUTE TO THE TUNNEL! OR SOMETHING THAT REPELS FLYING GOAT HEADS.
POLICE
ARE THERE ANY BODIES OF WATER NEARBY? OR SNAKES? GOATS ARE AFRAID OF WATER AND SNAKES.
POLICE
OKAY, COOL. IF I RUN INTO ONE OF THOSE MANY, MANY URBAN SWAMPS, I'LL BE SET.
I'M JUST TRYING TO HELP. NO NEED TO BE SNIPPY.
JESUS CHRIST!
THUMP!
WHAT THE HELL ARE YOU DOING?
DOESN'T THAT HURT?
DOESN'T WHAT HURT?

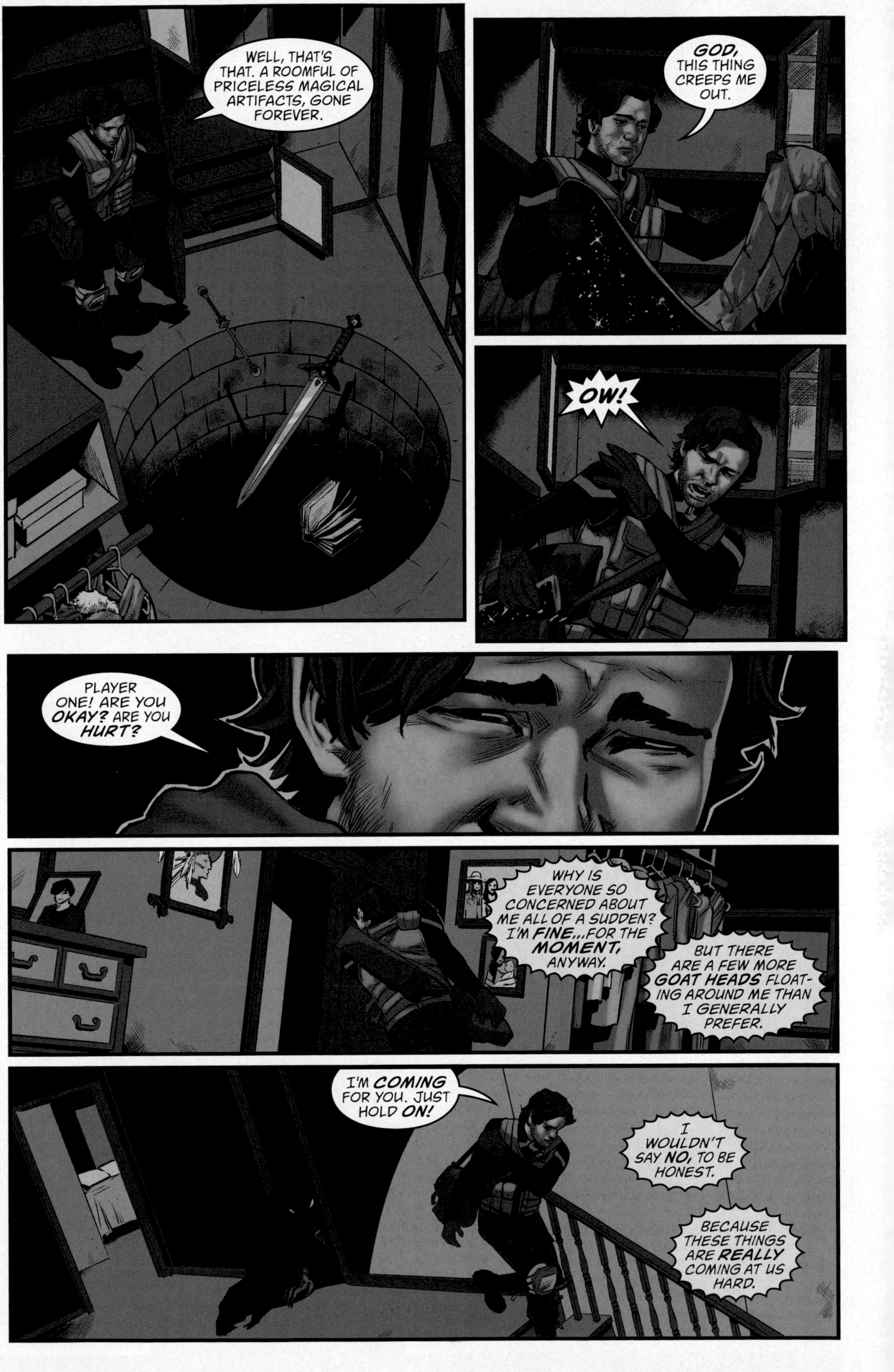
WELL, THAT'S THAT. A ROOMFUL OF PRICELESS MAGICAL ARTIFACTS, GONE FOREVER.
GOD, THIS THING CREEPS ME OUT.
OW!
PLAYER ONE! ARE YOU OKAY? ARE YOU HURT?
WHY IS EVERYONE SO CONCERNED ABOUT ME ALL OF A SUDDEN? I'M FINE...FOR THE MOMENT, ANYWAY.
BUT THERE ARE A FEW MORE GOAT HEADS FLOATING AROUND ME THAN I GENERALLY PREFER.
I'M COMING FOR YOU. JUST HOLD ON!
I WOULDN'T SAY NO, TO BE HONEST.
BECAUSE THESE THINGS ARE REALLY COMING AT US HARD.

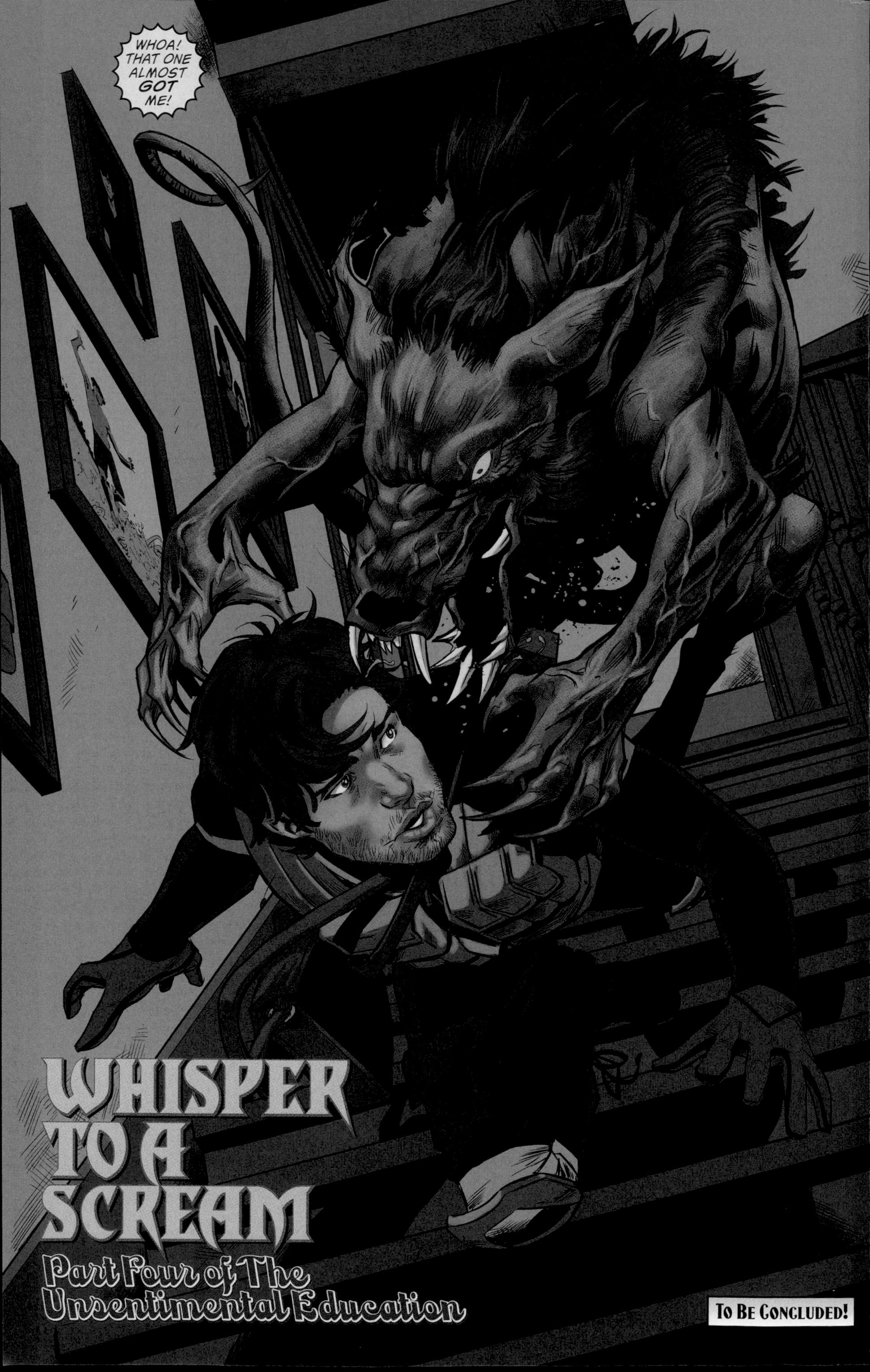
WHOA! THAT ONE ALMOST GOT ME!
WHISPER TO A SCREAM
Part Four of The Unsentimental Education
TO BE CONCLUDED!

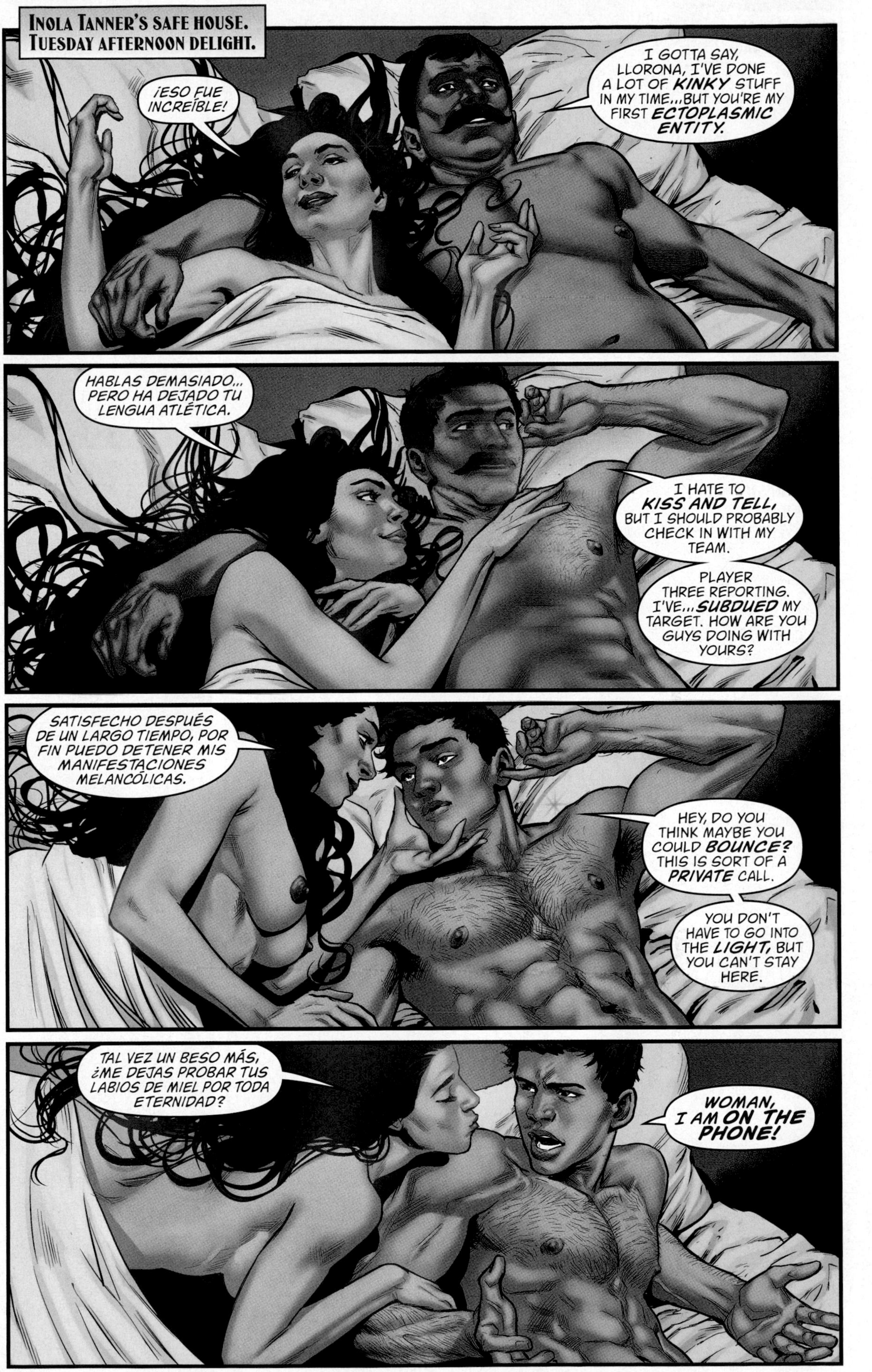
INOLA TANNER'S SAFE HOUSE. TUESDAY AFTERNOON DELIGHT.
¡ESO FUE INCREÍBLE!
I GOTTA SAY, LLORONA, I'VE DONE A LOT OF KINKY STUFF IN MY TIME...BUT YOU'RE MY FIRST ECTOPLASMIC ENTITY.
HABLAS DEMASIADO... PERO HA DEJADO TU LENGUA ATLÉTICA.
I HATE TO KISS AND TELL, BUT I SHOULD PROBABLY CHECK IN WITH MY TEAM.
PLAYER THREE REPORTING. I'VE... SUBDUED MY TARGET. HOW ARE YOU GUYS DOING WITH YOURS?
SATISFECHO DESPUÉS DE UN LARGO TIEMPO, POR FIN PUEDO DETENER MIS MANIFESTACIONES MELANCÓLICAS.
HEY, DO YOU THINK MAYBE YOU COULD BOUNCE? THIS IS SORT OF A PRIVATE CALL.
YOU DON'T HAVE TO GO INTO THE LIGHT, BUT YOU CAN'T STAY HERE.
TAL VEZ UN BESO MÁS, ¿ME DEJAS PROBAR TUS LABIOS DE MIEL POR TODA ETERNIDAD?
WOMAN, I AM ON THE PHONE!

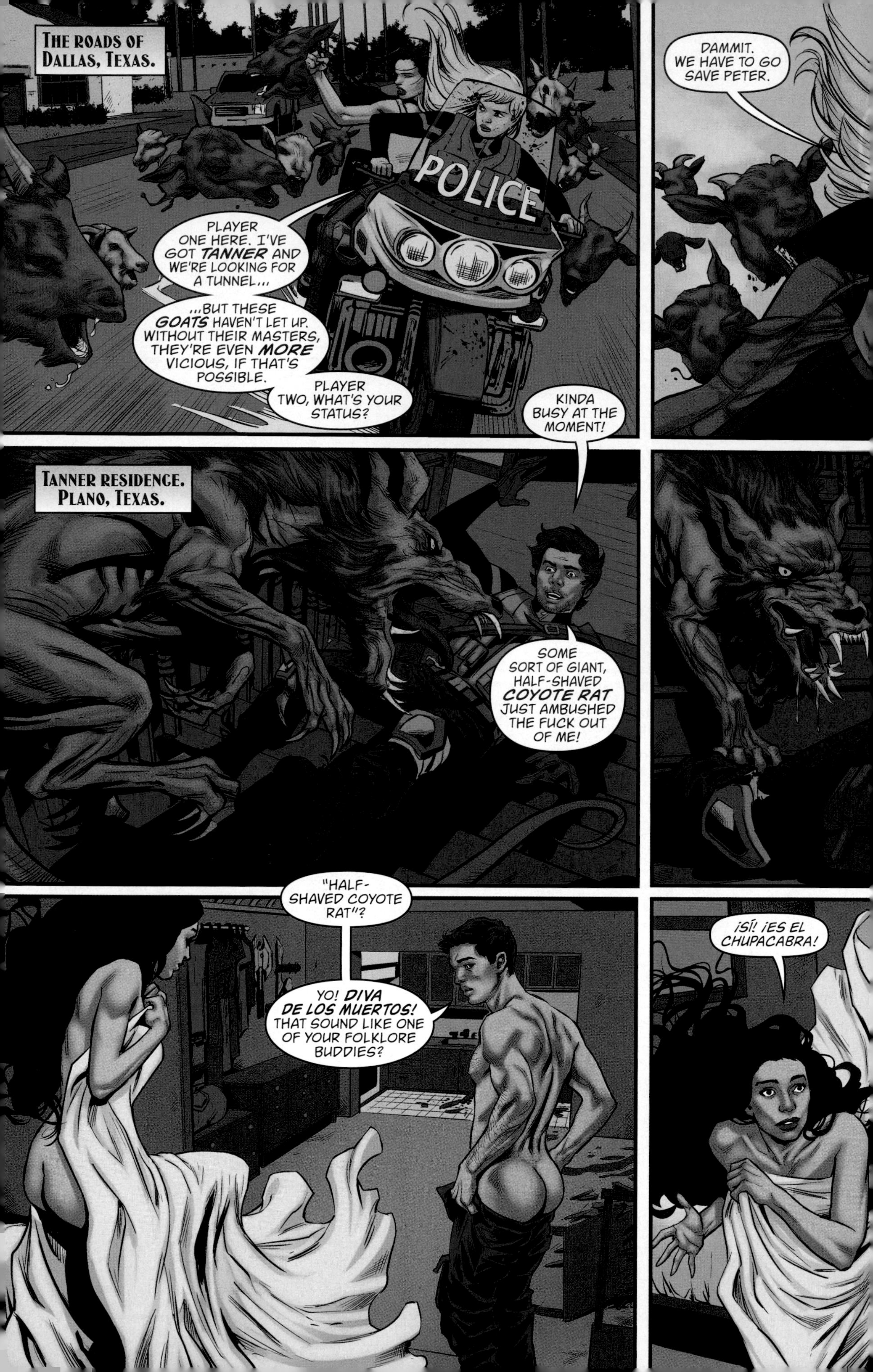
THE ROADS OF DALLAS, TEXAS.
PLAYER ONE HERE. I'VE GOT TANNER AND WE'RE LOOKING FOR A TUNNEL...
...BUT THESE GOATS HAVEN'T LET UP. WITHOUT THEIR MASTERS, THEY'RE EVEN MORE VICIOUS, IF THAT'S POSSIBLE.
PLAYER TWO, WHAT'S YOUR STATUS?
POLICE
DAMMIT. WE HAVE TO GO SAVE PETER.
KINDA BUSY AT THE MOMENT!
TANNER RESIDENCE. PLANO, TEXAS.
SOME SORT OF GIANT, HALF-SHAVED COYOTE RAT JUST AMBUSHED THE FUCK OUT OF ME!
"HALF-SHAVED COYOTE RAT"?
YO! DIVA DE LOS MUERTOS! THAT SOUND LIKE ONE OF YOUR FOLKLORE BUDDIES?
¡SÍ! ¡ES EL CHUPACABRA!

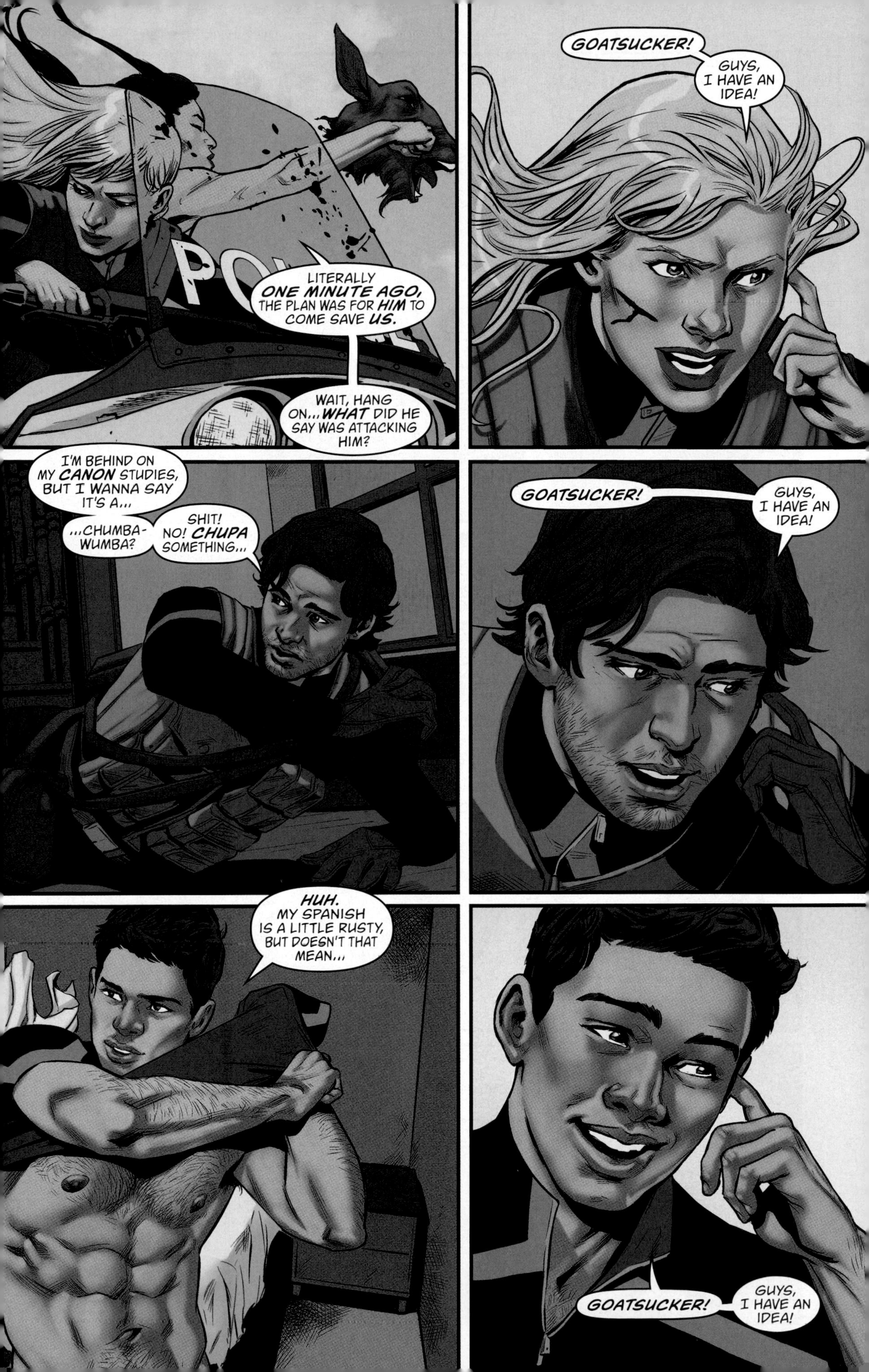
LITERALLY ONE MINUTE AGO, THE PLAN WAS FOR HIM TO COME SAVE US.
WAIT, HANG ON... WHAT DID HE SAY WAS ATTACKING HIM?
GOATSUCKER!
GUYS, I HAVE AN IDEA!
I'M BEHIND ON MY CANON STUDIES, BUT I WANNA SAY IT'S A...
...CHUMBA-WUMBA?
SHIT! NO! CHUPA SOMETHING...
GOATSUCKER!
GUYS, I HAVE AN IDEA!
HUH. MY SPANISH IS A LITTLE RUSTY, BUT DOESN'T THAT MEAN...
GOATSUCKER!
GUYS, I HAVE AN IDEA!

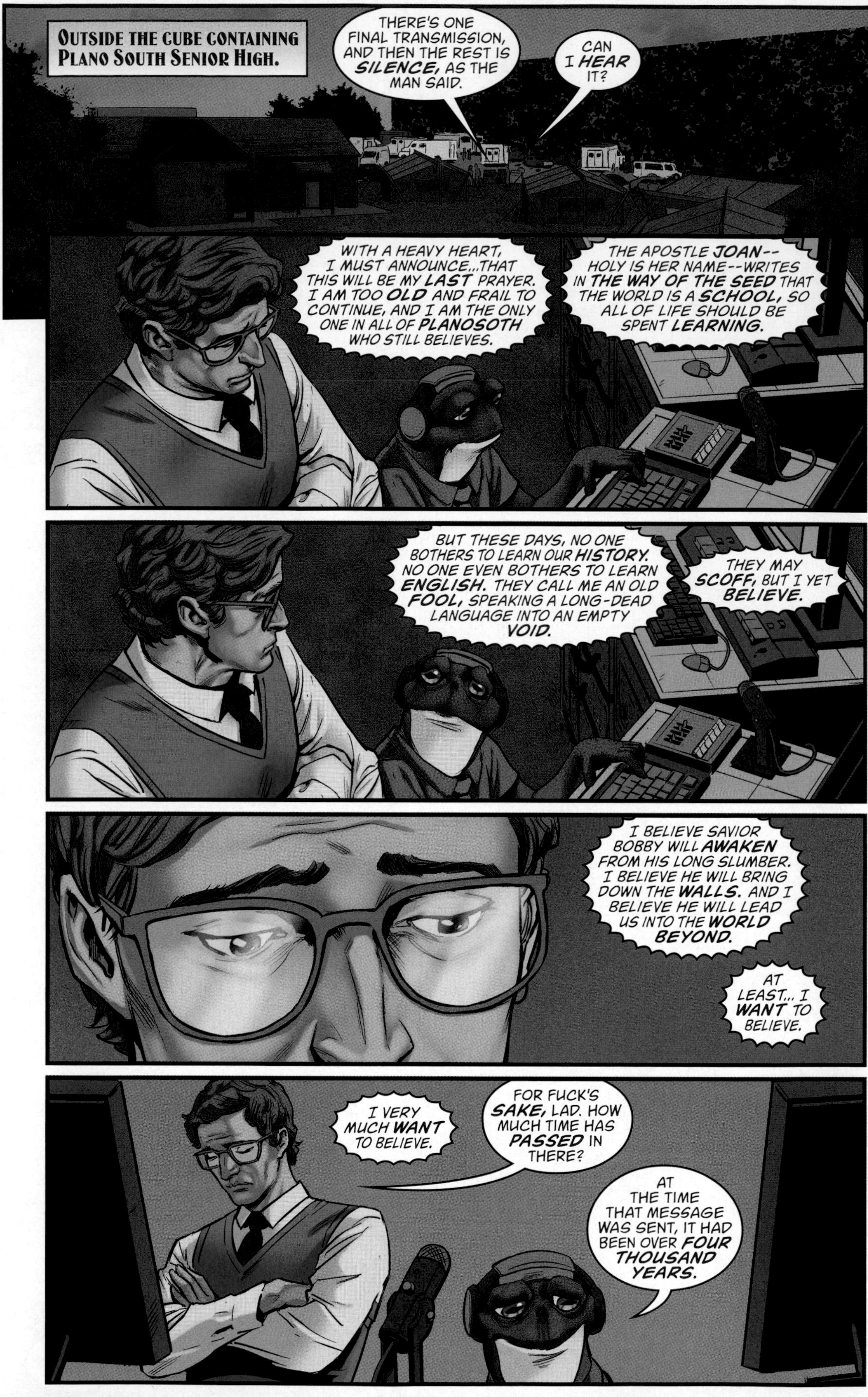
OUTSIDE THE CUBE CONTAINING PLANO SOUTH SENIOR HIGH.
THERE'S ONE FINAL TRANSMISSION, AND THEN THE REST IS SILENCE, AS THE MAN SAID.
CAN I HEAR IT?
WITH A HEAVY HEART, I MUST ANNOUNCE...THAT THIS WILL BE MY LAST PRAYER. I AM TOO OLD AND FRAIL TO CONTINUE, AND I AM THE ONLY ONE IN ALL OF PLANOSOTH WHO STILL BELIEVES.
THE APOSTLE JOAN--HOLY IS HER NAME--WRITES IN THE WAY OF THE SEED THAT THE WORLD IS A SCHOOL, SO ALL OF LIFE SHOULD BE SPENT LEARNING.
BUT THESE DAYS, NO ONE BOTHERS TO LEARN OUR HISTORY. NO ONE EVEN BOTHERS TO LEARN ENGLISH. THEY CALL ME AN OLD FOOL, SPEAKING A LONG-DEAD LANGUAGE INTO AN EMPTY VOID.
THEY MAY SCOFF, BUT I YET BELIEVE.
I BELIEVE SAVIOR BOBBY WILL AWAKEN FROM HIS LONG SLUMBER. I BELIEVE HE WILL BRING DOWN THE WALLS. AND I BELIEVE HE WILL LEAD US INTO THE WORLD BEYOND.
AT LEAST... I WANT TO BELIEVE.
I VERY MUCH WANT TO BELIEVE.
FOR FUCK'S SAKE, LAD. HOW MUCH TIME HAS PASSED IN THERE?
AT THE TIME THAT MESSAGE WAS SENT, IT HAD BEEN OVER FOUR THOUSAND YEARS.

HOW LONG HAS IT BEEN SINCE THEN?

IT'S HARD TO MAKE A PRECISE CALCULATION WITHOUT THE RADIO TRANSMISSIONS AS A GAUGE, BUT... LONGER THAN *THAT*. A *LOT* LONGER.

HELLOOOO, *TEXAS!*

YOU KNOW, FEATHERTOP, I *JUST* BROUGHT YOU A PERFECTLY GOOD WIZARD, AND YOU COULDN'T HOLD ON TO HIM FOR *ONE SINGLE DAY.*

SO, IF YOU WOULDN'T MIND, PLEASE TAKE *BETTER* CARE OF *ERWIN?* HE'S A *DEAR* OLD FRIEND.

NICE TO SEE YOU AGAIN AS WELL, *MADDIE.*

HE'S IN THE CARRIER?

WELL... *YES* AND *NO.*

COLE, WOULD YOU MIND DOING THE HONORS?

HMPH. I FIND YOUR "FRIEND" A BIT *UNNERVING,* IF I'M BEING PERFECTLY HONEST, BUT...

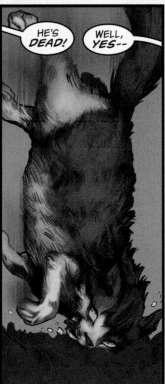

HE'S *DEAD!*

WELL, YES--

--AND NO.

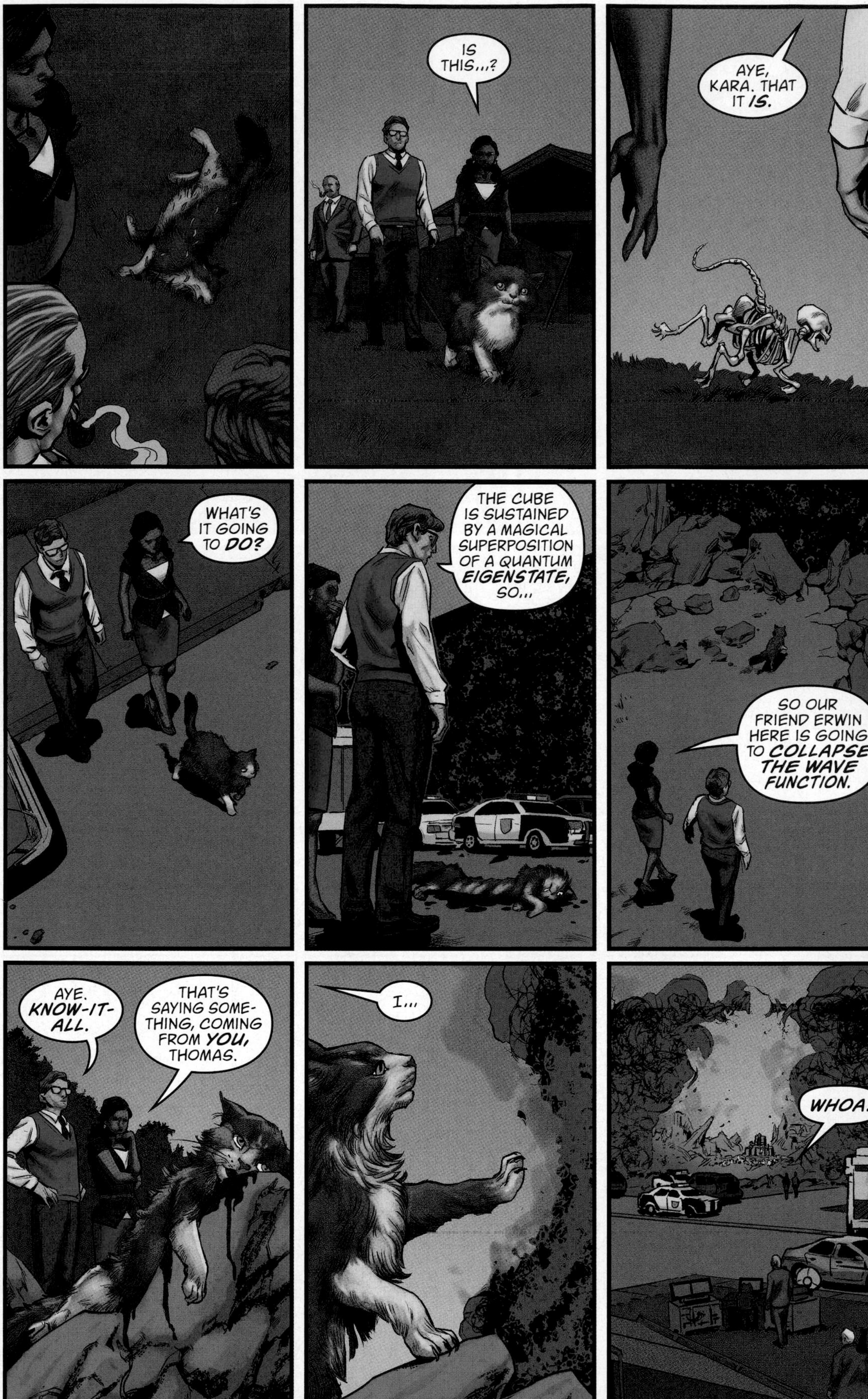
IS THIS...?
AYE, KARA. THAT IT IS.
WHAT'S IT GOING TO DO?
THE CUBE IS SUSTAINED BY A MAGICAL SUPERPOSITION OF A QUANTUM EIGENSTATE, SO...
SO OUR FRIEND ERWIN HERE IS GOING TO COLLAPSE THE WAVE FUNCTION.
AYE. KNOW-IT-ALL.
THAT'S SAYING SOME-THING, COMING FROM YOU, THOMAS.
I...
WHOA.

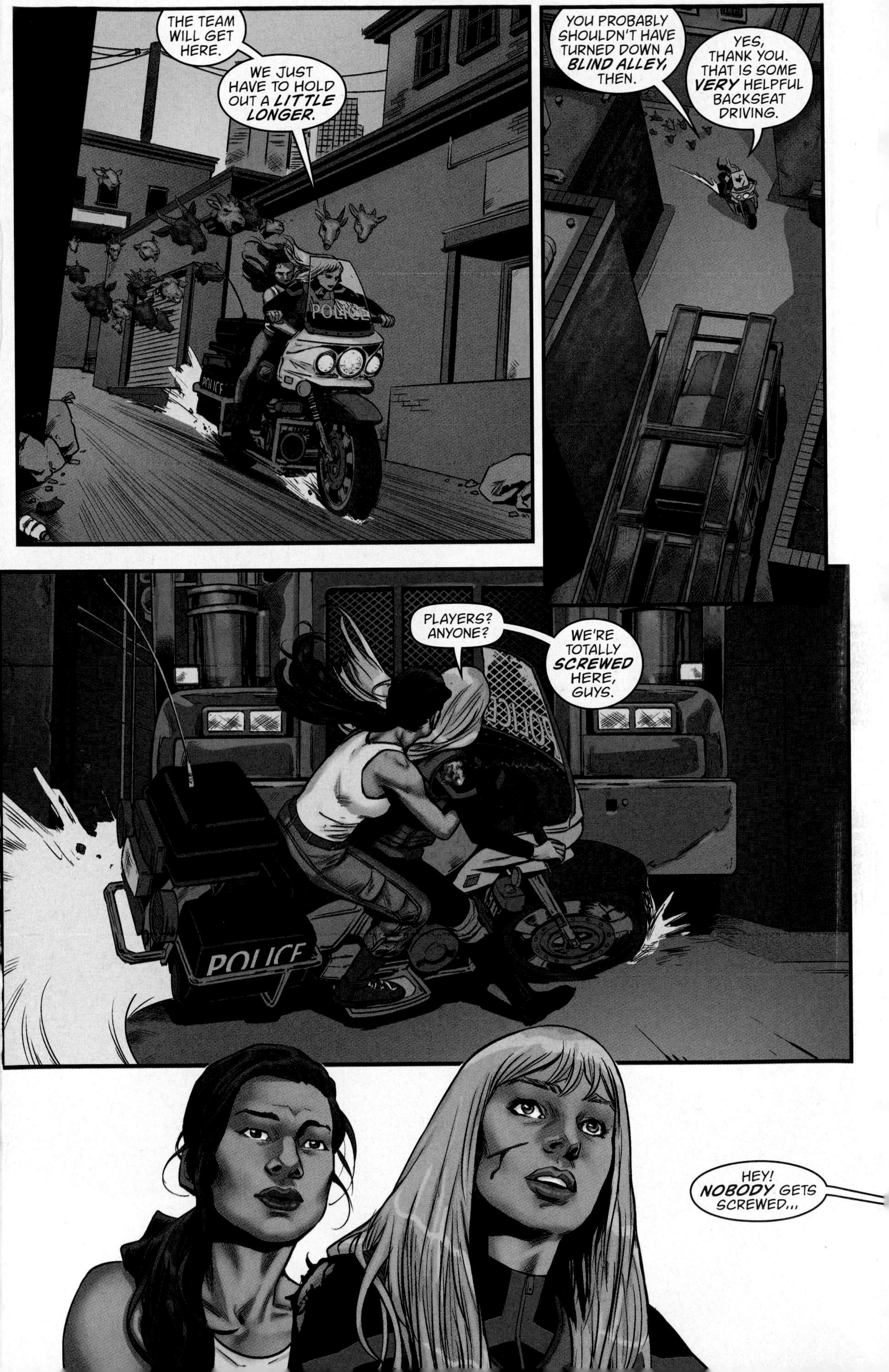
THE TEAM WILL GET HERE.
WE JUST HAVE TO HOLD OUT A LITTLE LONGER.
YOU PROBABLY SHOULDN'T HAVE TURNED DOWN A BLIND ALLEY, THEN.
YES, THANK YOU. THAT IS SOME VERY HELPFUL BACKSEAT DRIVING.
PLAYERS? ANYONE?
WE'RE TOTALLY SCREWED HERE, GUYS.
HEY! NOBODY GETS SCREWED...

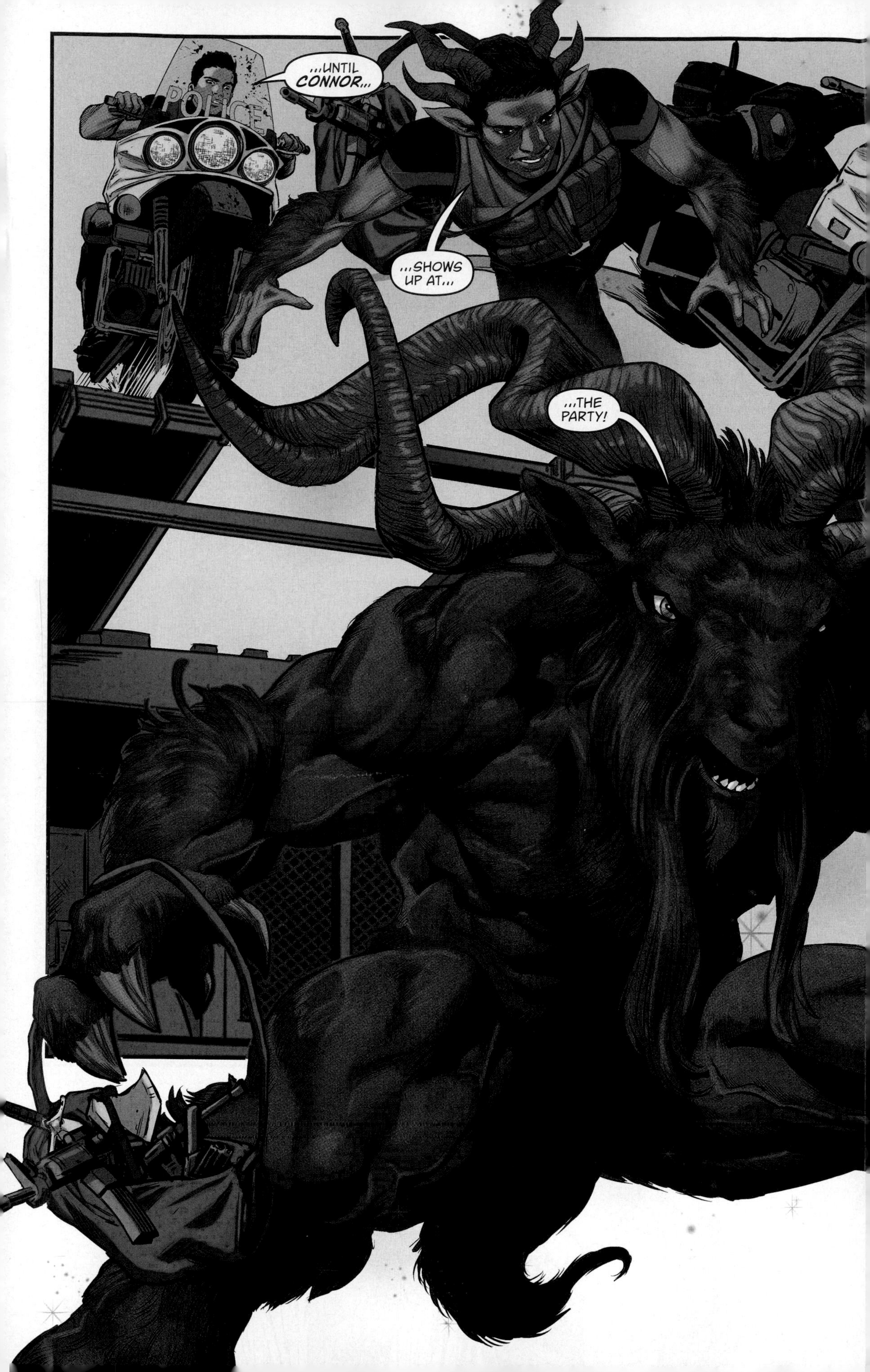

...UNTIL CONNOR...
...SHOWS UP AT...
...THE PARTY!
POLICE

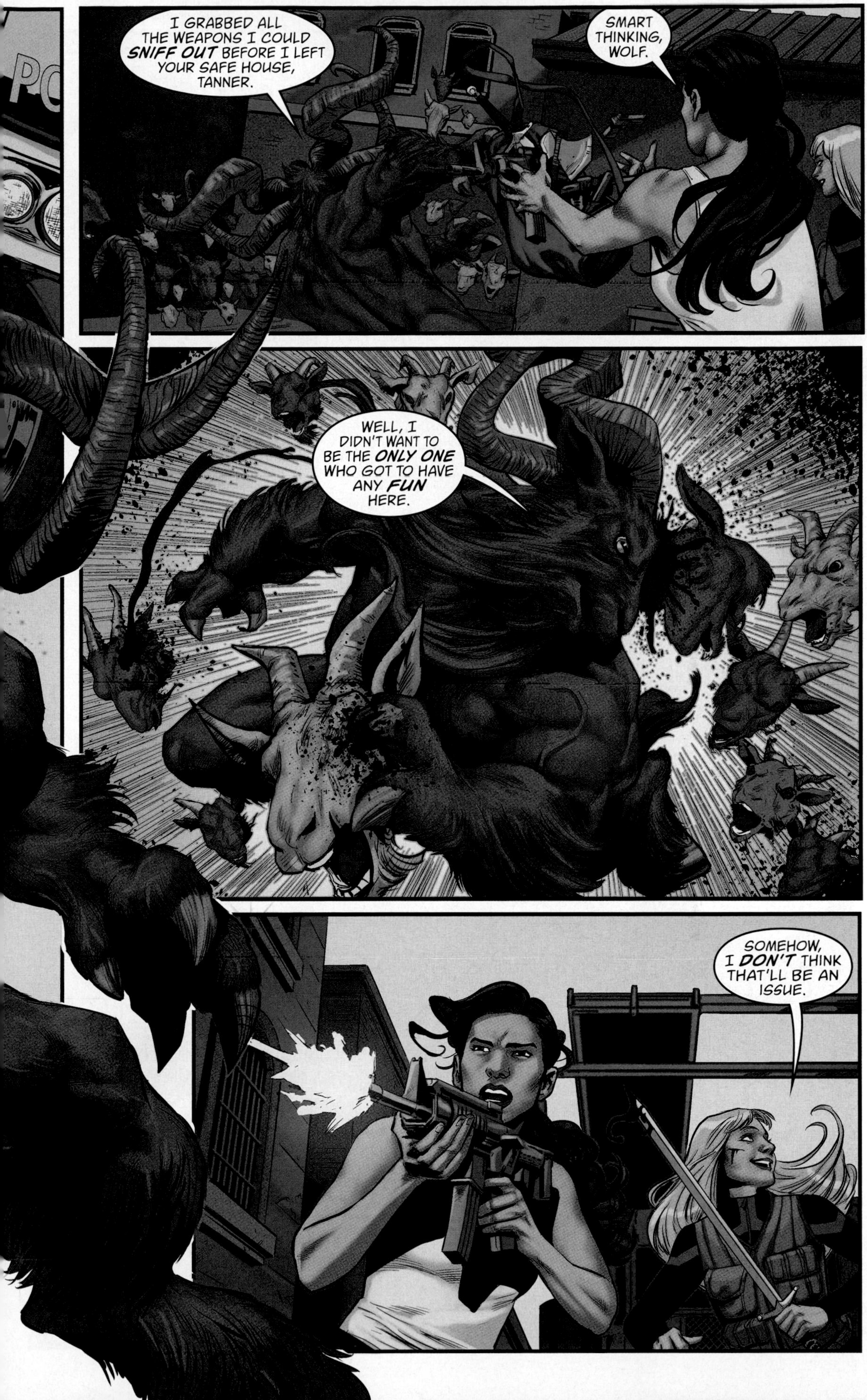
I GRABBED ALL THE WEAPONS I COULD **SNIFF OUT** BEFORE I LEFT YOUR SAFE HOUSE, TANNER.
SMART THINKING, WOLF.
WELL, I DIDN'T WANT TO BE THE **ONLY ONE** WHO GOT TO HAVE ANY **FUN** HERE.
SOMEHOW, I **DON'T** THINK THAT'LL BE AN ISSUE.

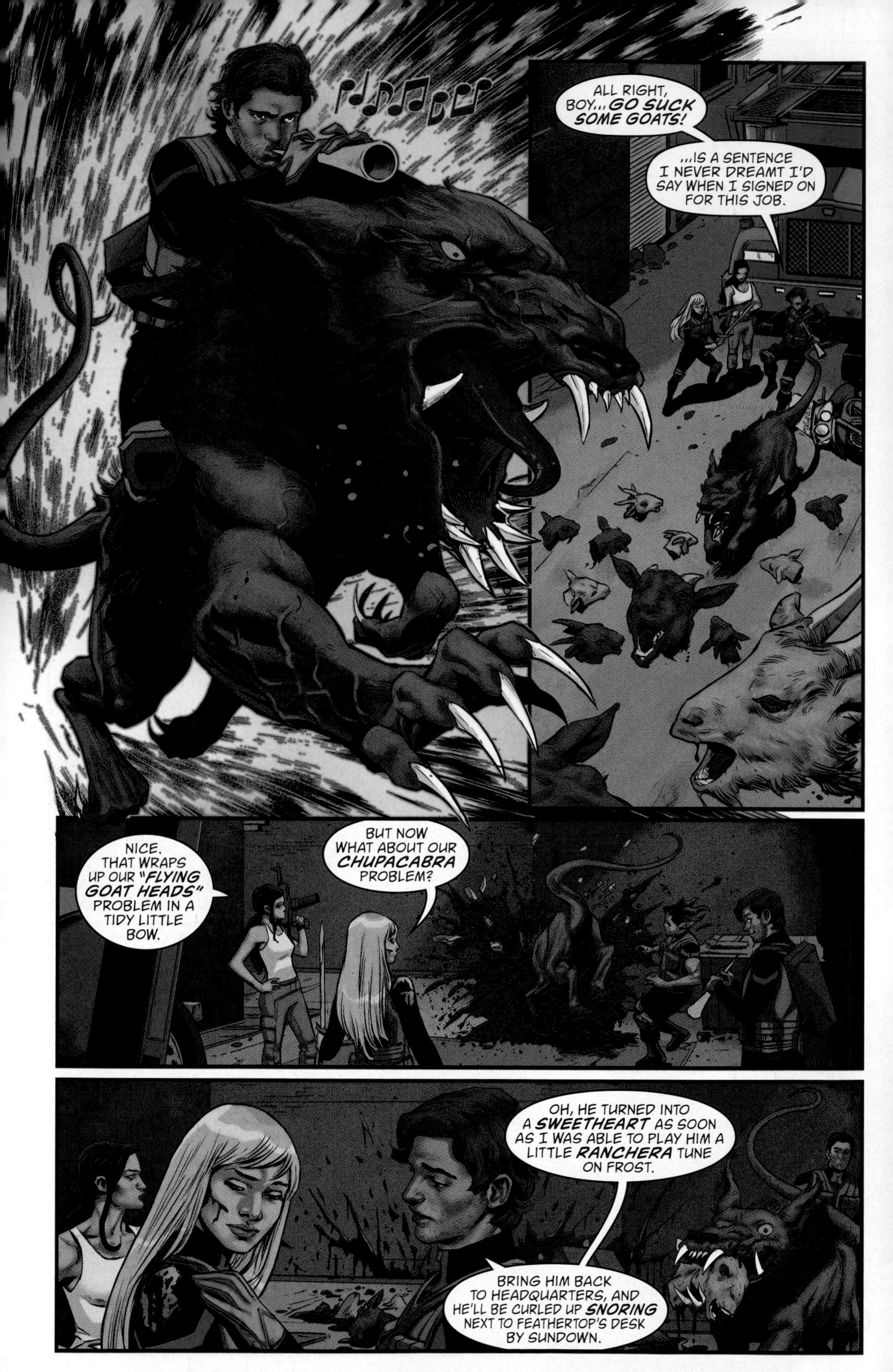
ALL RIGHT, BOY... GO SUCK SOME GOATS!
...IS A SENTENCE I NEVER DREAMT I'D SAY WHEN I SIGNED ON FOR THIS JOB.
NICE. THAT WRAPS UP OUR "FLYING GOAT HEADS" PROBLEM IN A TIDY LITTLE BOW.
BUT NOW WHAT ABOUT OUR CHUPACABRA PROBLEM?
OH, HE TURNED INTO A SWEETHEART AS SOON AS I WAS ABLE TO PLAY HIM A LITTLE RANCHERA TUNE ON FROST.
BRING HIM BACK TO HEADQUARTERS, AND HE'LL BE CURLED UP SNORING NEXT TO FEATHERTOP'S DESK BY SUNDOWN.

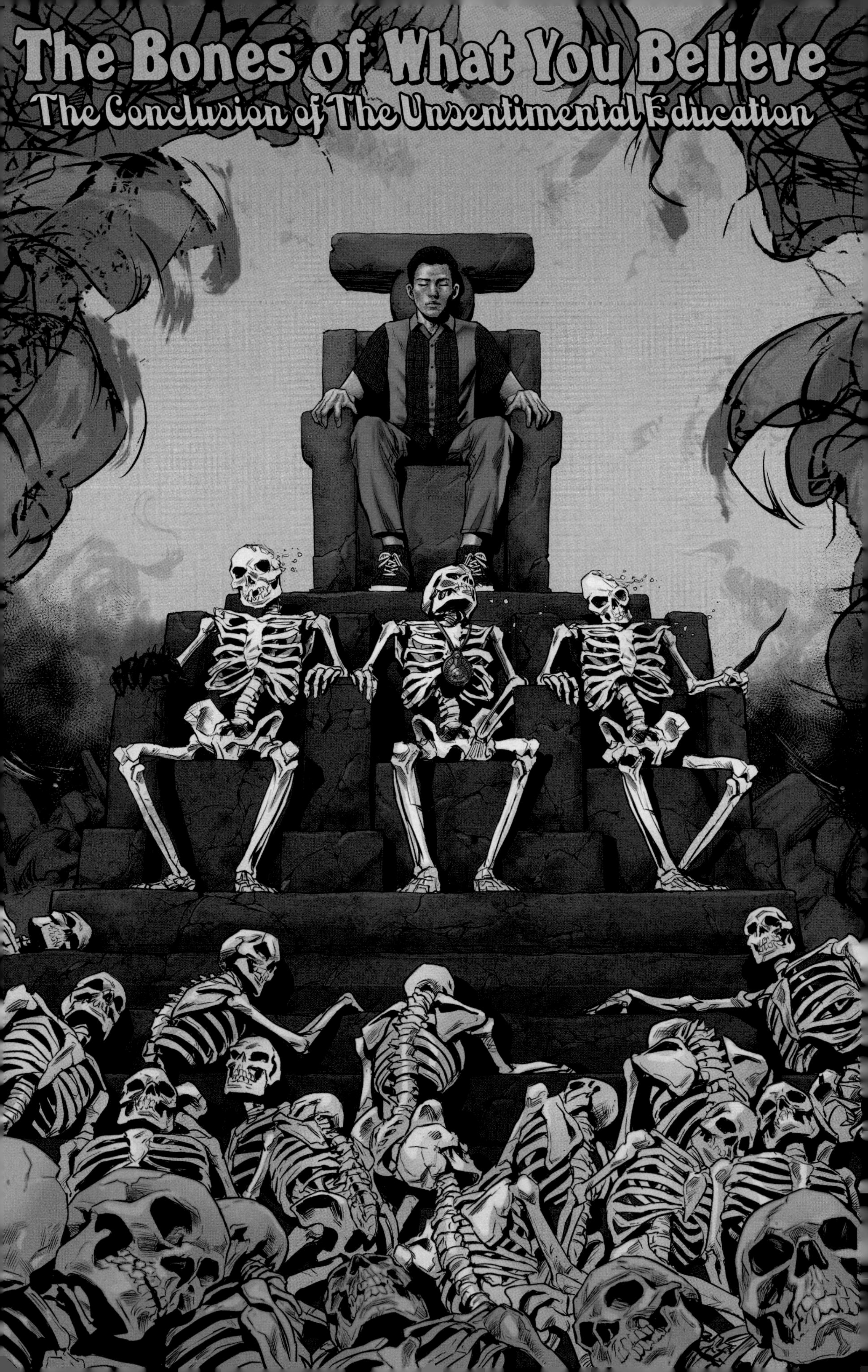
The Bones of What You Believe
The Conclusion of The Unsentimental Education

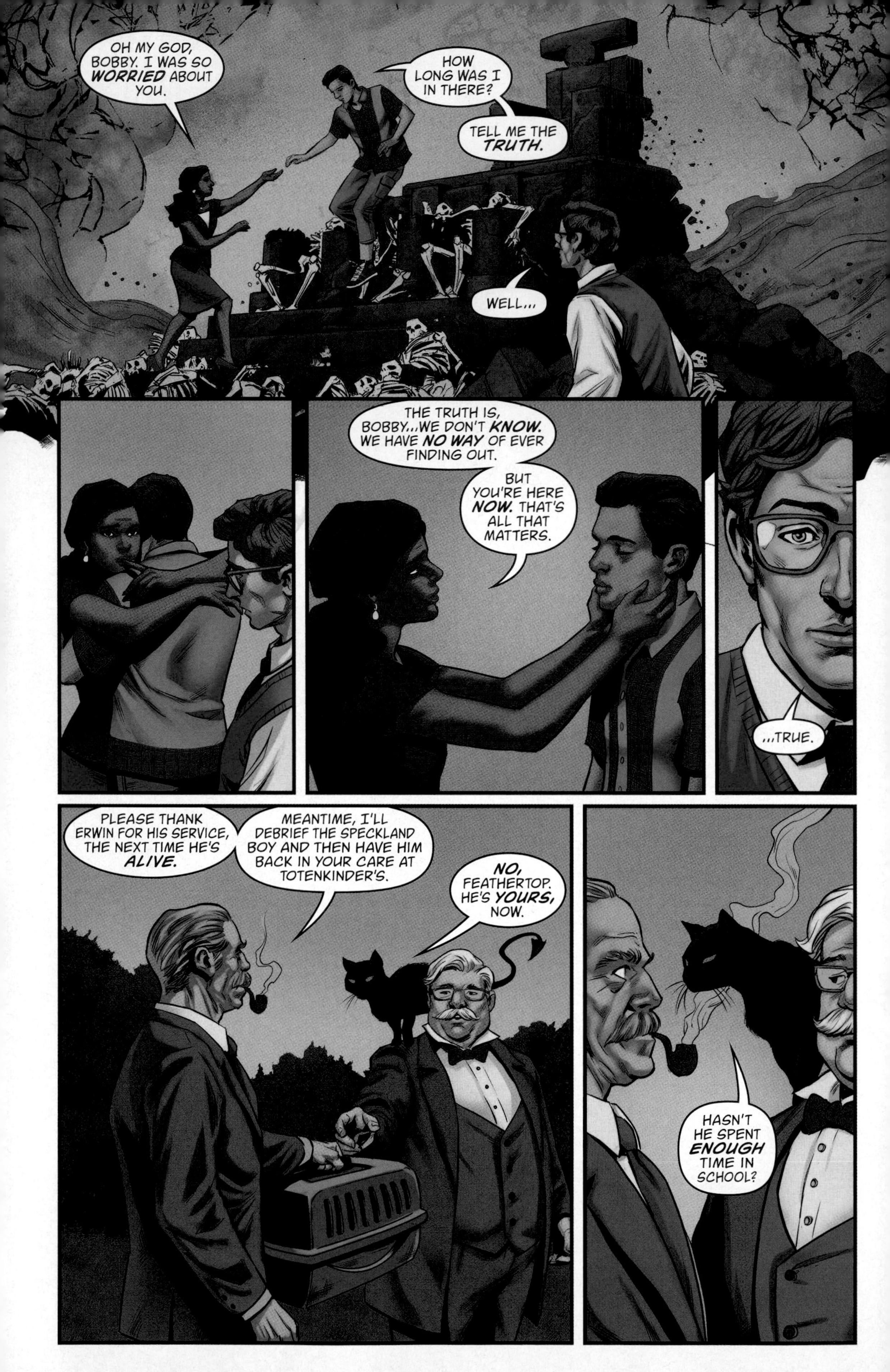
OH MY GOD, BOBBY. I WAS SO WORRIED ABOUT YOU.
HOW LONG WAS I IN THERE?
TELL ME THE TRUTH.
WELL...
THE TRUTH IS, BOBBY...WE DON'T KNOW. WE HAVE NO WAY OF EVER FINDING OUT.
BUT YOU'RE HERE NOW. THAT'S ALL THAT MATTERS.
...TRUE.
PLEASE THANK ERWIN FOR HIS SERVICE, THE NEXT TIME HE'S ALIVE.
MEANTIME, I'LL DEBRIEF THE SPECKLAND BOY AND THEN HAVE HIM BACK IN YOUR CARE AT TOTENKINDER'S.
NO, FEATHERTOP. HE'S YOURS, NOW.
HASN'T HE SPENT ENOUGH TIME IN SCHOOL?

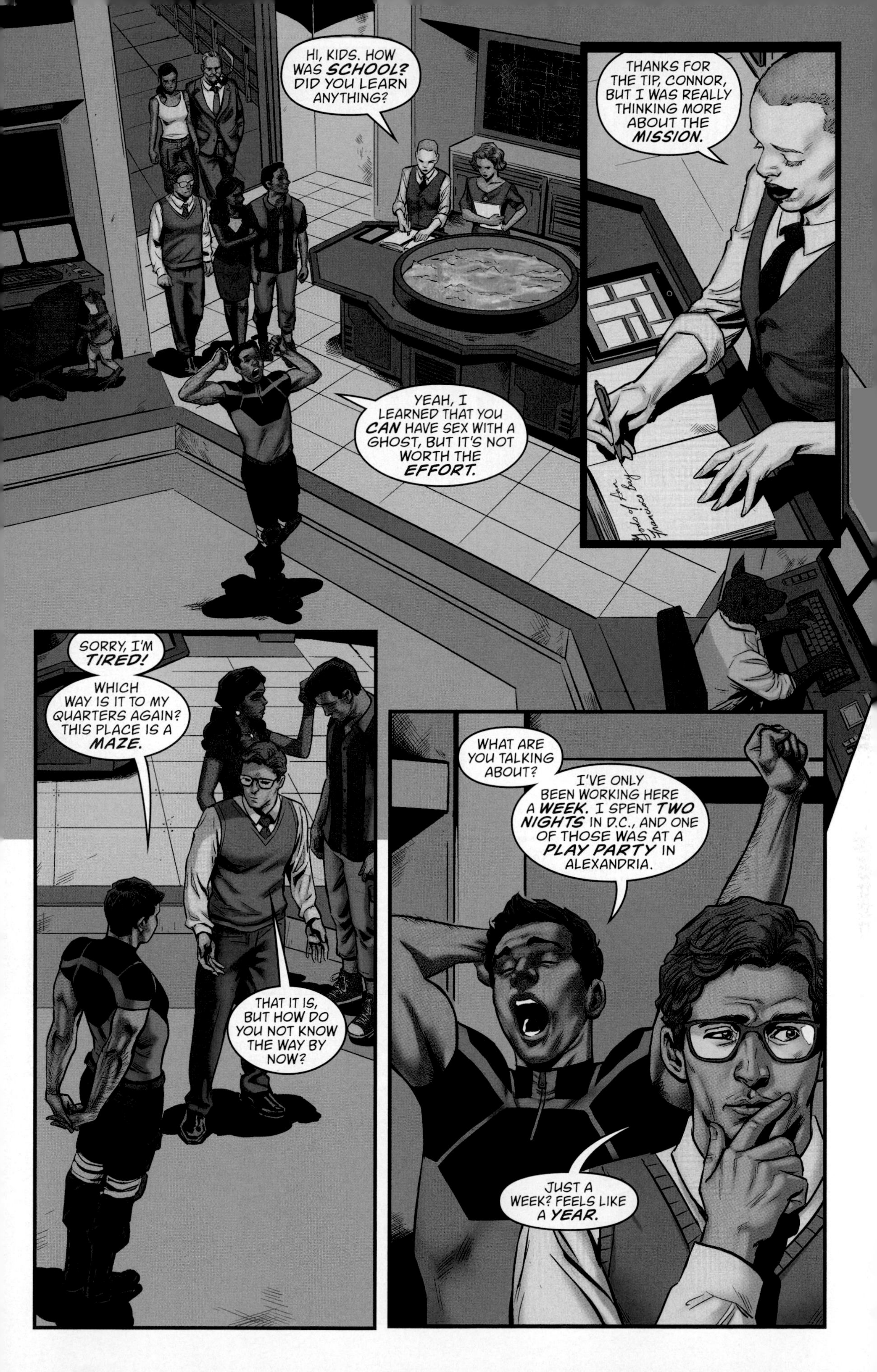
HI, KIDS. HOW WAS SCHOOL? DID YOU LEARN ANYTHING?
THANKS FOR THE TIP, CONNOR, BUT I WAS REALLY THINKING MORE ABOUT THE MISSION.
YEAH, I LEARNED THAT YOU CAN HAVE SEX WITH A GHOST, BUT IT'S NOT WORTH THE EFFORT.
SORRY, I'M TIRED!
WHICH WAY IS IT TO MY QUARTERS AGAIN? THIS PLACE IS A MAZE.
THAT IT IS, BUT HOW DO YOU NOT KNOW THE WAY BY NOW?
WHAT ARE YOU TALKING ABOUT?
I'VE ONLY BEEN WORKING HERE A WEEK. I SPENT TWO NIGHTS IN D.C., AND ONE OF THOSE WAS AT A PLAY PARTY IN ALEXANDRIA.
JUST A WEEK? FEELS LIKE A YEAR.

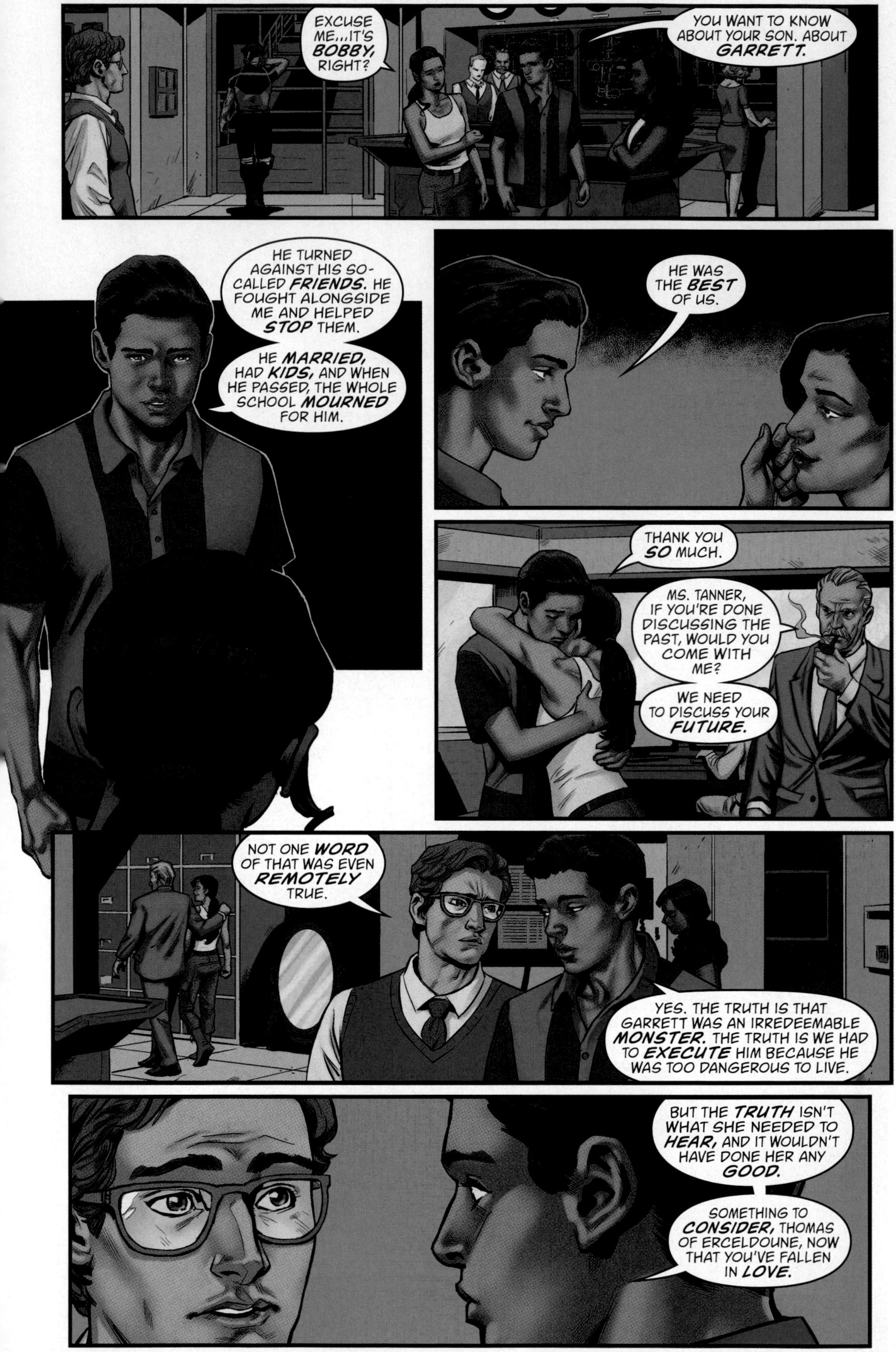
EXCUSE ME...IT'S BOBBY, RIGHT?
YOU WANT TO KNOW ABOUT YOUR SON. ABOUT GARRETT.
HE TURNED AGAINST HIS SO-CALLED FRIENDS. HE FOUGHT ALONGSIDE ME AND HELPED STOP THEM.
HE MARRIED, HAD KIDS, AND WHEN HE PASSED, THE WHOLE SCHOOL MOURNED FOR HIM.
HE WAS THE BEST OF US.
THANK YOU SO MUCH.
MS. TANNER, IF YOU'RE DONE DISCUSSING THE PAST, WOULD YOU COME WITH ME?
WE NEED TO DISCUSS YOUR FUTURE.
NOT ONE WORD OF THAT WAS EVEN REMOTELY TRUE.
YES. THE TRUTH IS THAT GARRETT WAS AN IRREDEEMABLE MONSTER. THE TRUTH IS WE HAD TO EXECUTE HIM BECAUSE HE WAS TOO DANGEROUS TO LIVE.
BUT THE TRUTH ISN'T WHAT SHE NEEDED TO HEAR, AND IT WOULDN'T HAVE DONE HER ANY GOOD.
SOMETHING TO CONSIDER, THOMAS OF ERCELDOUNE, NOW THAT YOU'VE FALLEN IN LOVE.

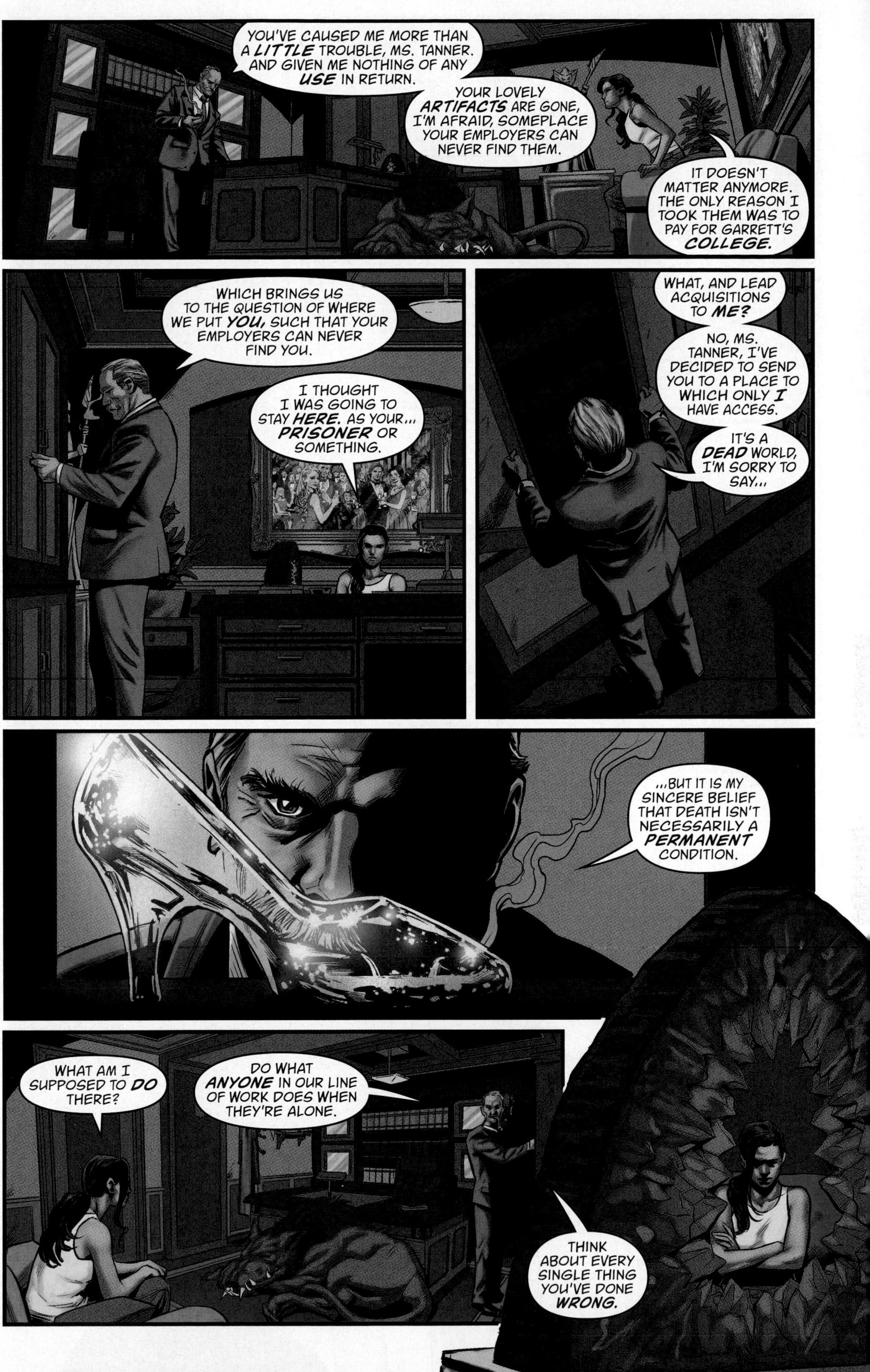
YOU'VE CAUSED ME MORE THAN A LITTLE TROUBLE, MS. TANNER. AND GIVEN ME NOTHING OF ANY USE IN RETURN.
YOUR LOVELY ARTIFACTS ARE GONE, I'M AFRAID, SOMEPLACE YOUR EMPLOYERS CAN NEVER FIND THEM.
IT DOESN'T MATTER ANYMORE. THE ONLY REASON I TOOK THEM WAS TO PAY FOR GARRETT'S COLLEGE.
WHICH BRINGS US TO THE QUESTION OF WHERE WE PUT YOU, SUCH THAT YOUR EMPLOYERS CAN NEVER FIND YOU.
I THOUGHT I WAS GOING TO STAY HERE. AS YOUR... PRISONER OR SOMETHING.
WHAT, AND LEAD ACQUISITIONS TO ME?
NO, MS. TANNER, I'VE DECIDED TO SEND YOU TO A PLACE TO WHICH ONLY I HAVE ACCESS.
IT'S A DEAD WORLD, I'M SORRY TO SAY...
...BUT IT IS MY SINCERE BELIEF THAT DEATH ISN'T NECESSARILY A PERMANENT CONDITION.
WHAT AM I SUPPOSED TO DO THERE?
DO WHAT ANYONE IN OUR LINE OF WORK DOES WHEN THEY'RE ALONE.
THINK ABOUT EVERY SINGLE THING YOU'VE DONE WRONG.

YOU NEED TO CHANGE THE **DRESSING** ONCE A DAY, AND TAKE THE **FULL COURSE** OF ANTIBIOTICS.

LET ME GRAB YOU A LITTLE SOMETHING FOR THE **PAIN**.

OH, I'LL BE FINE, DOCTOR...

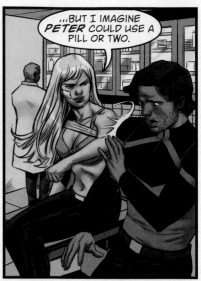

...BUT I IMAGINE **PETER** COULD USE A PILL OR TWO.

HOW LONG HAVE YOU KNOWN...?

THAT YOU MUST HAVE USED YOUR **SIGNING BONUS** TO TAKE **MY PAIN** ON YOURSELF?

IT TOOK ME WAY TOO LONG. AND NOW THAT I KNOW, I'M **FURIOUS** WITH YOU.

WHAT IN THE WORLD WOULD MAKE YOU DO SOMETHING SO **STUPID**?

LOVE, PEEP.

THE WAY THE BONUS SPELL HAD TO BE WORDED, **YOUR PAIN** IS TRANSFERRED TO THE ONE **YOU** LOVE THE MOST.

DAMMIT, PIPER.

IN THAT CASE, YOU'RE GOING TO SUFFER FOR **ETERNITY**.

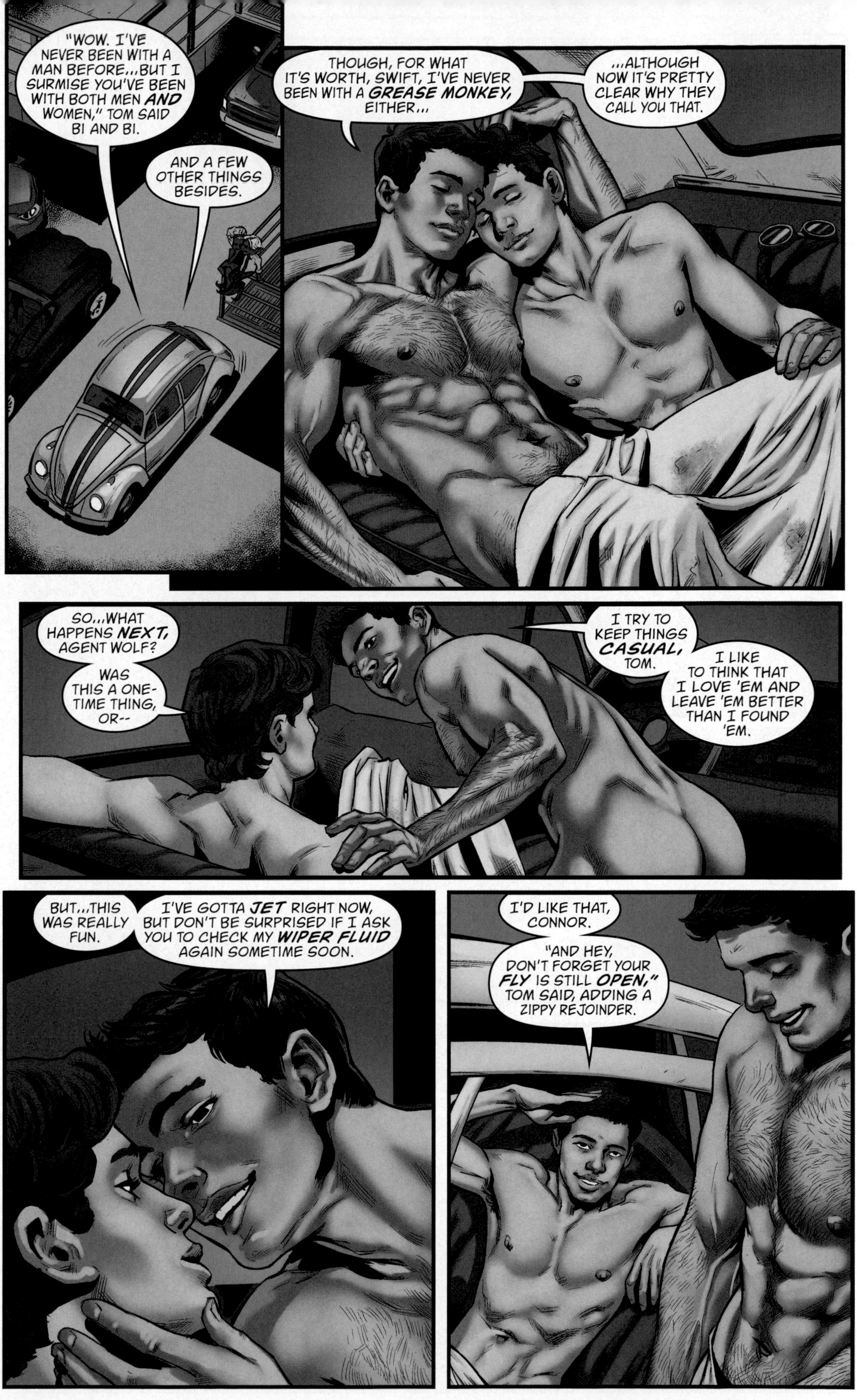
"WOW. I'VE NEVER BEEN WITH A MAN BEFORE...BUT I SURMISE YOU'VE BEEN WITH BOTH MEN AND WOMEN," TOM SAID BI AND BI.
AND A FEW OTHER THINGS BESIDES.
THOUGH, FOR WHAT IT'S WORTH, SWIFT, I'VE NEVER BEEN WITH A GREASE MONKEY, EITHER...
...ALTHOUGH NOW IT'S PRETTY CLEAR WHY THEY CALL YOU THAT.
SO...WHAT HAPPENS NEXT, AGENT WOLF?
WAS THIS A ONE-TIME THING, OR--
I TRY TO KEEP THINGS CASUAL, TOM.
I LIKE TO THINK THAT I LOVE 'EM AND LEAVE 'EM BETTER THAN I FOUND 'EM.
BUT...THIS WAS REALLY FUN.
I'VE GOTTA JET RIGHT NOW, BUT DON'T BE SURPRISED IF I ASK YOU TO CHECK MY WIPER FLUID AGAIN SOMETIME SOON.
I'D LIKE THAT, CONNOR.
"AND HEY, DON'T FORGET YOUR FLY IS STILL OPEN," TOM SAID, ADDING A ZIPPY REJOINDER.

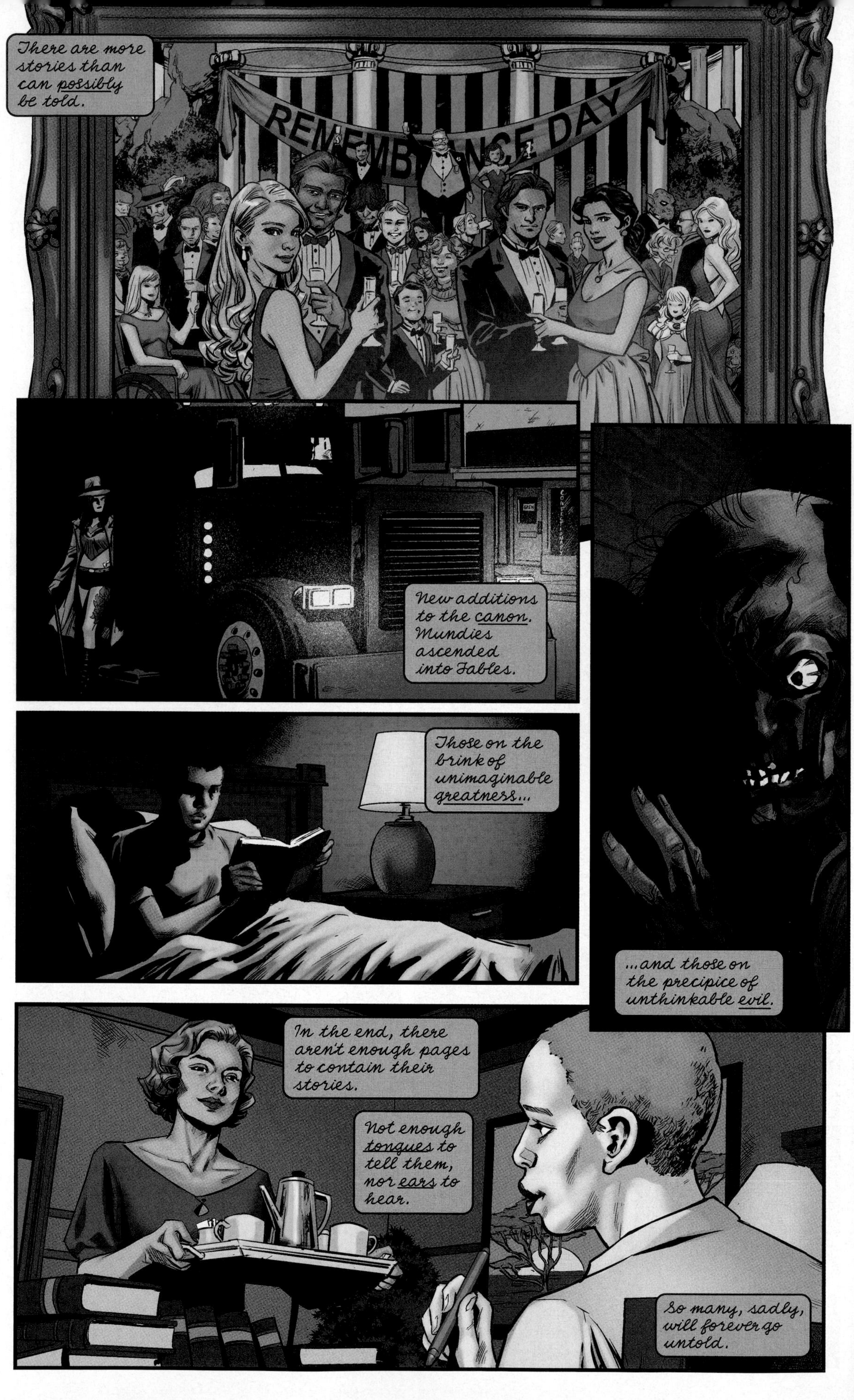

There are more stories than can possibly be told.
REMEMBRANCE DAY
New additions to the canon. Mundies ascended into Fables.
OPEN
Those on the brink of unimaginable greatness...
...and those on the precipice of unthinkable evil.
In the end, there aren't enough pages to contain their stories.
Not enough tongues to tell them, nor ears to hear.
So many, sadly, will forever go untold.

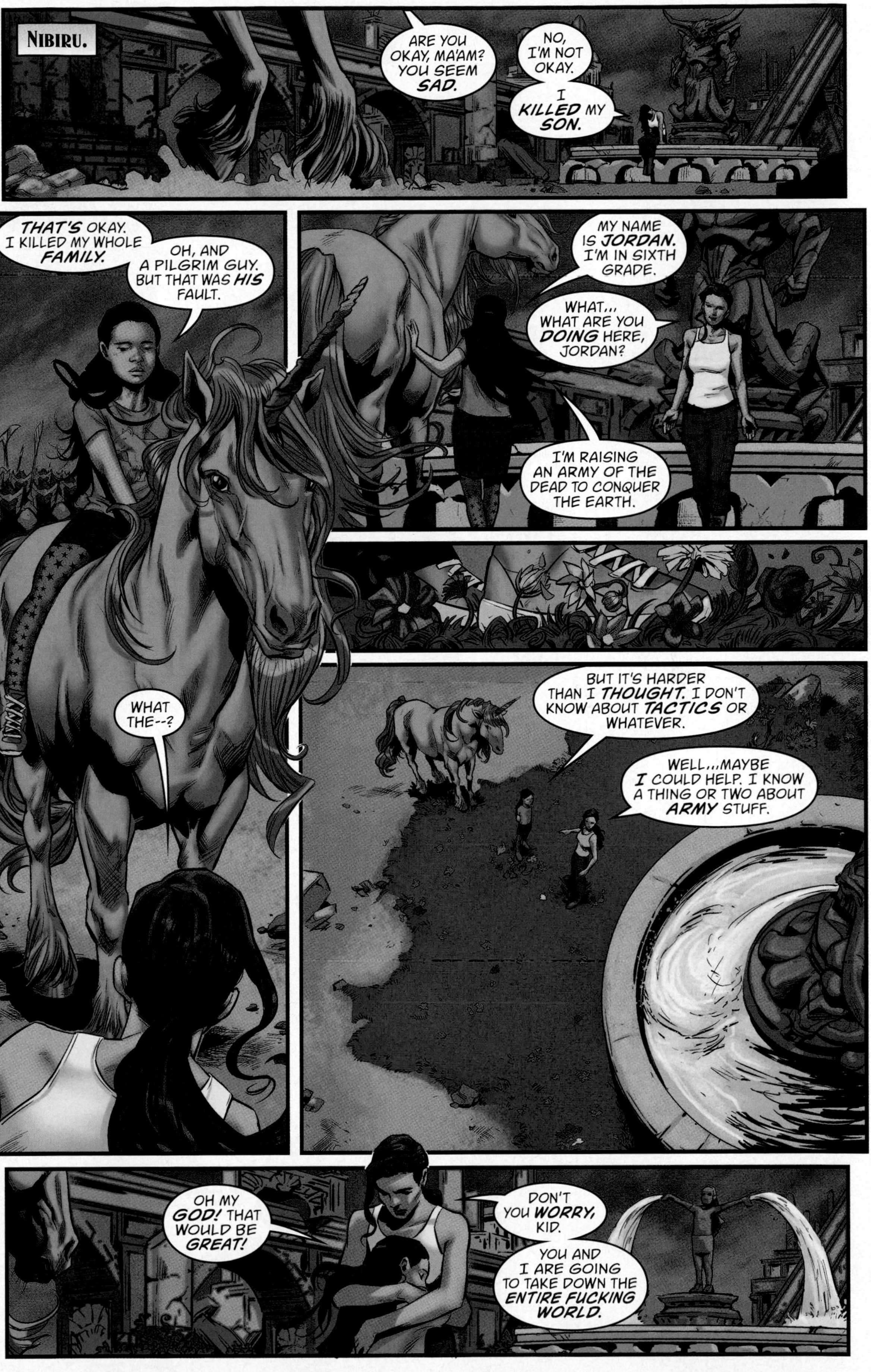
NIBIRU.
ARE YOU OKAY, MA'AM? YOU SEEM SAD.
NO, I'M NOT OKAY.
I KILLED MY SON.
THAT'S OKAY. I KILLED MY WHOLE FAMILY.
OH, AND A PILGRIM GUY. BUT THAT WAS HIS FAULT.
MY NAME IS JORDAN. I'M IN SIXTH GRADE.
WHAT... WHAT ARE YOU DOING HERE, JORDAN?
I'M RAISING AN ARMY OF THE DEAD TO CONQUER THE EARTH.
WHAT THE--?
BUT IT'S HARDER THAN I THOUGHT. I DON'T KNOW ABOUT TACTICS OR WHATEVER.
WELL...MAYBE I COULD HELP. I KNOW A THING OR TWO ABOUT ARMY STUFF.
OH MY GOD! THAT WOULD BE GREAT!
DON'T YOU WORRY, KID.
YOU AND I ARE GOING TO TAKE DOWN THE ENTIRE FUCKING WORLD.

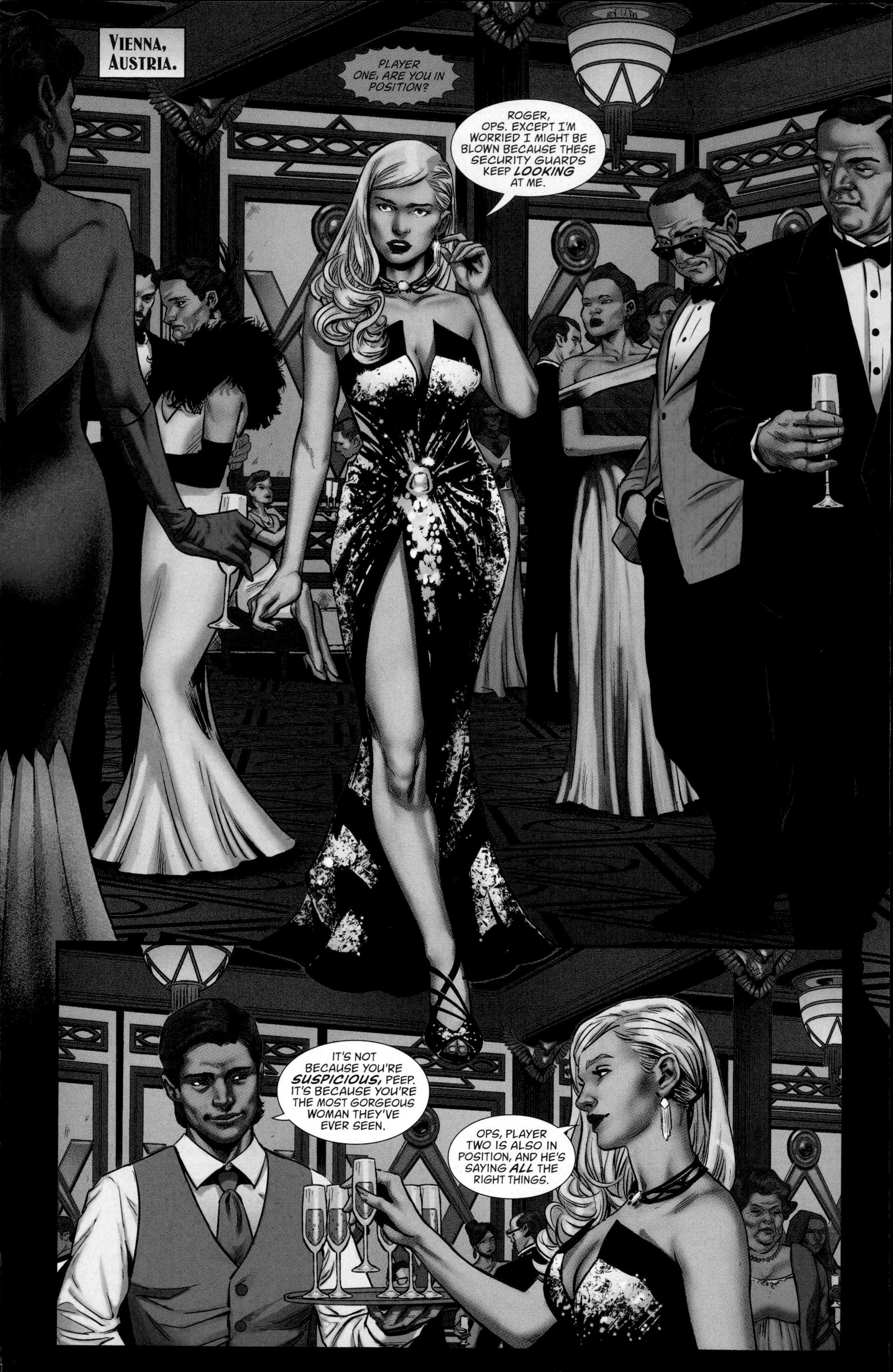
VIENNA, AUSTRIA.
PLAYER ONE, ARE YOU IN POSITION?
ROGER, OPS. EXCEPT I'M WORRIED I MIGHT BE BLOWN BECAUSE THESE SECURITY GUARDS KEEP LOOKING AT ME.
IT'S NOT BECAUSE YOU'RE SUSPICIOUS, PEEP. IT'S BECAUSE YOU'RE THE MOST GORGEOUS WOMAN THEY'VE EVER SEEN.
OPS, PLAYER TWO IS ALSO IN POSITION, AND HE'S SAYING ALL THE RIGHT THINGS.

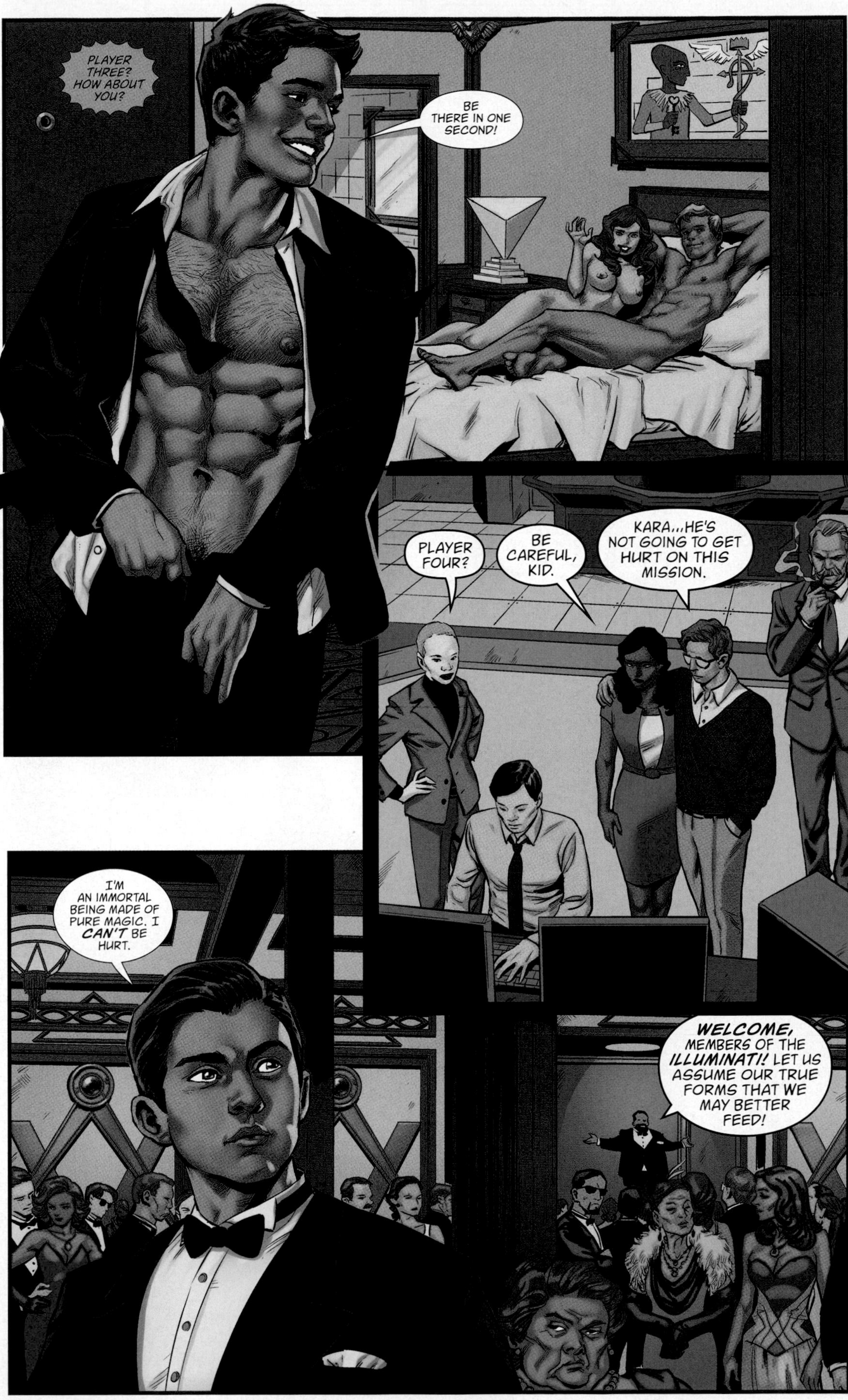
PLAYER THREE? HOW ABOUT YOU?
BE THERE IN ONE SECOND!
PLAYER FOUR?
BE CAREFUL, KID.
KARA...HE'S NOT GOING TO GET HURT ON THIS MISSION.
I'M AN IMMORTAL BEING MADE OF PURE MAGIC. I CAN'T BE HURT.
WELCOME, MEMBERS OF THE ILLUMINATI! LET US ASSUME OUR TRUE FORMS THAT WE MAY BETTER FEED!

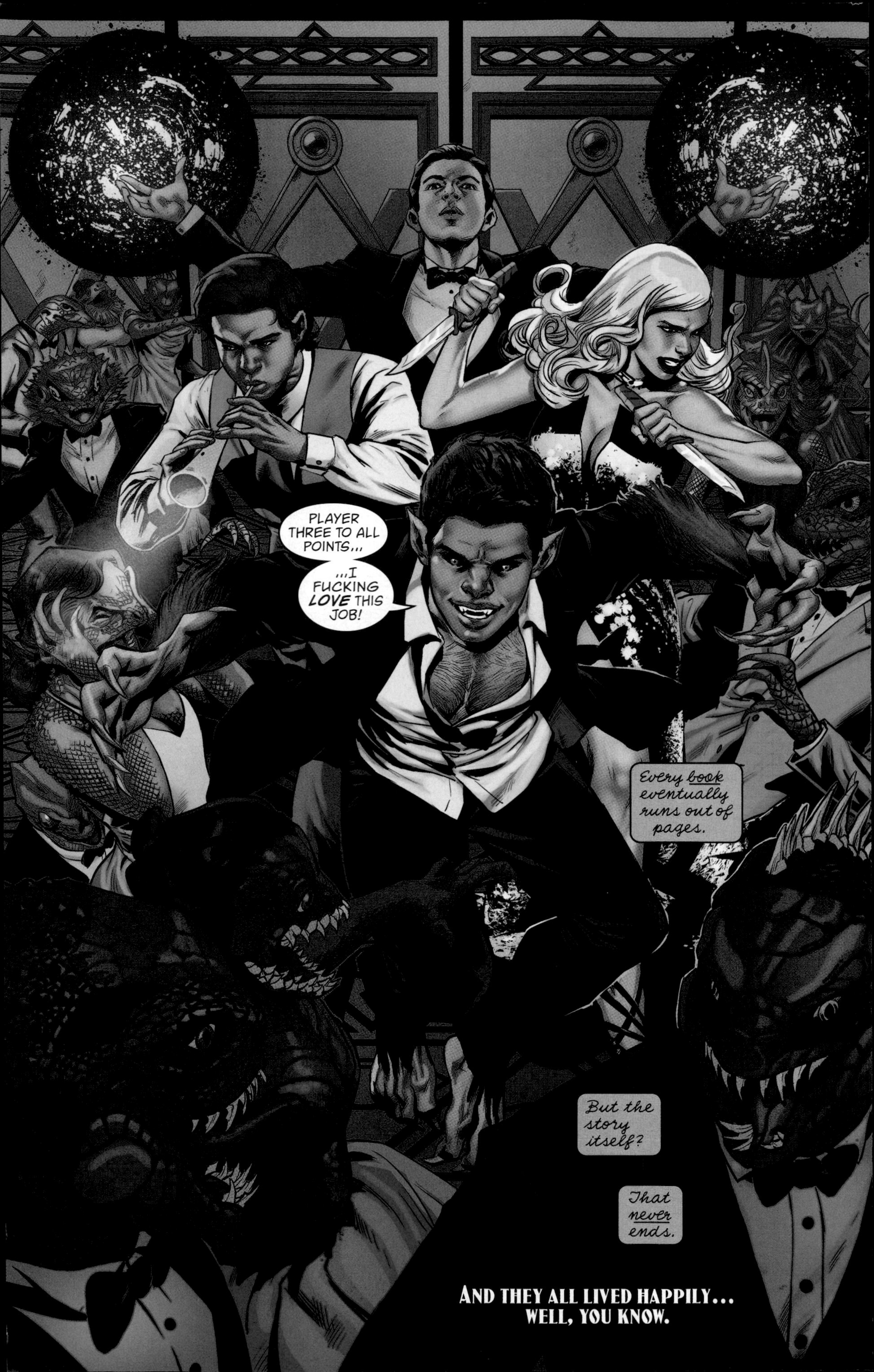
PLAYER THREE TO ALL POINTS...
...I FUCKING LOVE THIS JOB!
Every book eventually runs out of pages.
But the story itself?
That never ends.
AND THEY ALL LIVED HAPPILY... WELL, YOU KNOW.

Cover art for issue #7 by Tula Lotay

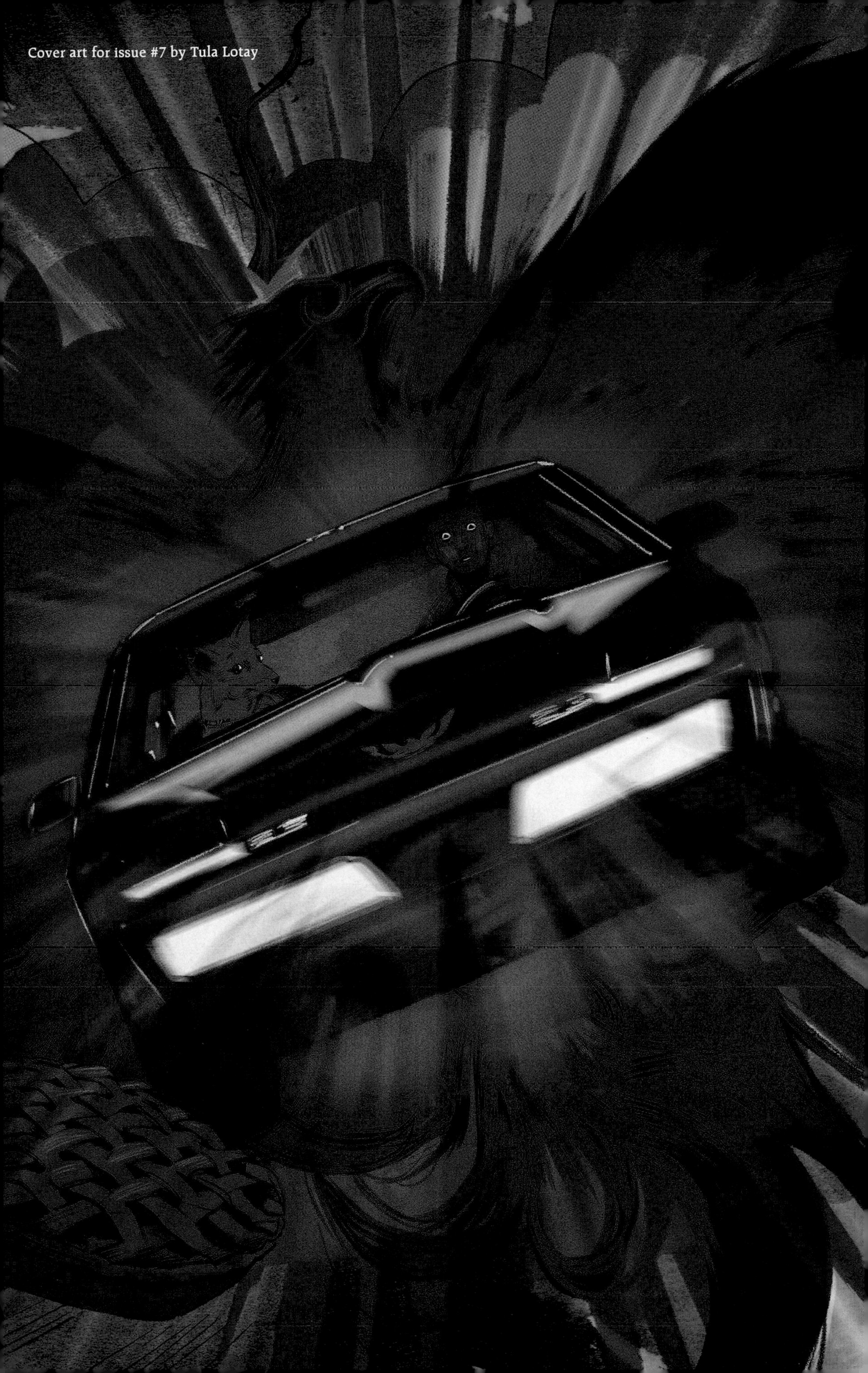

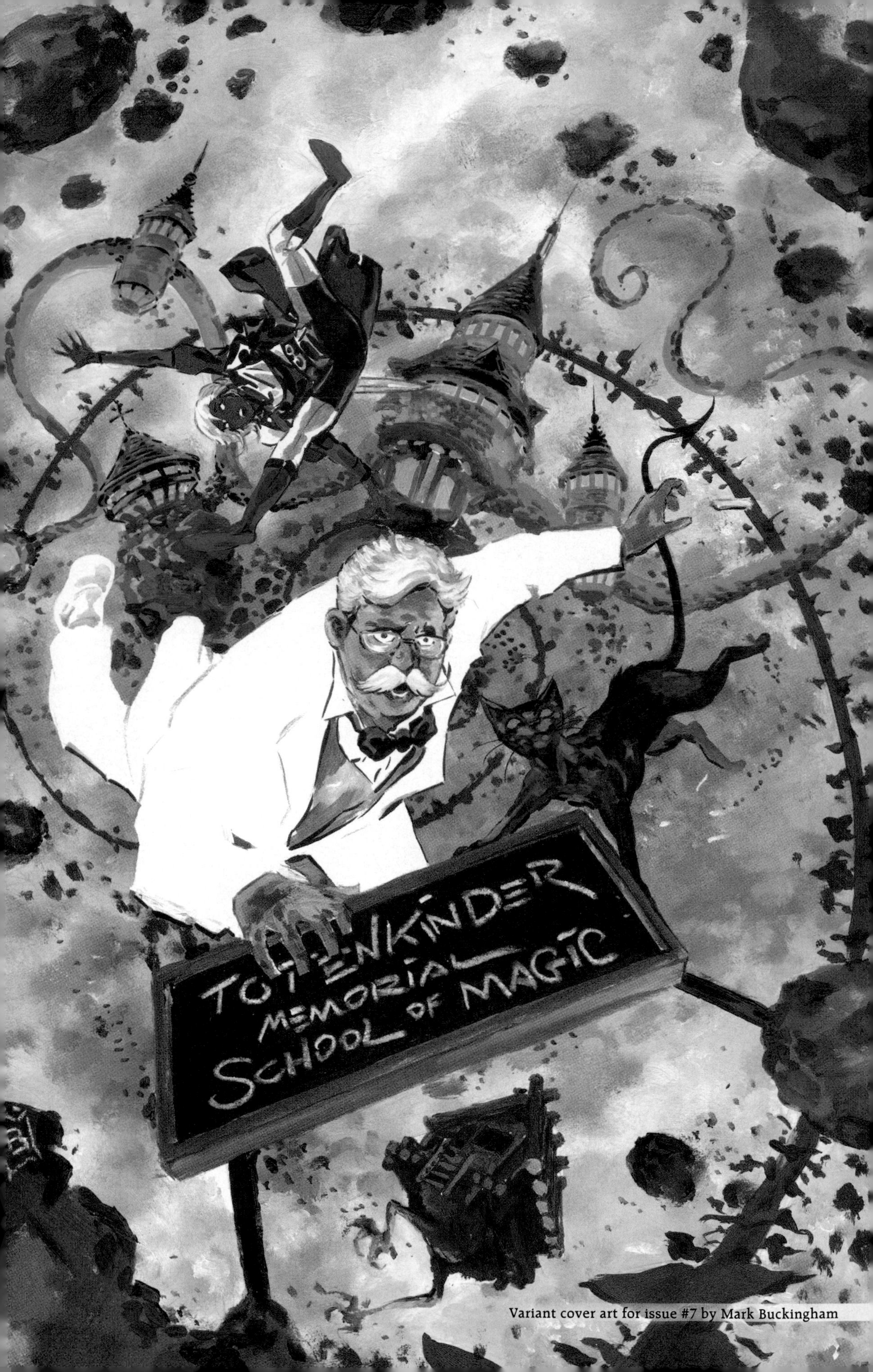
TOTENKINDER
MEMORIAL
SCHOOL OF MAGIC
Variant cover art for issue #7 by Mark Buckingham

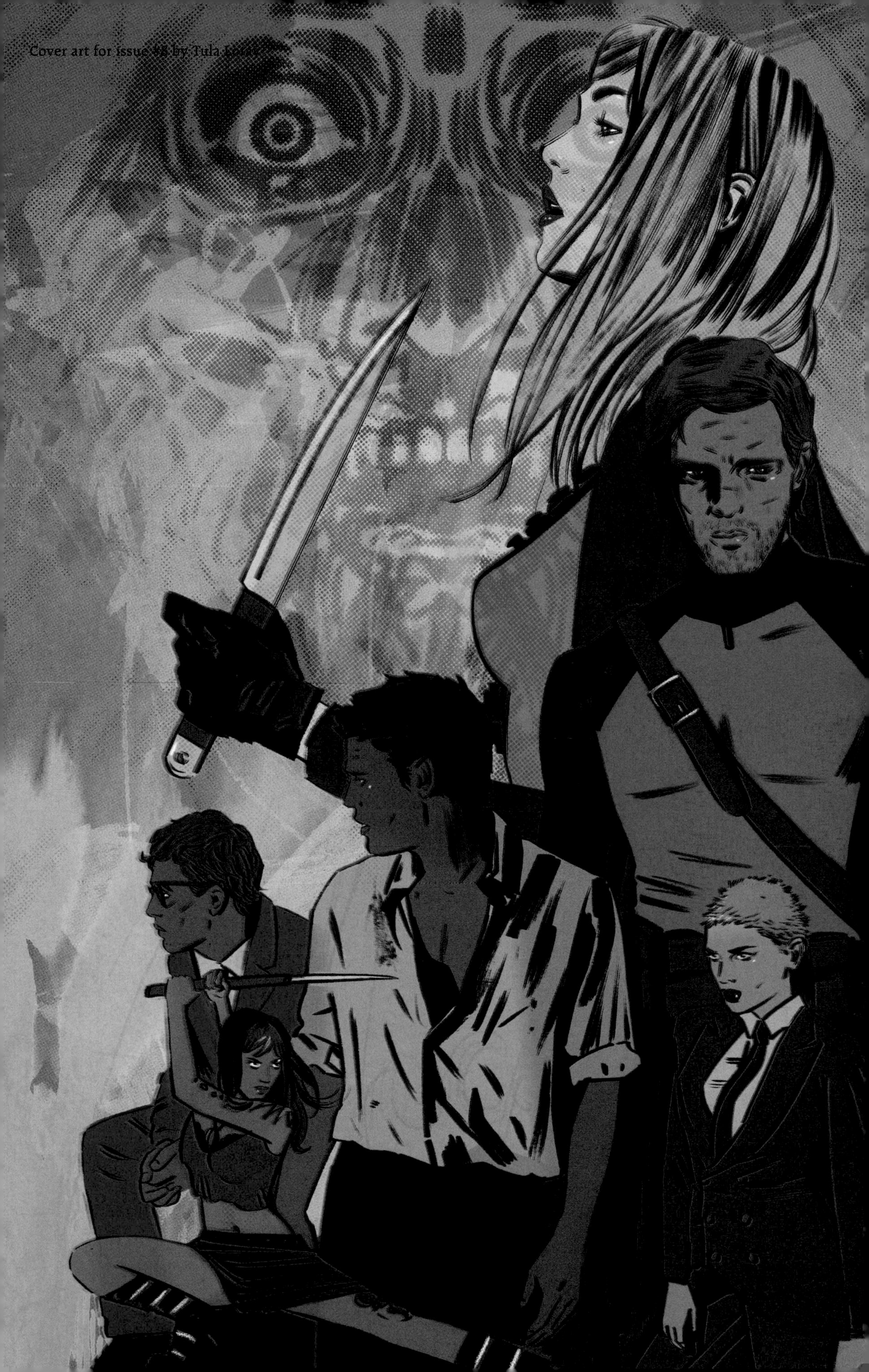

Cover art for issue #8 by Tula Lotay

Cover art for issue #9 by Tula Lotay

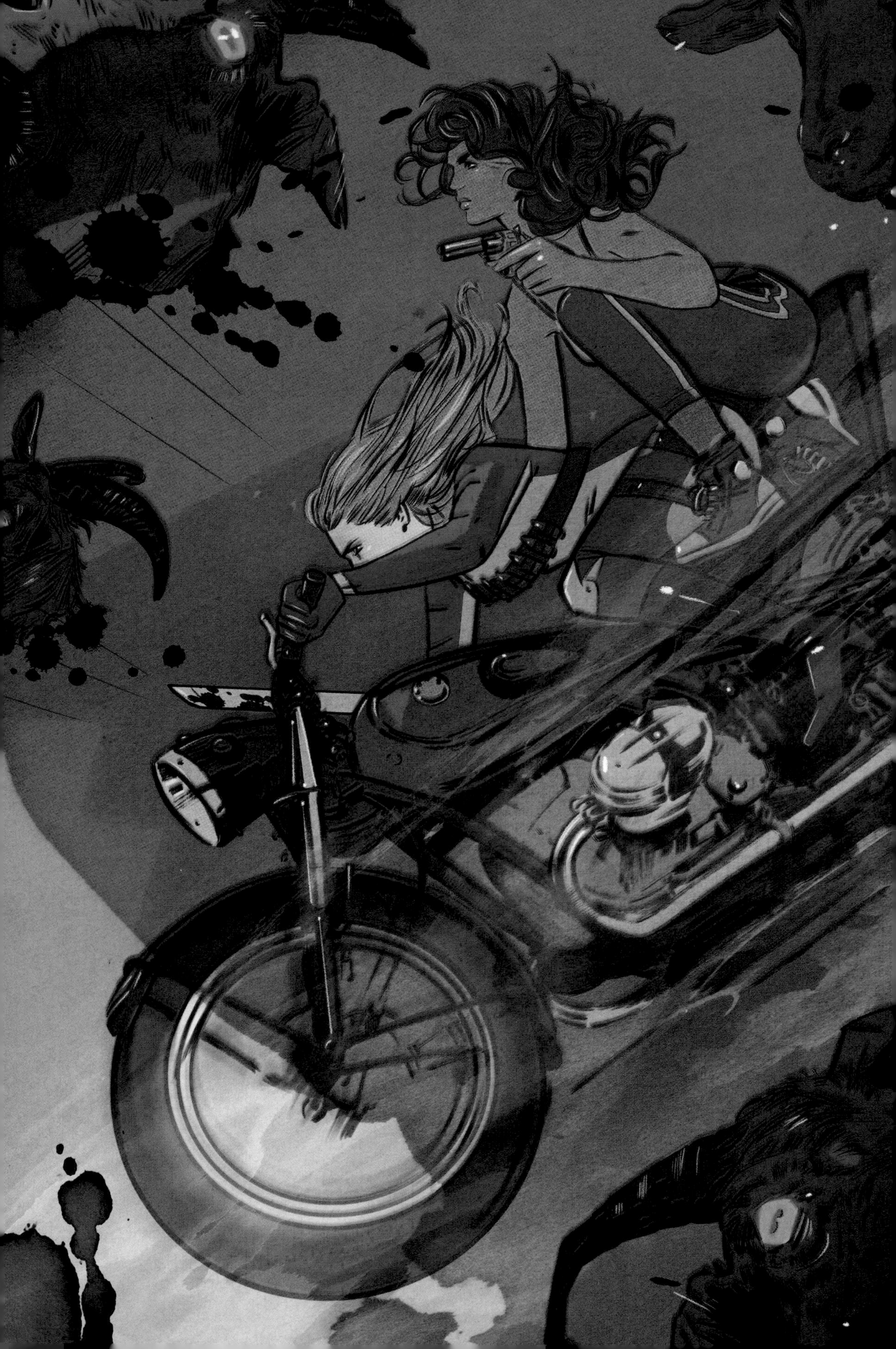

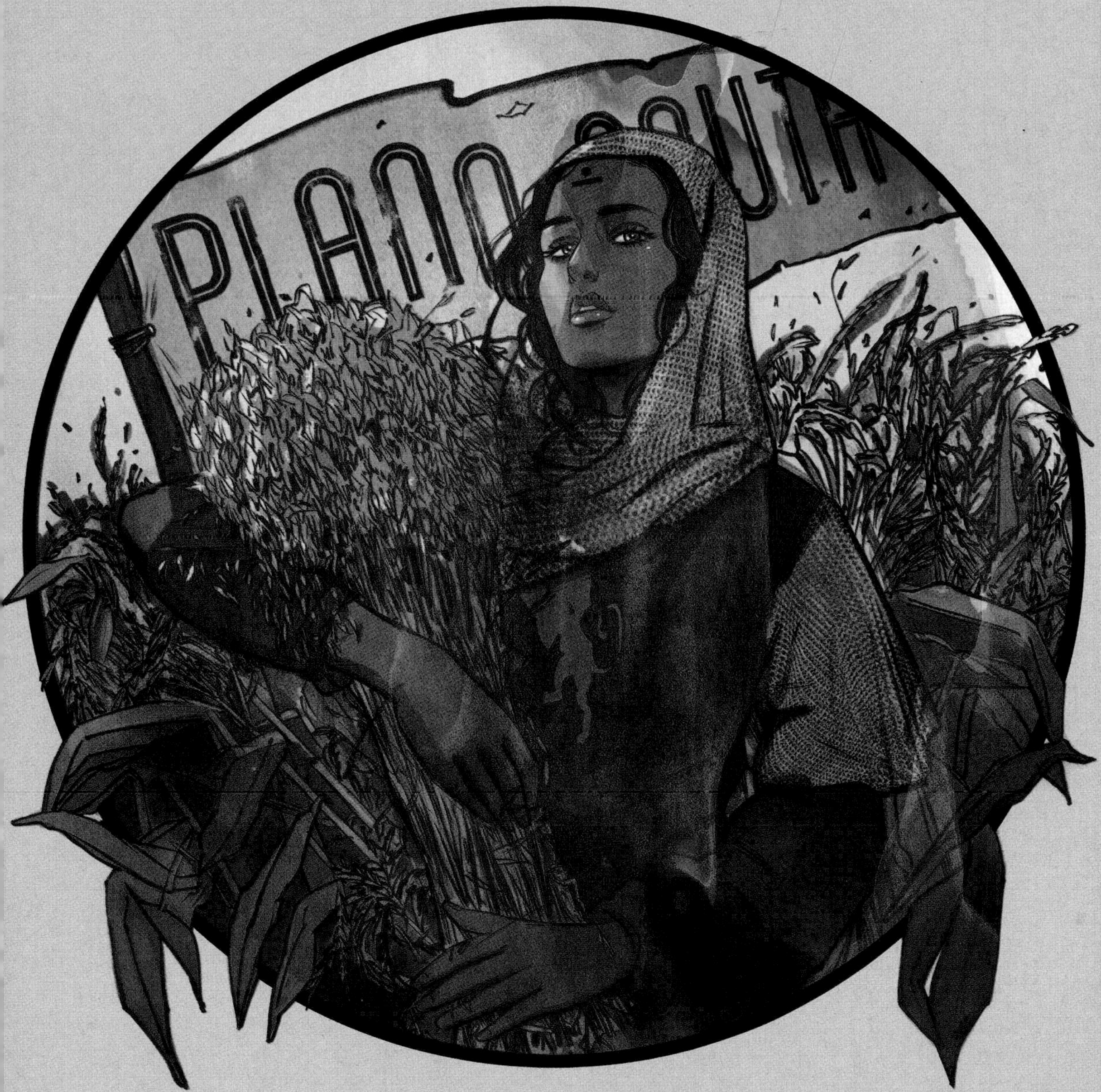
PLANO

Cover art for issue #10 by Tula Lotay

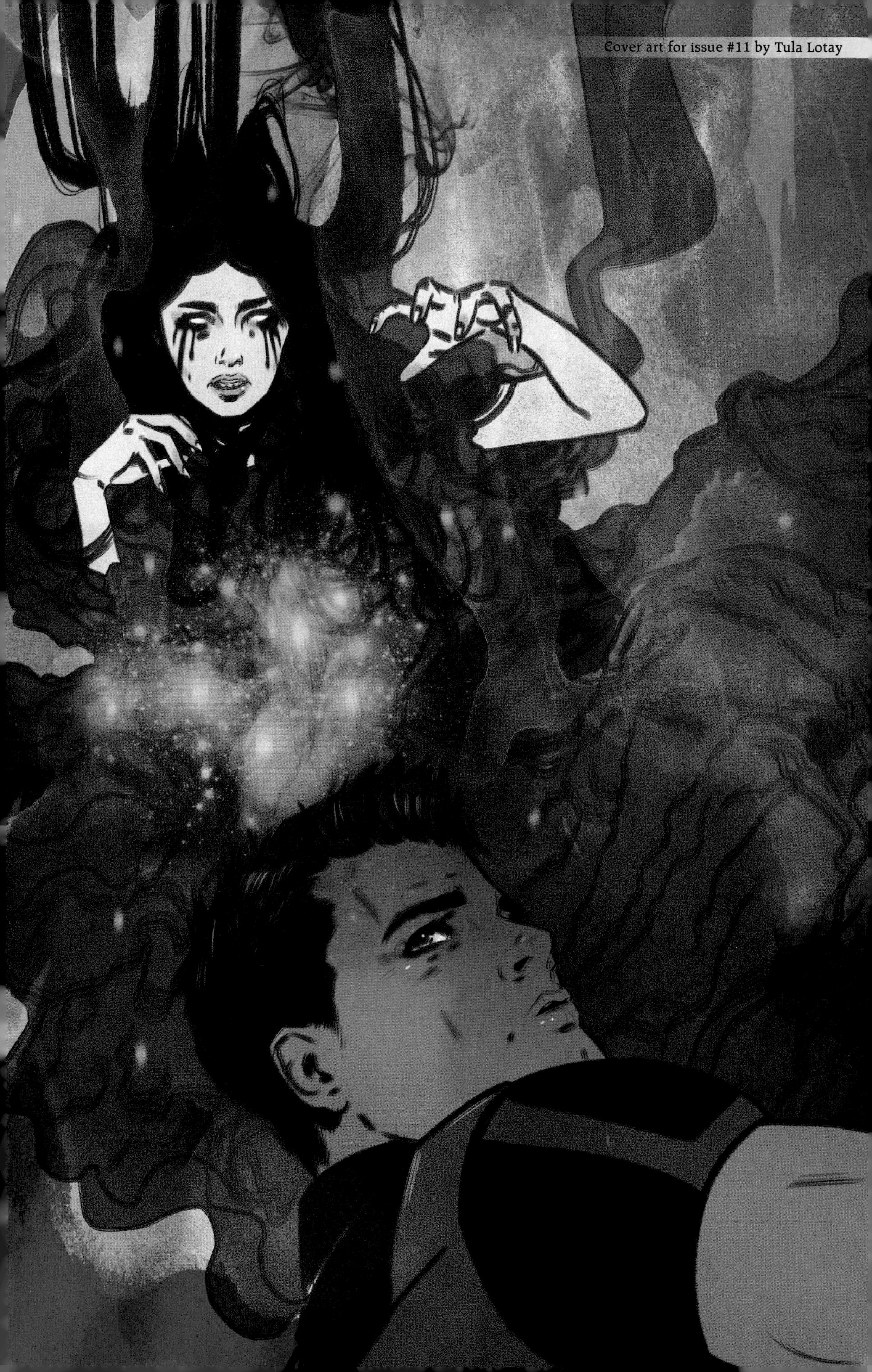

Cover art for issue #11 by Tula Lotay

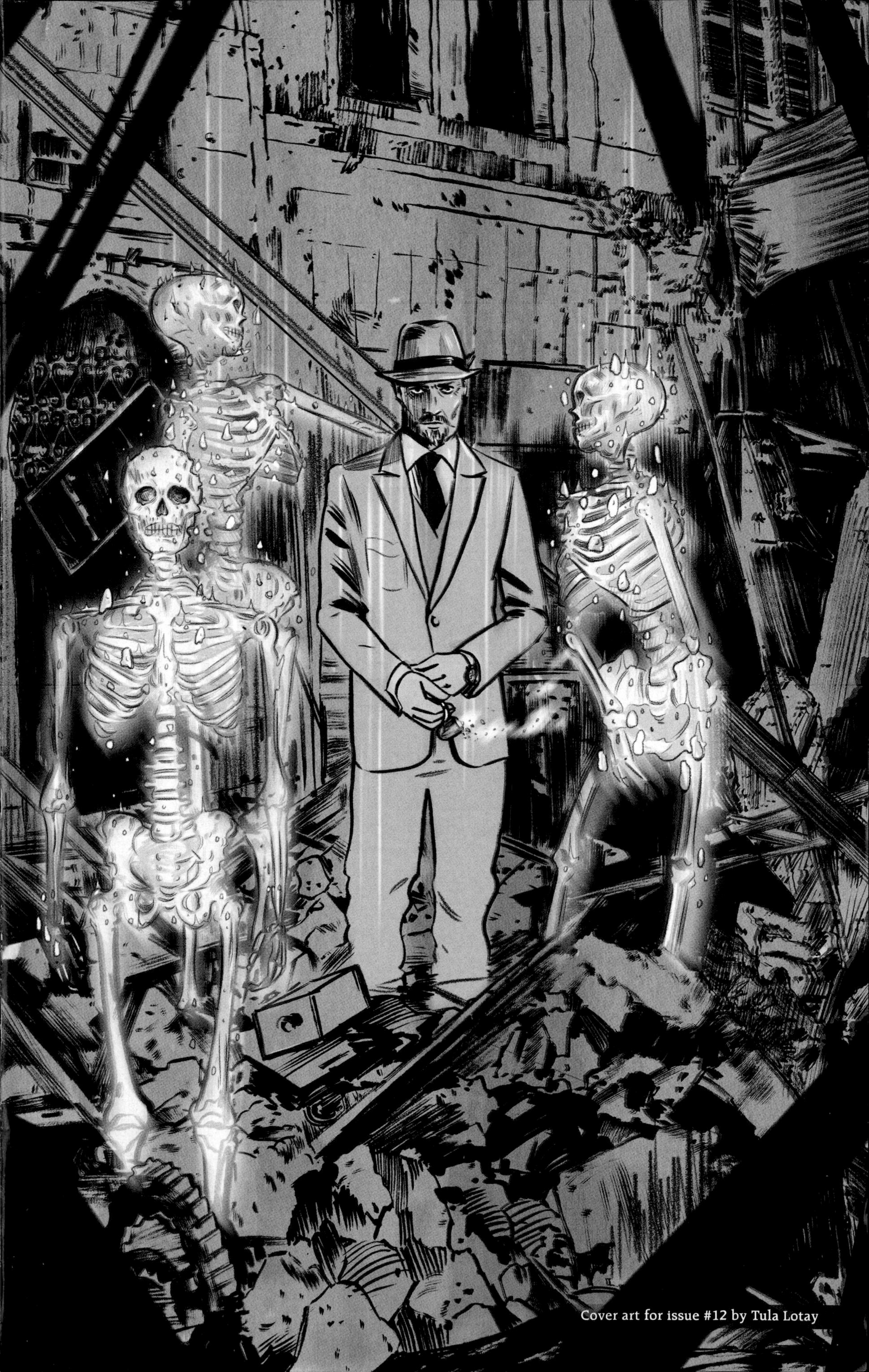

Cover art for issue #12 by Tula Lotay

Promotional art by Travis Moore

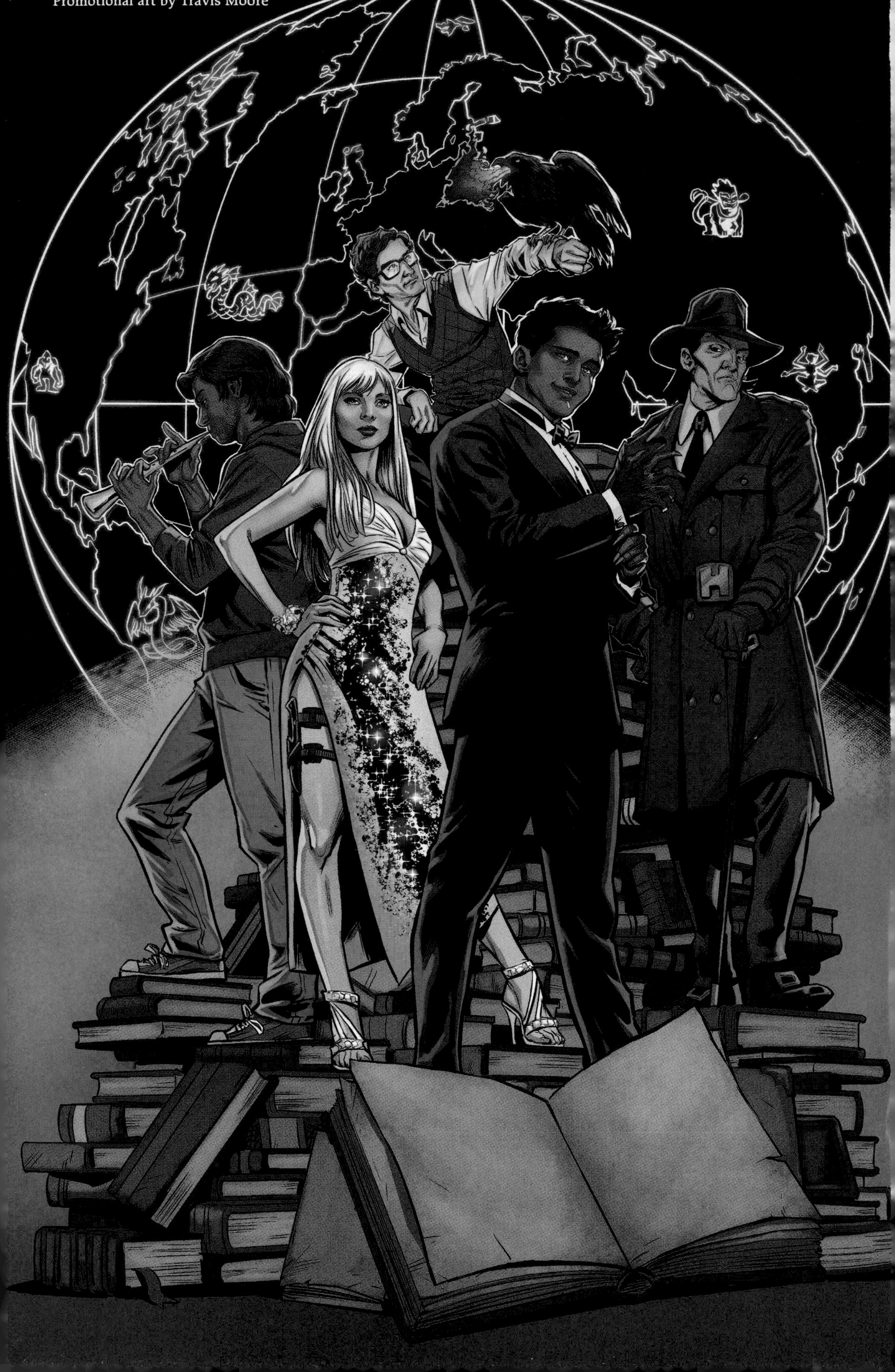